RESHAPING LOCAL WORLDS

Sponsored by the
JOINT COMMITTEE ON SOUTHEAST ASIA
of the
SOCIAL SCIENCE RESEARCH COUNCIL
and the
AMERICAN COUNCIL OF LEARNED SOCIETIES

RESHAPING LOCAL WORLDS

FORMAL EDUCATION AND CULTURAL CHANGE IN RURAL SOUTHEAST ASIA

Edited by
Charles F. Keyes

With the assistance of
E. Jane Keyes and Nancy Donnelly

Monograph 36/Yale Southeast Asia Studies
Yale Center for International and Area Studies

TABLE OF CONTENTS

PREFACE

This volume originated in a conference on "Cultural Change and Rural Education in Southeast Asia" held in July 1983 in Penang, Malaysia and sponsored by the Joint Committee on Southeast Asia of the American Social Science Research Council and the American Council of Learned Societies. This conference was part of a larger project on "Agrarian Change in Southeast Asia" undertaken by the Joint Committee.

Scholars from diverse backgrounds came together in Penang, with three from Malaysia, two from Vietnam, one each from Thailand, Indonesia, the Philippines, Japan and the United Kingdom as well as five from the United States (see list of contributors). The collection presented here has captured only a small part of the richness of exchange of ideas which took place in Penang. In the quest for coherence—that chimera which is used as a standard for determining whether written work should achieve temporary immortality in the shape of a book—a radical pruning has occurred. I can but hope that in the end this book embodies some of the spirit which was generated at the conference. While something has been lost in the movement between conference and book, something has also been gained. The volume includes papers by Alexander Woodside and Chayan Vaddhanaphuti who, although invited to the conference, were unfortunately unable to attend.

I should like to thank the Rockefeller Foundation for providing funding for the conference out of which this volume has grown. I am especially grateful to Lim Teck Ghee who handled often complicated and time-consuming local arrangements in Penang. I wish also to thank David Szanton, then Staff Associate for the Joint SSRC/ACLS Committee on Southeast Asia, who provided his usual excellent help in arranging the logistics for the conference as well as taking a very active role in the discussions.

I am deeply grateful to Jane Keyes and Nancy Donnelly for the considerable assistance they provided me during the editing of the book. I would also like to acknowledge the help which Kay Mansfield at the Southeast Asian Studies Program at Yale and Nancy Pollock and Larry Epstein at the University of Washington have given in preparing the manuscript for publication. Valuable suggestions from David Marr, Toby Volkman, James Scott and especially Ruth McVey helped me gain a critical perspective on how to shape the contributions into this volume.

STATE SCHOOLS IN RURAL COMMUNITIES: REFLECTIONS ON RURAL EDUCATION AND CULTURAL CHANGE IN SOUTHEAST ASIA

Charles F. Keyes

Introduction

During the 1950s and 1960s, many social theorists saw state school education in Third World countries as a primary instrument for transforming "traditional" peasants into "modern" men and women. Such theorists assumed that "modern" men (women were rarely mentioned) would inevitably also be economic men who would automatically engage in productive activities that would in turn increase the nation's GNP.[1]

Alex Inkeles, among the most ardent and articulate proponents of this view, claimed that centralized state school systems were essential for producing what he characterized as "a psychological syndrome of modernity" in developing nations. This syndrome, he argued, had four main components, namely "a sense of efficacy (high achievement), ... an openness to new experience, ... an emphasis on individual autonomy, and ... an orientation towards higher occupational achievement, especially in those occupations which are technologically modern" (Southeast Asia Development Advisory Group, n.d.:4). Drawing on work carried out by several of his associates in six developing countries (Argentina, Chile, East Pakistan—now Bangladesh—India, Israel, and Nigeria), Inkeles established scales which he claimed could be used to measure a nation's modernity syndrome (Inkeles 1974). At a Southeast Asian Development Advisory Group conference held in Chiang Mai in 1972, Inkeles sought to extend his theory to Southeast Asia.[2]

Although Inkeles's view that state schools were the most significant institutions for promoting economic development was very influential, by the early 1970s other scholars, many of them drawing on Marxist theory, especially as reformulated in the work of Gramsci, Althusser, and Poulantzas, were advancing very different views.[3] Their critiques of "development" theories regarding the role of formal education in Third World countries centered on the ethnocentric values that they saw as implicit in the conception of "modernity." These scholars maintained that schools should, rather, be seen as a means whereby dominant elites inculcate in the citizenry ideologies which buttress the orders they control. In a paper about the relationship between education and village "development" John Simmons, for example, argues that education, far from enabling the poor, especially those in rural areas, to participate in development, actually relegates them to marginal economic roles. "In most [developing] countries, the poor *are resigned* to letting the educational establishment decide their fate and legitimize their poverty" (Simmons 1980:289; emphasis added).

Although the Marxist approach to the study of education provided a much needed corrective to the roseate view of the role of schools put forward by modernization theorists in the 1960s and early 1970s, Simmons and others arguing in a similar vein go too far, I believe, in assuming that students are merely passive recipients of elite-determined socialization patterns. Insofar as formal education, whether of a traditional type or that sponsored by modern states, has been institutionalized culturally in a local community, it will shape for participants the perspective on the world in which they live.[4] Formal schooling has clear kinship to initiation rites (cf. Keyes 1986). This is perhaps most evident in the case of traditional religious schools discussed in this volume, such as temple-monastery Buddhist schools or the *pesantren/pondok* Islamic schools, which prepare students for specific adult roles such as community leader, curing practitioner, or entertainer, but above all for places within a religious realm. State schools also prepare students to enter an adult world, but one defined in political and economic rather than in religious terms.

In Southeast Asian rural communities, state education is not, however, the only cultural process molding children as they become adults. Rather, these children draw on two distinctive traditions as they go out into the adult world and enter the work force. On the one hand, they carry with them beliefs drawn from localized cultural traditions, say from customary practices associated with agricultural and ritual cycles, from folklore and folk dramatic performances, or from customary law; on the other, they hold views on their place in the nation and outside world drawn from their school experience. Because of the tension between these different processes, one cannot assume that all students who have been exposed to the same cultural messages in state schools will emerge with an identical perspective on the world, nor even that they will be imbued with the ideological outlook designed for them by those who created the national curriculum.

The state may assume it controls the student body through state schools, but students, or their parents, sometimes place local community needs over the objectives of the state-sponsored school. For example, a rural family may require a child's labor in the rice fields, leading that child to play truant and thus to resist school demands. Or, again, students may indirectly engage in passive resistance to state-imposed schooling by, for example, performing in ways that reflect poorly on their teachers, causing the latter to lose their promotions or pay raises. Even if students do not on their own or in concert with their parents act in ways which undermine school aims, they may still misunderstand the messages which the state seeks to convey to them through the formal education process. For example, the emphasis on national ideological symbols may make students conscious that valued aspects of local culture are being ignored or deprecated, thus leading them to be more rather than less conscious of their ethnic heritage than they otherwise would have been. Rural children may also learn that, in the larger world, their schooling prepares them for only the lowest level of a national hierarchy of educational attainment, a recognition that can contribute directly to the emergence of class consciousness.

Although villagers in Southeast Asia, like those in other Third World countries, do not, simply as a function of attending state schools, become the "modern men" predicted by modernization theory nor yet become members of a passive subordinate class as some Marxist theorists would have it, they have, nevertheless, seen their worlds transformed by the institution of state-sponsored compulsory mass education. In this new understanding of the world in which they live, students juxtapose what they learn in state schools with ideas appropriated from local traditions. The essays in this volume all demonstrate that the reshaping of local worlds in Southeast Asia resulting from the introduction of formal state schooling must be seen as a dialectical product of the interplay of local and national culture.

The Development of State Schools in Southeast Asia

Although indigenous schools have long existed in Southeast Asia, modern state schools in the region are relatively recent in origin, and emerged primarily from institutions introduced into the area from the West. Christian missionaries established the first Western schools in Southeast Asia in the sixteenth century (see Watson 1982b:71). Additional missionary schools were set up throughout the seventeenth and eighteenth centuries, especially in the Spanish-ruled Philippines,[5] but it was not until the following century that they began to assume an important place within Southeast Asian societies. During the nineteenth century, as colonial powers established control over all of Southeast Asia save for Siam, they encouraged missionaries to establish additional schools to provide education for natives who might be recruited into the colonial service.

Nineteenth-century Western, and especially Protestant missionaries, who went to Southeast Asia were strongly influenced by post-Enlightenment thought. This entailed making a fundamental distinction between knowledge of God and knowledge of nature and society whose laws, while ultimately derived from God, could be understood in their own terms. Although the primary objective of Christian schools in Southeast Asia was the preparation of students to understand and accept the Gospel, they also provided significant instruction in "naturalistic" knowledge. Indeed, missionary teachers, again especially in Protestant schools, deemed it essential to dispel what they considered "superstitious" understandings of the world in order that the true hand of God might be seen as present in the world. Even when they failed in their ultimate goal of conversion, missionary schools often led students to reject or question cosmological perspectives embedded in their traditional cultures and to acquire secular perspectives.

Christian missionaries also introduced what, for Southeast Asia, was the novel idea of providing education for girls as well as for boys (see Watson 1982a:13, 16; and compare Furnivall 1956:128). For example, in the early nineteenth century the Society for Promoting Female Education in the East (SPFEE) and the London Missionary Society (LMS) opened schools for girls in Malacca, Penang, and Singapore (Watson 1982b:78; also see p. 85). Catholic nuns opened similar girls' schools. Both Protestant and Catholic missionaries also established schools for some of the ethnic minorities in the societies in which they worked. This was especially the case in Burma where, from the mid-nineteenth century on, missionaries gave Karen tribal people, who had previously been marginal to Buddhist Burman and Shan civilizations, equal or greater access to Christian schools than the dominant Burmans.

Western missionaries also developed the first presses for printing in indigenous languages, again with the intention of making the Gospel widely available. Once set up, however, these presses were used to produce a variety of works which went far beyond solely Christian scriptures and tracts. By the late nineteenth century the literate public of Southeast Asia, now expanded by those who had gone to missionary schools, had grown significantly. The demand of this public for printed works stimulated the rise of "print capitalism" (see Anderson 1983:66ff) and led to the establishment of numerous small presses which produced newspapers and other nontraditional publications.

Mission school teachers shared one important characteristic with their counterparts in indigenous religious schools, namely their dedication to a sacred vocation. Missionary teachers, like Buddhist monk-teachers and Islamic *kyai* or *guru*, were (and often still are) as concerned with the ultimate salvation of their pupils as with their preparation for places within this world. They thus differ significantly from teachers in state schools today who lack this sacred commitment, and who prepare their students to assume roles within a national and secular rather than a universal and sacred order.

At the outset of the colonial era, Western officials often sought to introduce a Christian-based civilization into those areas they had come to rule. This was true not only of Catholics, such as the Spanish in the Philippines, but also of Protestants, as with the British in Burma, Malaya, and Singapore. Furnivall (1956:123) quotes one British official, H. M. Durand, as having argued for the annexation of Lower Burma on the grounds that "it would have 'a blessed effect by spreading civilization and the Gospel'."

As colonial governments turned their attention away from "pacification" and towards integrating subject populations within uniformly and efficiently administered systems, the need developed for "loyal" natives capable of serving in administrative posts; and as the colonial regimes began to "develop" their domains, they generated yet additional needs for natives with the requisite skills and language competencies to work for construction and trading firms. Even in independent Siam, comparable administrative and development changes generated a need for skilled workers. By the end of the nineteenth century, colonial governments in Southeast Asia, together with the government of Siam had, however, come to realize that the type of training provided through missionary schools was no longer adequate to meet these newly emerging state needs. They therefore began to devise and implement policies whereby the governments themselves assumed responsibility for "the promotion, direction and control of education" (Furnivall 1956:373).

In most Southeast Asian countries—Siam and the American-administered Philippines being exceptions—these policies exacerbated growing divisions between classes and communities. In Vietnam, for example, reforms were instituted in 1917 aimed at creating "a unitary educational system for all Vietnamese" (Kelly 1982:13). These reforms entailed the elimination at the village level of most indigenous schools where students acquired a minimal literacy in Chinese characters. The new "Franco-Vietnamese" schools substituted five years of primary schooling conducted in French. They differed, however, from schools that were open primarily to French citizens, and which were tied directly to the system in France itself. Thus, from the very outset, a division was created between what Furnivall (1956:373), speaking of British Burma and the Netherlands Indies, has called "European schools" and schools for native peoples. In Vietnam, as elsewhere in colonial Southeast Asia, the schools established for natives were not, moreover, integrated within a unitary system. By the early 1920s, the French colonial government was forced to recognize that French-medium schools had proved ineffectual in much of rural Vietnam. As a result, a new system was instituted which "effectively created two separate educational systems: one in Vietnamese, for rural youth; the other in French, destined for urban populations" (Kelly 1982:34–35). Similar developments took place in British Burma and the Netherlands Indies where instruction was provided in what Furnivall (1956:373) terms either "Western" or "vernacular" schools. "Vernacular" schools in Southeast Asia were further differentiated according to which vernacular was used. In Vietnam, for example, Montagnard peoples attended schools in which the medium of instruction was either one of the major tribal languages or French, but not Vietnamese (Hickey 1982:302, 331–34, 413–16). The most significant divisions among "vernacular" schools were in Malaya where authorities allowed schools to teach in Malay, Chinese, or Tamil as well as in English (see Seng 1975).

The history of state-sponsored education in the Philippines and Siam stands in contrast to those of other countries in Southeast Asia during the colonial period. When Americans took control of the Philippines at the end of the nineteenth century they found the educational system primarily in the hands of Catholic priests, most of whom were Spanish. The more than 200 primary schools which existed in 1898 (Chafee et al. 1969:121) served primarily to inculcate in the local populace some basic understanding of Spanish Catholicism. The new American rulers were antagonistic toward the Catholic Church and favored Protestant missions, especially in non-Catholic areas. In 1907 the colonial government created a new school system which, in theory at least, was to provide secular education at the primary level for all the populace. In practice, most of the elite continued to attend Catholic schools while Protestant missionary schools dominated in non-Catholic areas.[6] By the 1920s, however, the American administration had succeeded in ending Catholic domination of the school system. English now became the sole medium of instruction, and the education system was designed to inculcate in the diverse peoples of the islands a sense of common citizenship within the colonial state. The government forced even elite Catholic schools to shape their curricula to fit state-determined ends, especially since many of the graduates of these schools were destined for employment in the colonial bureaucracy. The government also did not, as in other countries, allow schools for expatriates to be separate from the school system for indigenous peoples. In practice, however, the general use of

English as the medium of instruction led to significant differences between those urban schools where teachers had a good command of English and rural schools where they usually did not.

In Siam during the nineteenth century three new types of schools developed along with the traditional monastic schools. Missionaries established a number of schools in different parts of the country. These differed not only according to whether they were Catholic or Protestant but also, because they were set up to serve different ethnic and regional communities, according to the various languages used as the media of instruction. Chinese immigrants set up a second type of school modeled on schools in China and employing teachers from there. The palace established yet another type of school for members of the royal family and certain nobles belonging to the court circle. New Western subjects, especially English language and science, were introduced, in part to prepare these privileged students for study in Western countries. By the end of the nineteenth century, many members of the nobility had come to recognize that the type of education offered at the palace or at mission schools was a prerequisite for gaining access to the new bureaucratic positions which were being created, and thus they began to turn away from the older monastic schools. Although the elite schools in Siam resembled, in certain respects, the "European" schools found in the Southeast Asian colonial dependencies, they were distinguished from them in that Thai—the indigenous language—rather than a European language served as the principal medium of instruction.

At the end of the nineteenth century, King Chulalongkorn and his advisors established a state-wide educational policy for reasons similar to those followed by the rulers of neighboring colonial states (see, in this regard, Wyatt 1969). They based this policy on the premise that all citizens, regardless of their ethnic origin or class background, should receive the same basic education and that this should be given in Thai, the national language. By the 1930s, the Siamese government had established state schools throughout most of the country, and had forced missionary and Chinese schools to follow the state-prescribed curriculum, permitting them to offer religious or Chinese instruction only outside regular school hours. Initially the Siamese government grafted state schools onto traditional monastic schools, but altered the character of the latter by insisting on a curriculum devised for national rather than religious purposes.

By the eve of World War II, state education significantly affected the lives of rural peoples only in Thailand and the Philippines. Throughout the rest of Southeast Asia colonial governments had succeeded in extending state-supported education to only a small part of the population (cf.

Furnivall 1943). Thus, most rural people in the area had not yet begun
to experience any challenge to the understanding of the world that they
derived from their local traditions.

This situation was to change radically in the postwar period. As
the countries of Southeast Asia gained independence, so their governments
adopted educational policies which sought to replace the pluralism of colonial education with uniform national systems that extended to all their
peoples. In time, Burma, Vietnam, Laos, and Cambodia abolished all
schools that were not run by the state. Even where governments—such as
in Thailand—have allowed non-governmental schools (such as those affiliated with religious institutions) to continue, they have made them conform
to government-decreed standards. Although all postcolonial governments,
save that of the Philippines, have dictated that an indigenous, but now "national" language, be substituted for a Western language as the medium of
instruction, none (with the partial exception of Laos[7]) have modeled state
schools on older indigenous forms. Contemporary schools in Southeast
Asia, whether in socialist or capitalist societies, retain a set of fundamental
cultural characteristics that evolved during the colonial period and which
have their roots in Western rather than indigenous concepts of education.
The government school, as Mojares puts it in his chapter, brokers a world
very different from that projected by such folk cultural institutions as Buddhist temple-monasteries, Vietnamese communal halls, Islamic schools, or
Filipino morality plays.

Cultural Molding in State Schools

Like their religious counterparts, state schools everywhere are designed
to impart literacy. Literacy has, of course, long been a primary goal of
indigenous schools in Southeast Asia, although it was often acquired in
languages very different from those taught today. Although instruction in
traditional Buddhist and Islamic schools was oriented toward the inculcation of basic literacy that would enable students to gain access to sacred
texts, such education was not exclusively "other worldly." Religious leaders renowned for their ability to read and interpret sacred texts, especially
those written in the sacred languages of Pali (in the Buddhist case) and
Arabic (in the Islamic case) were believed to have attained magico-religious
powers that could be used for mundane purposes. Those who did not follow the religious life after attending religious schools nevertheless put their
literacy to use as folk medical practitioners, folk drama or shadow play
performers, composers of love poetry and songs, and so on. In other words,
the traditional education provided by Buddhist and Islamic schools, while

instilling an understanding of the sacred cosmos, also served to reproduce valued roles within the local rural society.

In contemporary state schools, students acquire literacy in those languages and writing systems that are deemed "national," to the exclusion of other languages in which literacy was available traditionally. In determining a national language policy, each of the governments of Southeast Asia has had to choose among the many languages spoken by peoples living within its domains. In addition Southeast Asian language policy planners have had to consider what place, if any, should be accorded to written languages associated with indigenous religions and traditional civilizations. Finally, these planners have had to determine what relevance to assign to the linguistic legacy of the colonial past.[8]

In Vietnam, for example, all instruction today, including in minority areas, is carried out in *quoc ngu*, the romanized Vietnamese script, rather than in *chu nom*, a demotic script, or Chinese, which had been used prior to French colonial rule. In Indonesia and Malaysia, state schools use romanized forms of the national languages of Indonesian and Malay, while Islamic schools continue to use *jawi*, a form of Arabic script. In Burma and Thailand, only local literati and scholars now make use of once significant written languages such as Shan and Mon in Burma and Lao and Yuan (northern Thai) in Thailand; the vast majority in these countries now learn only standardized Burmese and Thai. The mandatory use of national languages by all public school students clearly entails a form of cultural dominance even, or perhaps especially, for those Southeast Asians who still acquire literacy in traditional languages.

State schools in contemporary Southeast Asia offer students not only literacy in a language which is often different from the one which they would have traditionally learned to read, but also a view of the world quite different from the one they would have acquired through traditional cultural practices. Although the content varied, throughout Southeast Asia such practices provided a view of a hierarchically structured world in which the place each human occupied was determined by underlying cosmic principles.[9] State school curricula throughout the region are all predicated on a very different assumption, first introduced into the region through missionary schools: that there are laws or patterns or principles structuring certain domains of the world that can be understood independently of one's knowledge of God's or Allah's will or the law of Karma or of the Tao.

Intrinsic to this naturalistic perspective of the world is a notion of time that is quite different from that which underlies everyday life. In everyday life, time flows, punctuated by natural changes such as sunrise and sunset, or social events such as a wedding. In school, time is divisible into discrete units—course periods, school days, school years. School children learn how to "organize" their lives with reference to these units of time. Inkeles's observation is well-taken in this regard: "School starts and stops at fixed times each day. Within the school day there generally is a regular sequence for ordering activities: singing, reading, writing, drawing, all have their scheduled and usually invariant time. Teachers generally work according to plan. ... The pupils may have no direct knowledge of the plan, but its influence palpably pervades the course of their work through school day and school year" (Inkeles 1974:21).[10]

Numeracy is also intrinsic to a naturalistic perspective. Although manipulation of numbers is an ancient skill, numeracy entails something rather different than the method of manipulation associated with rituals or even found in indigenous forms of schooling. Traditional manipulation was often numerological; that is, particular numbers were assumed to have an intrinsic quality about them. Buddhists, for example, associate the number three with "The Three Gems" (the Buddha, the Dhamma, and the Sangha) and the three aspects of existence (birth, pain, and death) that one seeks to transcend by following the Path. The Path itself is thought to be divided into three parts (morality, mental concentration, and wisdom). When goods are offered in a ritual, a Buddhist will often think not of simple addition, but in terms of threes and multiples of threes. All traditional cultures contain similar ideas. Modern schools inculcate skills of numeracy which assume that the principles of manipulation are the same no matter to what domain of experience the numbers apply.

Equipped with a naturalistic perspective which entails seeing the world as predicated on underlying patterns in nature, organizing action according to consciously-recognized temporal divisions, and manipulating experience in terms of principles of numeracy, humans can control or be made to control the consequences of their work. This potential for humans to participate "actively ... in natural life in order to transform and socialize it more and more deeply and extensively," as Antonio Gramsci (1971:34) observed, became the basic educational principle of compulsory education. Every government seeks through its educational policies to ensure that its citizens will work in ways which produce and reproduce the social order which it rules.

The World of the School

In state schools, students are taught to think of the world they will enter as adults as having continuity with "a suitable historic past" (Hobsbawm 1983:1), that is, a past which they share with others as members of the same "nation." It is now well recognized that nation-building entails the promotion of an interpretation of the past designed to suit the interests of the dominant elite as the legitimate national past for all those living within the boundaries of the state. Compulsory education is arguably the most effective tool used by governments for inculcating in citizens a sense of national consciousness. Students appropriate an understanding of "their" national past from school texts and from participation in such "invented traditions" (Hobsbawm and Ranger 1983) as school rituals and celebrations of national holidays.

State schools propose "national" worlds characterized by distinctive statewide divisions of labor. In this regard I find especially pertinent Gramsci's observations, and the theories of those who have followed him, about the way in which schooling prepares a person for creating or recreating himself through work. Any system of formal state-sponsored education entails the establishment of a uniform system of credentials which are distributed among all citizens (compare, in this connection, Bourdieu and Passeron 1977 and Bourdieu and Boltanski 1977). Depending on the credentials a person has acquired—for example, completion of the lowest or compulsory level of education, obtaining a secondary school certificate, or gaining a university degree—he or she will be considered qualified or not qualified to seek access to particular occupations.

Because rural people recognize that the credentials acquired through schooling have state-wide salience, they often see formal education as their major means for achieving upward mobility. But while a few members of poor rural families in Southeast Asia have succeeded in moving up the social ladder after attaining higher levels of education, the vast majority find themselves at the bottom of a social order structured on educational attainment. The only jobs outside of their local communities open to those with the lowest level of required formal schooling are proletarian ones.

One of the most striking changes in social structure that has come about with the introduction of compulsory education has been that females as well as males have been given access to schooling. Although such education has by no means undermined traditional patterns of male dominance, there is no question but that formal education has enabled Southeast Asian women to visualize a world very different from that known by their grandmothers. Southeast Asian women have entered many new job areas, with school teaching being certainly one of the most significant. The female school teacher, who is becoming especially common in Thailand, Vietnam, and the Philippines, provides a very different role model for village girls

than any traditionally known in Southeast Asia. This said, several contributors to this book note that, even today, women teachers are not vested
with the authority held by traditional male literati such as Buddhist monks,
Islamic teachers, Catholic priests, or Confucian scholars.

Whether filled by women or men, the role of state school teacher
is itself a wholly new status. Whereas Buddhist monks, Islamic school
teachers (*kyai* in Java, *guru* in Malaya), Confucian literati in Vietnam,
or Catholic priests in the Philippines drew their moral authority from
tradition, teachers embody for villagers, and especially for village children,
the authority of the state as it is encountered on a day-by-day basis. Yet,
while local teachers speak with the authority of the state in instructing their
pupils, they are such lowly members of the state system that they lack
any ability to influence policy makers on how to adapt state-determined
curricula to local cultures. Throughout Southeast Asia, educational policy-
making and curriculum construction are highly centralized. Local teachers
are permitted almost no freedom to choose from among alternative texts or
to adapt instruction to local conditions. Teachers in local state schools
have been trained in normal schools or teachers' colleges according to
standardized programs designed to ensure that they will teach the same
curriculum no matter where they happen to be posted.

Rural teachers are often acutely aware of the tensions between local
traditions and the "national" culture they are employed to impart. Although there are some cases, such as in Malay-speaking villages in southern Thailand, where the village school teacher is truly an outsider and thus
an unambiguous representative of the state, the more typical case is the
teacher who comes from a rural background, receives teacher-training in
a town, and then returns to a nearby village to become a teacher. Some
teachers have sought to resolve the tension inherent in their role by accen-
tuating their position as government representatives; others have turned
in an opposite direction, and a few have even joined movements opposed
to the state. Most, however, remain betwixt and between, confronting on
an almost daily basis but never fully resolving situations which reflect the
tensions between national and local views of the world.

Reshaping Local Worlds

Although state systems of education have undoubtedly altered Southeast Asian villagers' worlds, nowhere has the state school preempted all
processes of cultural transmission through which rural (or urban) children
learn to orient themselves toward the practical world they will enter as
adults. For villagers, the social order they learn about in school is only one

of the "proposed" orders they encounter while growing up. Instead of state schools, some rural people continue to attend traditional religious schools, such as the *pesantren/pondoks* found in parts of Java and elsewhere in Indonesia, in northern Malaysia, and even in southern Thailand, or Buddhist monastic schools found in parts of Burma. Most rural people continue to participate in religious rituals presided over by local *imams*, monks, or priests. Even in Vietnam, where the state has unquestionably been more successful than in any other Southeast Asian country in curbing the influence of non-state institutions, villagers continue, as do their counterparts elsewhere in the region, to derive alternative views of the world from a folk culture transmitted in the form of songs, stories, and festivals.

Each of the contributors to this volume discusses the dialectical relationship between local or religious cultures and national culture as mediated through state schools. Despite the very different political systems found in Southeast Asia, there is some degree of similarity, from country to country, in the culture introduced through state schools. However, there still is no way to predict how a local social world may be transformed by the interaction between the world of the state, as proposed by schools, and the local worlds projected by traditional rituals, folklore, or religious schools. It is possible, however, to conclude that everywhere villagers take an active role in determining the outcome of the process.

Notes

1 In the language of the time, those who were to be transformed were often referred to as "human resources," and the quality to be maximized
as "human potential." For example, Wong (1973:22), speaks of the
withdrawal of students from school before completion of compulsory
primary schooling in Malaysia, Singapore, Thailand, Indonesia, and
the Philippines as "a tremendous waste of human potential." In this
language Wong explicitly echoes that of a 1967 UNESCO report, *The
Problem of Educational Wastage.*

2 The Southeast Asia Development Advisory Group (SEADAG) was created in the 1960s by the United States Agency for International Development with the intention of drawing on the advice, and sometimes
the criticism, of scholars who were either Southeast Asian specialists or
experts in development fields. SEADAG was administered by the Asia
Society in New York. The conference brought together about a dozen
social scientists, a number of whom were themselves Southeast Asians,
USAID personnel, and SEADAG administrators. For a summary of
Inkeles's position at the conference, see Southeast Asia Development
Advisory Group (n.d., esp. p. 26).

3 Martin Carnoy's (1982) essay, "Education, Economy and the State,"
provides a good review of this literature. See also Carnoy (1984).

4 Institutionalized schooling is one type of what I have termed a "work
of culture," that is, a structured process of cultural learning through
which individuals acquire pragmatically coherent meaning for some
domain of experience (see Keyes 1985). For a similar view of schooling
as a distinctive process of cultural learning, see Wexler (1982, esp. pp.
280–81).

5 In the Philippines, at least prior to the middle of the nineteenth century, Catholic schools were more comparable to indigenous schools
found elsewhere in Southeast Asia than they were to the type of
missionary schools introduced in conjunction with the expansion of
British, French, Dutch, and American empires.

6 See, in this connection, Bentley's (1989) paper on the relationship
between Protestant missionary work and government education among
the Maranao in the early years of American rule.

7 On trips to Laos in 1989 and 1990 I learned that many, perhaps most,
rural schools in lowland Lao communities are still located in Buddhist
temple-monasteries, and monks are still employed as teachers in some

of these schools. These monk-teachers are required, however, to teach a modern rather than traditional religious curriculum.

[8] On the development of national languages in Indonesia and Malaysia, see Wong (1971), Rafferty (1983) and Mead (1988). On the relationship between national and local languages used in schools in Thailand and Cambodia, see Kalab (1982).

[9] The interconnectedness of rural social structure and religious cosmology has been well described by Tambiah in his 1970 study of a rural northeastern Thai village.

[10] I do not, however, follow Inkeles in the next line in the passage quoted: "Thus, principles directly embedded in the daily routine of the school teach the *virtue* of planning ahead and the importance of maintaining a regular schedule" (Inkeles 1974: 21, emphasis added). Inkeles unfortunately couples significant insights into the nature of the schooling process with ethnocentric ideas about what schooling *should* produce.

References

Anderson, Benedict. *Imagined Communities: Reflections on the Origin and Spread of Nationalism.* London: Verso, 1983.

Bentley, G. Carter. "Implicit Evangelism: American Education among the Muslim Maranao." *Filipinas: A Journal of Philippine Studies,* 12(1989):73–96.

Bourdieu, Pierre, and L. Boltanski. "Formal Qualifications and Occupational Hierarchies." In *Reorganizing Education,* ed. by E. J. King, 61–69. London and Beverly Hills: Sage Publications. 1977.

Bourdieu, Pierre, and Jean-Claude Passeron. *Reproduction in Education, Society and Culture.* London and Beverly Hills: Sage Publications, 1977.

Carnoy, Martin. Education, Economy and the State. In *Cultural and Economic Reproduction In Education,* ed. by Michael W. Apple, 79–126. London: Routledge & Kegan Paul, 1982

——. *The State and Political Theory.* Princeton: Princeton University Press, 1984.

Chafee, Frederic H., et al. *Area Handbook for the Philippines.* Washington, D. C.: U. S. Government Printing Office, 1969.

Furnivall, J. S. *Educational Progress in Southeast Asia.* New York: Institute for Pacific Relations, 1943.

——. *Colonial Policy and Practice: A Comparative Study of Burma and Netherlands India.* New York: New York University Press, 1956. (First published, Cambridge: Cambridge University Press in cooperation with the International Secretariat, Institute of Pacific Relations, 1948.)

Giroux, Henry A. "Theories of Reproduction and Resistance in the New Sociology of Education: A Critical Analysis." *Harvard Educational Review,* 53.3(1983):257–93.

Gramsci, Antonio. *Selections from the Prison Notebooks,* ed. and tr. by Quintin Hoare and Geoffrey Nowell Smith. New York: International Publishers, 1971

Hickey, Gerald Cannon. *Sons of the Mountains: Ethnohistory of the Vietnamese Highlands to 1954.* New Haven: Yale University Press, 1982

Hobsbawm, Eric. "Introduction: Inventing Traditions." In *The Invention of Tradition,* ed. by Eric Hobsbawm and Terence Ranger, 1–14. Cambridge: Cambridge University Press, 1983.

——, and Terence Ranger, eds. *The Invention of Tradition.* Cambridge: Cambridge University Press, 1983

Ileto, Reynaldo Clemeña. *Pasyon and Revolution: Popular Movements in the Philippines, 1840–1910.* Quezon City: Ateneo de Manila University Press, 1979

Inkeles, Alex. "The School as a Context for Modernization." In *Education and Individual Modernity In Developing Countries,* ed. by Alex Inkeles and Donald B. Holsinger, 7–23. Leiden: E. J. Brill, 1974.

Kalab, M. "Ethnicity and the Language Used as Medium of Instruction in Schools." *Southeast Asian Journal of Social Science,* 10.1(1982):96–102.

Keyes, Charles F. "The Interpretive Basis of Depression." In *Culture and Depression,* ed. by Arthur Kleinman and Byron J. Good, 153–74. Berkeley and Los Angeles: University of California Press, 1985.

——. "Ambiguous Gender: Male Initiation in a Northern Thai Buddhist Society." In *Gender and Religion: On the Complexity of Symbols,* ed. by Caroline Bynum, Stevan Harrell, and Paula Richman, 66–96. Boston: Beacon Press, 1986.

Mead, Richard. *Malaysia's National Language Policy and the Court System.* New Haven: Yale University Southeast Asian Studies, Monograph No. 30, 1988.

Rafferty, Ellen. "National Language Ability: A Sociolinguistic Survey in East Java, Indonesia." *Journal of Southeast Asian Studies,* 14.1:34–48, 1983.

Seng Loh Fook, Philip. *The Seeds of Separatism: Educational Policy in Malaya, 1874–1940.* Kuala Lumpur: Oxford University Press, 1975.

Simmons, John. "The Political Economy of Education for Village Development." In *Village Viability In Contemporary Society,* ed. by Priscilla Copeland Reining and Barbara Lenkerd, Boulder, CO: Westview Press for the American Association for the Advancement of Science, AAAS Selected Symposium, 34, 1980.

Southeast Asia Development Advisory Group. *Education and Human Resource Development Panel Seminar.* New York: Southeast Asia Development Advisory Group of the Asia Society, SEADAG Reports, nd. (The conference was held from November 30–December 2, 1972.)

Tambiah, Stanley, J. *Buddhism and the Spirit Cults in North-East Thailand.* Cambridge: Cambridge University Press, Cambridge Studies in Social Anthropology, 2, 1970.

Watson, Keith. "Colonialism and Educational Development." In *Education in the Third World*, ed. by Keith Watson, 1–46. London and Canberra: Croom Helm, 1982a.

———. "The Contribution of Mission Schools to Educational Development in Southeast Asia." In *Education in the Third World*, ed. by Keith Watson, 71–87. London and Canberra: Croom Helm, 1982b.

Wexler, Philip. "Structure, Text, and Subject: A Critical Sociology of School Knowledge." In *Cultural and Economic Reproduction in Education*, ed. by Michael W. Apple, 275–303. London: Routledge and Kegan Paul, 1982.

Wong Hoy Kee, Francis. "The Development of a National Language in Indonesia and Malaysia." *Comparative Education*, 7.2(1971):73–80.

———. *Comparative Studies in Southeast Asian Education*. Kuala Lumpur: Heinemann Educational Books, 1973.

Wyatt, David K. *The Politics of Reform in Thailand*. New Haven: Yale University Press, 1969.

THE JAVANESE *PESANTREN*:
BETWEEN ELITE AND PEASANTRY

Sidney Jones

Introduction

Religious in nature, located in an isolated rural area, and central to the maintenance of a traditional belief system, the *pesantren* is in many ways the archetypical traditional educational institution. Like traditional schools throughout Southeast Asia, the *pesantren* has suffered from the expansion of a secular state school system and the popular demand for better and higher education. Enrollment has steadily fallen in all but the largest *pesantrens*. To survive, many *pesantrens* are either having to approximate the model of a secular school to retain their traditional clientele, or attract a new clientele by becoming alternatively a finishing school for girls, a halfway house for juvenile delinquents (see, for example, Castles 1966:37), a Sufi retreat for old women, a community development center, or the Muslim equivalent of "vacation Bible school" for urban middle-class youth. Even so, *pesantrens* still absorb a significant proportion of the school-age population, as high as 20 percent in the Muslim strongholds of East Java (see Geertz 1960).

Given the fate of traditional religious schools elsewhere in the region, it is remarkable that the *pesantrens* have managed to survive for as long as they have. Their longevity suggests that the impact of a secular government school system on traditional schools varies with four factors, namely: the degree to which the school has important non-educational functions in society; the degree to which the school becomes linked to the identity of a particular social group and the perceived power of that group; the degree to which educational pluralism is permitted by the state and the degree of coercion it is willing to bring to bear to make attendance at state schools compulsory; and lastly the degree to which employment for "graduates" of traditional schools exist. In this chapter, after a brief note on the historical development of the *pesantren*, I will analyze each of these factors with an emphasis on the first.

The Historical Development of the Pesantren

The history of the *pesantren* goes back to Java's pre-Islamic past, to the Hindu-Buddhist *asrama* where disciples would gather to seek enlightenment from a master. As easily as Java absorbed Islam into its syncretic religious tradition, the *pesantren* changed faiths without changing functions, and became a center of Islamic mysticism where a *kyai*—a Muslim scholar, Sufi leader, and wise man—would lead his male followers in meditation and study. The function of a *pesantren*, until well into the eighteenth century, was less one of formal schooling than of progression through stages of knowledge under the guidance of a *guru* until the "secrets of being" were revealed (see Anderson 1972a:43). It was through seeking out a well-known *kyai* in the isolated, monastic, retreat-like atmosphere of a *pesantren* and pledging absolute obedience to him that an individual would have the opportunity to be initiated into the select group of savants who held the key to access to the divine and the supernatural.

Throughout the nineteenth and twentieth centuries, the mystic aura of the *pesantren* and the power of the *kyai* remained strong, but the former's function as a center of formal schooling gradually assumed greater importance. One factor involved in this change was the spread of printing facilities in Java, which made religious texts much more widely available for study. A second was the increased flow of Javanese pilgrims to Mecca, an indirect result of the opening of the Suez Canal in 1869, and the consequent rise in the number of trained religious scholars desirous of opening *pesantrens*. A final factor was the increasing popular demand for education, and the failure of the Dutch colonial administration to open schools for the indigenous population in any systematic fashion until 1915—and then only for children of aristocrats.[1] Until the early 1900s, the *pesantren* was, for all practical purposes, the only educational institution available to the Javanese, so it was to these rural boarding schools that children of nobility, entrepreneurs and traders, and wealthy peasants were sent. By definition a boarding school, the *pesantren* drew students from outside the village in which it was located, in keeping with the Islamic tradition of wandering in quest of knowledge.[2] The expense of sending a son to a distant village, providing for his upkeep, and foregoing his labor in the fields generally kept a *pesantren* education beyond the reach of all but the relatively wealthy (Dhofir 1980:16–18).[3]

Toward the end of the nineteenth century, growing divisions between the *priyayi* or aristocracy and pious Muslims (and within the pious Muslim community itself) and the emergence of new school systems corresponding to ideological and cultural divisions narrowed the appeal of the *pesantren* to those traditionalist Muslims who later formed a social organization-cum-political party called the Nahdlatul Ulama (NU).[4] By the 1920s the *pesantren* had become the traditionalist Muslim institution *par excellence*, and the overwhelming majority of *pesantrens* throughout Indonesia are today still affiliated with NU.

The 1920s also witnessed the adoption of the three major reforms in *pesantren* education, the direct result of competition between Dutch schools and Muslim reformist schools. The first was the opening of some *pesantrens* to female *santris* (*pesantren* students), beginning with Den Anyar, a well-known *pesantren* in Jombang, East Java, in 1924. There was no coeducation, however, and females and males were kept strictly segregated.

A second reform was the adoption of a classroom-style education for less-advanced students, based on the *madrasah* or Islamic school in Mecca[5] and the Western-style schools in Java that were steadily growing in number. The classroom system was used in addition to, not in place of, the two traditional methods of *pesantren* instruction.[6]

A third innovation was the adoption of a partially secular curriculum with instruction in mathematics, the Indonesian language, and other subjects. Not all *pesantrens* adopted this reform and those that did became set apart, so that today *pesantrens* are divided into two groups, the *salafiyyah* or "pure" *pesantrens* which teach only religious subjects, and the *khalafiyyah pesantrens* with a more diverse curriculum.

The Pesantren and Social Cohesion

The *pesantren* has contributed to the social cohesion of Javanese Muslims at two different levels. It has helped sustain vertical linkages between elite and peasantry at the local level, and historically, it has been the key institution for maintaining the group identity of traditionalist Muslims throughout Java in the face of competing cultural traditions.

The Integration of Elite and Peasantry

Both the agrarian elite and the peasantry have had a stake in the *pesantren*. The peasantry has derived a measure of economic and spiritual security, the elite a legitimation of their social status through the values that *pesantren* instruction upholds. Both rely on the *pesantren* and its leader to sustain the cycle of Islamic rituals that reinforces the social order. The *kyai* in turn depends on both elite and peasantry for his own reputation and economic well-being. To establish a *pesantren*, the *kyai* needs to attract students, generally the children of the agrarian elite. Only after the *pesantren* begins to grow does the community begin to attribute charismatic qualities and supernatural powers to the *kyai* (see Dhofir 1980). A reputation for such powers leads to an increase in students, and the cycle continues.

For the elite, the *pesantren* manages to instill values which accentuate the primacy of trading and farming, both through the curriculum and through the personal example of the *kyai*. Unlike Western schools where the focus on literacy first in Dutch and then in Indonesian was tied directly to the prospect of employment in the state bureaucracy, the content of the traditional *pesantren* curriculum was less important than the norms it conveyed.

The *pesantren* ethic of *watak mandiri*, or standing on one's own, placed a higher value on self-employment than on working in a bureaucracy.[7] In a *pesantren*, at least in the eyes of *santris* themselves, there were no superiors or subordinates, only each *santri* striving to improve himself individually, equal in status to every other *santri* (Asjari 1967:103).[8] The *pesantren* ethic of self-sufficiency was supported by studies of *hadith*, the sayings and actions of Mohammed, some of which were used to emphasize the value of working with one's own hands or the value of trade; of *akhlaq* or ethics; and of *fara'id* or inheritance law which implicitly emphasized the need to accumulate land so that one would have enough to divide among one's heirs. Furthermore the *pesantren* instilled the principle that one's entire life should be an act of *ibadat*, or worship. Self-employed, one was far less likely to be subject to the pressures and temptations that would lead one to stray from the path of total devotion to Allah.

Another way in which the traditional *pesantren* stressed commitment to the land and which in the process reinforced ties between the *pesantren* and the surrounding community was the tradition of *santris* hiring themselves out as agricultural labor to help contribute toward their upkeep. The practice was so common that "*pesantren*" came to have another meaning: "an agreement by which a limited right to harvest is granted to designated workers" in return for their performance of certain pre-harvest tasks for which no remuneration was made—hoeing, weeding, and transplanting (Wiradi 1978:3).

The Islamic precepts of self-sufficiency only confirmed and strengthened a long-standing antipathy of the *pesantrens* and their leaders toward the bureaucracy, and by extension, the ruling power. This antipathy went as far back as the latter part of the seventeenth century when the rulers of major Javanese states, like Mataram, allied with the Dutch in the latter's efforts to gain a stranglehold over north coast Javanese trade. Since this meant encroaching on lands held by the orthodox gentry, traders and landholders joined forces with *kyais* to resist (Pigeaud 1976:89–90). The infidel colonial rulers were despised as much for their religion as for their economic policies, and by the end of the nineteenth century, when the *priyayi* had become less traditional aristocrats than administrative and political agents of the Dutch (Sutherland 1979), *kyai* antipathy was directed against them as well.

A *pesantren* education also encouraged the accumulation of capital. Thoughts of the *santris* were never allowed to stray too far from the glory of going on the *haj*, the pilgrimage to Mecca, and the *haj* required savings, usually in the form of land investment.[9] Not only was the *haj* the culmination of a pious *santri*'s life, marking fulfillment of one of his obligations to Allah, not only was it a subject of Islamic law courses, but the mystique of the *haj* permeated the *pesantren*. Arabian robes, shoulder cloths, prayer-rugs, wall hangings, and books were prized above all other possessions. Furthermore, by the early part of this century, many of the parents of *santris* could be counted among the *haji*, and they as well as the *kyai* himself served as models for the *santri* to emulate. The focus on savings as opposed to conspicuous consumption of the *priyayi* marked another difference between the two groups (Geertz 1965).

Finally, the *pesantren* reinforced the idea of acquiring *pahala* or religious merit through religious works. Of the various forms of bequests or donations, land was most highly valued, through religious endowments (*wakf*), bequests (*wasiat*), voluntary alms (*sodaqah*) and so on. It was through such donations that the *kyai* frequently became one of the largest landowners of a village. The stress on religious merit thus served as an incentive to give either wealth on the part of the rich, or labor on land of *kyais* or *hajis* on the part of the poor. Either way, the rich were the beneficiaries. The *pesantren* thus served to legitimize the Muslim agrarian elite's economic position as one being sanctioned by Allah.

The Pesantren and the Peasantry

If education was for the elite, then social, political, and spiritual security were for the peasants. The authority of the *kyai* as teacher for the *santri* was of an entirely different order than his authority as ritual specialist for the villagers around him.

As curer, as provider of magical amulets, as diviner of the future, and even, at times, as sorcerer, the local kijaji comes to play a role not strictly Islamic, but one fused with the broader and quite heterodox status of *dukun*, the Javanese 'folk magician.' The kijaji thus brings together the general moral doctrine of Islam and the specific animistic notions of local tradition, the fragmented, barely conceptualized, practical religion of the ordinary peasant, the two playing into one another in such a way that his competence

in the first guarantees his effectiveness in the second. (Geertz
1960:239)

It was the *kyai's* reputed magical powers and capacity to confer in-
vulnerabilty through Quranic incantations combined with his antipathy toward the bureaucracy that made him a natural leader of the peasantry in
the agrarian rebellions that flared up in Java throughout the nineteenth and
early twentieth centuries. The rebellions are indicative of the common political and economic grievances of rich and poor peasants during this time,
for an increasing burden of rural taxation hurt both. In addition, the *santri*
population of a *pesantren* always dropped sharply in times of hardship as
the expenses became too great or the young men were needed to help out
at home. Hardship for the peasantry thus frequently put the survival of
the *pesantren* on the line. *Kyai*-led rebellions were frequently initiated by
the *kyai*, who then mobilized his following (Kartodirdjo 1972). It was not
usually a case of peasants banding together and approaching the *kyai* for
his support. At the same time, despite the *kyai's* own wealth relative to
those he led, he was immune from protests against the power structure,
local or national, since he was clearly outside it. Bitterness at economic
distress was far more likely to be directed against the Dutch, the *priyayi*
as their agents, or the Chinese.

The existence of the *pesantren* and the security it symbolized were
particularly important for the peasantry in times of societal or personal
crisis.

When society itself succumbed to chaos and disintegration, the
counter-institutions of the *pesantren* and the *djago*[10] band offered a model
of a transcendent order. As the meaning of the regular life-arc was undermined by war, oppression, or economic disaster, the asceticism and elan
within *pesantren*-like communities took on a general significance unimag-
inable in times of peace. Traditional deviant aspects of *santri* existence
—sexual abstinence, fraternal solidarity, selfless devotion, nomadic wandering, and dealings with the supernatural—were now seen as in harmony
with the times. The sense that everything was in suspension while disorder
raged in the cosmos seemed to be reflected in the suspended quality of the
pesantren's inner order. The society itself became the larger *pesantren*, in
which the *pesantren* life-style assumed the mode of normality and necessity.
(Anderson 1972b:10)

Another form of security was provided by the Sufi orders, or *tarekat*.
The *pesantren* was traditionally the center of a Sufi order, and by the turn
of the century most Sufi initiates seem to have been old people, rich and
poor alike, seeking to ready themselves for death by "cleansing their hearts"

through initiation into Sufi lore and removal from the material world.[11] The *pesantren* thus served to mediate not just between rich and poor, the divine and the mundane, but also between life and death.

Finally the *pesantren* provided social security of the traditional patronage variety, with the *kyai* lending sums of money as needed to villagers for ritual occasions, especially weddings and funerals. For the latter the *pesantren* also possessed the burial equipment needed, and this in addition to the *kyai*'s attendance, was of great importance in the village. For the destitute, the *pesantren* could usually provide some form of menial employment in exchange for meals; for travellers and traders it provided lodging. It also had the resources necessary to provide what has been termed "collective economic insurance" (Scott and Kerkvliet 1977:444). It alone could maintain the ritual order—the village could be cleansed yearly of evil spirits, the Muslim holidays celebrated with due pomp, the ritual feasts or *selametan* held as needed. Even if, as was frequently the case, the poorest of the village could not attend or were not invited to *pesantren* celebrations, there was widespread acceptance of the belief that *kyais*, and to a lesser extent, *hajis*, were closer to God, and that if their voices and requests for blessings, favors, or forgiveness were heard, the whole village would benefit.

The Pesantren and the Community: An East Javanese Example

Interests of elite and peasantry converge in the celebration of Islamic ritual in which the *pesantren* plays a key role. An example from a coeducational but otherwise traditional institution in East Java can serve as an illustration. The *pesantren* is Pondok Mayan, located on the banks of the Brantas River in Kediri, East Java, one of eighty-three such schools in the Kediri regency.

Mayan became the center for the village celebration of Id ul-Adha, the second most important holiday in the Muslim calendar which commemorates the prophet Ibrahim's sacrifice of his son. Before the ceremony, at which animals are ritually slaughtered and the meat distributed among members of the community, there was an informal competition among local mosques and *pesantrens* to see which would receive the most animals for sacrifice, from donors desirous of the religious merit to be had—fifty times the merit of a donation on an ordinary day. Pondok Mayan received nine goats from wealthy villagers, four to start with and five more after intensive soliciting.

Beginning at *maghrib* the night before, the *santris* started taking turns chanting the *takbir*, the repetition of "*Allahu Akbar, Allahu Akbar,*" as children and adult men of the village piled into trucks and minibuses and made the rounds of the villages, also chanting. The chanting continued through the night, and the generator was left on at the *pesantren*, keeping the lightbulbs lit and the *santris* awake. Early in the morning, over 100 village men gathered in the main mosque for morning prayer, with each head of household bringing a large metal bowl filled with rice and other dishes, and covered with a banana leaf. After prayers the food was brought to the kitchen where neighbors and the usual friends of the *pesantren* who provided volunteer labor for all major occasions divided it up into individual banana-leaf packets. About twenty women came to pray with the wife of the *kyai*, or *nyai*, and afterwards sat near the kitchen with her to share a meal. As soon as everyone had finished eating, the women who had come to pray departed, leaving behind their barely touched portions which were then rewrapped in banana-leaves and distributed to the village orphans along with small cash contributions.

Only after those who had gathered for the prayers had departed did the ritual butchering take place. As each major part of the body was cut up in the kitchen yard by a group of village men and senior *santris*, it was brought to the kitchen where the women would divide it into smaller parts. Choice meat, as from the leg, was cut into quarter-kilogram portions (*seperempat*) and wrapped in banana leaf. Bony parts were given to a young male *santri* who sat on the floor with a miniature butcher block and chopped up leg bones, ribs, and so on. Packets were then made up of one chunk of bone, some of the less choice meat, a piece of skin, and some of the innards. These were wrapped in banana leaf and again in teak leaf to distinguish them from the *seperempat*. The *nyai* had drawn up a list the day before of who was to receive the packets. There were over five hundred names on the list, and the packets were carefully counted as they came off the *santri* assembly line—butcher, chop, assemble, wrap. Every family in the hamlet surrounding the *pesantren* would get a share. Beyond that, it was friends of the *pesantren*—twenty-five families in another hamlet, fifteen families in the next village over, a few families elsewhere. This was not a ceremony to distribute food to the poor, but to distribute it to the religious community under the *kyai's* authority, with the scope of authority being implicitly defined by how far the meat would reach. Thus, "everyone" got a teak-leaf packet, but the *seperempat* went to those families who, because of wealth, position, or religious learning, were considered to be "almost-equals" of the *kyai* and *nyai*. This included all the local political officials.

In addition to the packets of meat, over 100 boat-shaped banana leaf packets containing yellow rice, some meat, and young jackfruit cooked in coconut milk were handed out to village children who swarmed around the kitchen door. A special meal was served in the evening to village women who flooded the *pesantren* for the weekly meeting of the Muslim party's women's association.

Several aspects of the ceremony are noteworthy. First, it served to reaffirm ties between the *pesantren* and the community around it, and in the distribution of meat, it functioned to demonstrate the boundaries of the *kyai*'s influence. Had the *pesantren* managed to solicit only two goats, with the distribution not even serving the entire hamlet, the *kyai* would obviously have been a less powerful person.

Second, the ceremony took place at the *pesantren* rather than elsewhere in the village, largely because the *pesantren* had the largest mosque. Solidarity of the *ummat*, or community of believers, expressed in numbers of people, is important on these occasions, and a small prayer-house would have been inadequate. Locally influential *kyais* without *pesantren* or with only very small *pondok* who otherwise would be treated as social equals of the *kyai* were, in this case, obliged to become part of the *kyai's* sphere of influence. Here it was clearly control over resources, in this case the mosque, that strengthened the *kyai's* authority.

Third, in donating their goats to the *pesantren*, the wealthy villagers were implicitly assigning the right of attribution of social rank to the *kyai* and *nyai*. It was they who redistributed the meat, they who determined who would receive the *seperempat*, and they who were thus clearly at the top of the status hierarchy.

Finally, the importance of food and food preparation underscores the role of the *nyai*, not only in this festival but on virtually any occasion involving the *kyai* and his followers where food is exchanged in some fashion—*santri* parents or other guests bringing in agricultural produce and in turn receiving a meal, or the ritual feasts, *selametan*, which are the major integrating force within Javanese society. One consequence of the *kyai's* having his own personal institution is that he exercises his authority through the structure of a household. He receives guests in his home, not in an office or mosque or school. His children are village children, his wife has the influence with the village women—and men—that he has, sometimes more so. Within the *pesantren*, the *kyai* may be a one-man show, but the *pesantren* is integrated into the community by virtue, in part, of its being a family unit.

The Pesantren and the Javanese Muslim Community

If the *pesantren* helped maintain the cohesion of the community at the local level, it was also instrumental in maintaining the cohesion of the Javanese *ummat* or community of believers more generally. The *pesantren* held the *ummat* together over time and space through the bond established between *kyai* and *santri*. This was particularly important given the absence of any focal point of Muslim culture in Java. There was no Muslim ruler, no predominant university center like al-Azhar in Cairo, no single shrine that could make one city the gathering place for pilgrims, no single authoritative Islamic office that could issue *fatwa* or decrees in the name of all Indonesian Muslims. There was only the network of *pesantrens*, with each school the personal property of its own, very independent *kyai*.

Just as in Islamic thought where the prosperity of the *ummat*, the Muslim community, depends on each individual fulfilling his obligations toward Allah, the cohesion of the orthodox landowning elite came to depend, in part, on a network of individual obligations of *santri* to *kyai* that endured long after the *santri* had left the *pesantren*—indeed, long after the *kyai* was dead.

The extension over time and space of this bond created a network, ideal for maintaining a society with no single territorial base and one interspersed with opposing cultural variants. Over time, the bonds were extended by means of intellectual genealogies —Z studied with *Kyai* Y who studied with *Kyai* X, back to one of the nine saints (Wali Songo) who are credited with having introduced Islam to Java, and through them back to Mohammed. By virtue of being the last link in the chain, Z not only became firmly anchored in the Javanese Islamic tradition, but his perceived obligations to his *kyai* had inherited the *barokah* or divine favor of the Prophet.

Over space, which was probably more important for social integration, the bonds were multiplied by means of *santri* mobility and the tradition of wandering from *pesantren* to *pesantren*. This meant that every *santri* developed bonds of loyalty to five or six *kyais* in different places, a system which furthered social integration at the same time it discouraged the emergence of any single leader.

The network was all the more effective in integrating the elite because the bond could be broken only by the death of the *santri*, not of the *kyai*. Ceremonies such as the *selametan haul*, a ritual feast in memory of the dead *kyai*, would attract hundreds, even thousands, of his former *santris*, and reinforce the power of the bond. If anything, the hold of the *kyai* over the *santri* became greater in death, for then the *kyai* was perceived as being better able to intercede for his followers with the Prophet. One result of the continuity of the bond in death is that whoever is in a position of authority is simultaneously in a position of deference, giving rise to an infinitely expanding system of dyadic bonds, such that for every individual there is always someone above and someone below.

Once the *santri* left the *pesantren*, his debt to his former *kyai* was in theory unlimited. The diffusion of *santris* that made the bond so important in holding *santri* society together also made it impossible for the obligations to be anything but unspecified and voluntary. This was no patron-client relationship. The *santri* was not required to pay anything to the *kyai*, the *kyai* was not obliged to offer any specific form of social security, although implicit in the bond was a promise of security in the next world if the *santri* was faithful in honoring his debt to the *kyai* throughout his (the *santri's*) lifetime. The bond was rather latent and contingent: *if* the *kyai* should ever ask a favor directly of the *santri*, the latter would be duty-bound to oblige. The importance of the *kyai-santri* bond, then, was to provide a sense of common background and common obligation to a geographically dispersed group of people, and to make religious obligation, rather than economic interests, the principal unifying factor among them.

Why the Pesantren Survived

The *pesantren* survived as an educational institution long after its counterparts in other Asian societies began to succumb to the appeal or imposition by the state of secular education. One factor contributing to this survival was clearly the role of the *pesantren* in binding traditionalist Muslim society both horizontally, linking together a wealthy agrarian elite, and vertically, across socioeconomic classes. The value of a *pesantren* education in that society remained high, as long as it was viewed as one way of resisting the challenge from competing cultural traditions and political ideologies. Unlike in Thailand where the move to replace traditional Buddhist monastic schools with secular education came from a monarchy and political elite that was itself Buddhist, in Indonesia, secular schools were associated with and promoted by a new generation of Javanese aristocrats-cum-civil servants whose value system was far different and often antagonistic to that of the traditionalist Muslims.

But there were other factors operating to prolong the life of the *pesantren*. One was very simply that the government never attempted to impose a single system of education on the populace. Educational pluralism in Indonesia was an outgrowth, in part, of developments in the late colonial period. The Dutch made little effort to satisfy a growing demand for education, and a multitude of indigenous schools, many subsidized by the colonial government, sprang up. Such schools were an important vehicle for the nationalist movement which had over three decades to simmer before breaking out into revolution in 1945. The nationalist movement was never a unified one, and different manifestations of it produced their own schools. To impose a unified school system immediately after independence would have been to deny the contributions of different nationalist groups or to give the lie to the unity-in-diversity motto of the new state. Accordingly, up until this day, several different school systems co-exist: the state secular school system run by the Ministry of Education; the state Islamic school system run by the Ministry of Religion; the Muhammadiyah or modernist Muslim system; the schools of the Protestant and Catholic minorities; the Java-centric Taman Siswa schools which stress Javanese art and culture; smaller networks of privately owned Muslim schools; and the *pesantrens*.

Except for the *pesantrens*, all other Muslim school networks were based on the institution of the *madrasah*, a graded day school introduced into Indonesia in the early twentieth century, probably influenced by Dutch schools. They offered a mixture of secular and religious courses, and for Indonesian children who had no access to Dutch schools, an opportunity to acquire a "modern" education.

The spread of the *madrasah* as an institution received a major impetus from the formation in 1912 and rapid growth of the Muhammadiyah, a Muslim modernist movement which found its greatest strength among the Muslim merchants and traders of Indonesian towns who were greatly taken with aspects of Islamic reformism reaching Indonesia from the Middle East. In Indonesia, Muhammadiyah schools were developed as a very conscious alternative to *pesantrens*, which were regarded as anachronistic, impractical, and more steeped in Javanese lore than in the fundamentals of Islam.

By the 1980s, the *form* of a Muslim school, *madrasah* or *pesantren*, was no longer an issue, as many *pesantrens* incorporated the *madrasah* into their "campuses." The word *pesantren* referred to the school as a whole—its physical complex as well as the total environment where praying, eating, sleeping, and working took place. Within this environment, the *madrasah* came to mean the place where classroom-style lessons were conducted.

The differentiation today among Muslim schools in Indonesia, then, rests not on the form education takes but largely on degree of government control and influence. *Pesantrens* continue to be owned and run for the most part by the *kyai*'s family, and are relatively free from government interference. The state Islamic school system (a tiny fraction of Muslim schools) is funded by the Ministry of Religion and uses the established government curriculum, consisting of thirty percent religious subjects and seventy percent secular subjects. Between the *pesantrens* and the state

Islamic schools are various networks of *madrasahs* sponsored by Islamic organizations which adapt the government curriculum to their own needs and may receive partial government funding.

If there is unprecedented pressure now on all private schools from the government of President Suharto to follow the state curriculum and at least obtain equivalency with state secular schools, it is in part because the state now has unprecedented resources at its disposal and an unprecedented desire to impose a state ideology which it can best do through the education system.[12]

A third factor in the *pesantren's* longevity has been politics. After independence, the traditionalist *kyai*-led organization called Nahdlatul Ulama (NU) emerged as an independent political party and, after the 1955 national parliamentary election, became the third largest party in the country. A *pesantren* background became the hallmark of NU leaders, and the success of the party was reflected in the importance of the *pesantren's* political role. Party branch meetings and traditional prayer-meetings became indistinguishable, and party strategists often used the seclusion of the *pesantren* for planning sessions. The political process infused new life—and new wealth—into *pesantrens*. Moreover, the political success of NU gave additional security to the *pesantren*. With NU representing the Islamic element of Sukarno's hallowed ideological triad called NASAKOM (Nationalism, Religion, Communism), the central government was not about to offend an important coalition partner by placing curbs on its schools.

The political system could not prevent an increasing demand for secular education, but it buffered the impact of that demand. It did so by enhancing the value of a *pesantren* education for members of the party, by encouraging the adoption of a partially secular curriculum within *pesantrens*, and by taking advantage of party control over the Ministry of Religion to expand a religious school system which fed the *pesantrens*.[13]

Finally, the *pesantren* survived because, until very recently, there was a place in society for its "graduates." As long as the *pesantren* was the only educational institution available, the problem of placement was not an issue. And as long as NU was politically influential and in charge of the Ministry of Religion, as it was through 1971, *pesantren* graduates could find jobs in the Ministry and its provincial and district offices, and in the party itself. They could continue on to the state Islamic universities, which the organization also controlled through its hold over the Ministry, establish their own *pesantrens*, or return to the traditional occupations of trading and farming. It was primarily after the loss of political power that *pesantren* education became more of a liability than an asset, and today there are far fewer opportunities for *santris* once their *pesantren* education is complete.

The Process of Change

How will change affect the *pesantren*? Despite the rapid pace of so-cial and political change in Indonesia through the fifties and sixties, or perhaps because of it, the appeal of the *pesantren* as an educational insti-tution remained surprisingly unaffected. Even in 1981 in Kediri, *pesantrens* accounted for roughly twenty per cent of the post-elementary student pop-ulation.[14]

The political changes that have come with the establishment of the New Order government of Suharto and subsequent clampdown on party activity have affected *pesantren* in four ways. When the party could no longer accord the *pesantren* an honored role, nor guarantee jobs for those *pesantren* alumni who sought jobs outside or in addition to farming and trading, the inadequacies of the *pesantren* education were made starkly apparent. Erosion, indeed, had begun well before the change in regime. Castles, in a study of a major *pesantren* in East Java, noted that in 1964 "Gontor's clientele is being eroded at the top as higher education becomes increasingly necessary to social status and perhaps also at the bottom as Indonesia's economy runs downhill" (Castles 1966:40).

Despite the introduction of secular courses into major *pesantrens* as early as 1916, most still had a primarily religious curriculum. The most glaring shortcoming was the lack of training in and achievement of func-tional literacy in Indonesian—most classes were conducted in Javanese rather than the national language. The lack of an equivalency with pub-lic schools meant that further education was virtually impossible; for most *santris*, the *pesantren* education was the last schooling they would have. Accordingly, enrollment began to decline, particularly among the smaller *pesantrens*.[15] The decline sharpened in recent years. Between 1976 and 1981 *pesantren* enrollment in Kediri regency dropped by roughly twenty percent and by thirty percent in the capital city.[16]

Second, the *pesantren's* traditional invulnerability from government intervention began to decrease. This was related in part to the decline in enrollment which brought economic pressures in its wake. Those *pesantrens* which chose to stem the exodus of students by offering a secular curricu-lum were forced to hire government teachers on salary, leading to a vastly increased overhead for the schools whose teachers were traditionally taken from the ranks of senior *santris* and were not paid. Hiring government teachers usually entailed accepting government aid. The Suharto govern-ment, wary of the political independence of *pesantrens*, also embarked on a program to upgrade the schools by offering vocational education programs. This marked another incursion of government, an influx of government aid, and the possibility of government control. Four *pesantrens* became pilot projects for the vocational training programs in 1974; the number was increased to 42 in 1975, 92 in 1976, and 500 in 1977 (Kafrawi 1978:78). Likewise, government officials began a concerted attempt to woo *kyais* into membership in the government party GOLKAR with promises of "presidential aid" or extra-budgetary assistance for their *pesantrens*. In some cases, the blandishments worked; one impact of government aid was to reduce the moral force of the *kyai* as a voice independent and defiant of the government.

Third, the clientele of the *pesantren* began to change. As secular education has become the key to social and economic advancement (and as land and population pressures make traditional occupations less attractive) many families seem to be making the choice of sending their sons to secular schools and their daughters to religious schools. What were traditionally schools whose students were almost exclusively male are now becoming schools with increasing percentages of females. At the same time, while regular *santris* are still heavily drawn from the agrarian elite, many of the large *pesantrens*, especially those in or on the outskirts of cities, are attracting sons and daughters of urban civil servants, both for the full year as well as for the concentrated Quranic study offered during the fasting month of Ramadhan when many public and private schools are on holiday. The *pesantren's* role in defining a specific sociocultural group is thus beginning to change, albeit slowly.

Finally the nature of a *pesantren* education itself has begun to change. There seems to be a greater propensity to stay in one *pesantren*, especially in those which have adopted a secular program, rather than to wander among several. Those who still attend *pesantrens* also appear likely to stay a shorter time than did those who went to them even in the recent past. Whereas many men now in their forties spent ten to fifteen years in *pesantrens*, the average time now seems to be about five or six years (the equivalent of secular secondary education). In the long run, this may have serious implications for the regeneration of *kyais*, for the propagation of a distinctively Javanese variant of Islam, and for the solidarity of an elite that once relied on the *kyai-santri* bond for cohesion. The shorter duration of *pesantren* stay and commitment to one *pesantren* rather than several may mean that religious expertise is less and less indigenously acquired. Rather than rely on the *pesantren* network to acquire sufficient religious knowledge to open a *pesantren*, a would-be *kyai* may find it increasingly necessary to

acquire the balance of his education in the Middle East. In a sense, this
has always been true as most well-known *kyais* traditionally spent several
years of study in Mecca. They usually studied, however, with important
sheikhs of the "Jawa" (Malay archipelago, including Java) community. Now
opportunities for study come increasingly with access to scholarships made
available by many Middle Eastern governments, particularly Saudi Arabia,
but also including Egypt, Syria, Iraq, and even Libya. Study takes place
not in a one-to-one tutorial with a well-known sheikh, but in a university
with other Muslim students from around the world. The trend toward
Saudi study may mean a break with Javanese tradition, leading to the
"internationalization" of Javanese Islam, and also a steady reduction in the
number of *kyais* produced. The effect on the reproduction of *kyais* will be
particularly pronounced in the allotment of scholarships. There is a policy
of giving preferential treatment to *kyais'* sons, traditionally their heirs, who
are considered to have a greater likelihood of becoming *kyais* themselves.
For many of these scholarship recipients, the attraction lies less in the
opportunity to advance one's religious learning than in the chance, given
the generosity of the Saudi stipend, to travel abroad during the holidays.

Change and the Peasantry

All of the above changes have affected the *pesantren* in relation to
its elite clientele. What of the peasantry? Will the *pesantren*, in the
face of major transformations of its educational function, continue to serve
the poorer strata of rural Javanese society in providing social, economic,
religious, and political security? And if not, what then will the *pesantren*
mean for the peasantry?

The influx of government aid, the decline in enrollment, and the change
in student clientele have not affected the fact that the *pesantren* is still
a village institution. But the changes—and this is speculation since the
pesantren is only in transition, not dead, not even necessarily moribund—
may profoundly affect village society in two ways.

First, to the extent that the elite move on to secular schools and
become one step removed from the *pesantren*, feelings of solidarity with
peasants who shared their allegiance to *kyais* may decline. This is, of course,
intimately bound up with the political system. When the NU, the party
led by *kyais*, was strong and in constant competition with other parties,
there was a prevalent ethic that only *orang kita*, "our people," should be
patronized. Wealthier landlords made an effort to hire NU peasants, or
conversely, those peasants who worked for NU landlords were more likely
to identify themselves as NU. Today, the notion that a landlord should hire

agricultural labor affiliated with NU is greeted with ridicule. Business and profit, rather than religio-political ties, now take precedence in the elite's communication with the poor peasantry, and a move toward secular schools will only further this trend.

More importantly, the mystique and moral force of the *kyai* are being eroded by the twin trends of declining enrollment and increased truck with government officials. As noted above, the *kyai's* influence derived not just from his charismatic qualities, but from his independence of the state. Without the latter, the charisma has little value, as *kyais* and their followers who have joined the government party have belatedly realized. Acceptance of government aid does not necessarily brand a *kyai* a traitor. It may even, in the short run, contribute to his reputation as a worthy opponent of the state who can cunningly milk it of resources without conceding anything in return. But the increased intervention of the government in the *pesantren* in the long run may well mean a decline of the influence of the *kyai* with the peasantry, if it means that a traditional channel of voicing dissent is closed off.

Likewise, part of the *pesantren*'s influence and staying power in Indonesian society has lain in the difference between the *pesantren* community and the world around it, the fact that it represents the secret and the mysterious rather than the known and the palpable, wisdom rather than knowledge (Anderson 1972:5–6). This mystique is likely to be compromised the more the *pesantren* takes on the qualities of a full-fledged school, with vocational training, volleyball courts, a television in the *kyai*'s home, and a car in his garage. If the mystique is undermined, so may be the acceptance of social stratification that the *kyai* has traditionally inspired. This role is described well by Horikoshi:

> As the *ulama* do not enforce the collection of the principle owed to them or ask the villagers for labor services for the *ulama's* family's personal economic operations, the indebted villagers maintain a continuous sense of 'balance due' to the *ulama*. Whether it is economic or social favors, the consequent indebtedness serves a social function to preserve the *ulama's* superiority and influence. On the one hand, the *ulama's* careful avoidance of any abuse of this trust for their own personal gain serves as a reference point of the *ulama's* expected high moral credibility and thereby prestigious status. On the other hand, it eliminates any opportunity for villagers to return their 'balance due' to the *ulama*. (Horikoshi 1976:225)

The pervasive belief that to be poor and less fortunate is partly caused by lack of faith and diligence in both religious and economic activities makes the continually indebted villagers feel ashamed of themselves.

Mystique and morality are intertwined; the *kyai* maintained his "moral credibility" in part by his removal from the rest of society. As he becomes more integrated into that society, in part as the result of educational change, his activities as landowner and businessman may come increasingly into public view and his wealth become a source of skepticism or resentment. In Kediri only thirty-two percent of households in the regency own or sharecrop over half a hectare of land. The average land controlled by the nineteen leaders of the subdistrict of NU who represent the highest stratum of the *pesantren*-trained agrarian elite in 1981 was 10.1 hectares. The leading *kyai* controls fifty hectares, and has three cars, including one Mercedes which his unlicensed children drive about the town with great abandon. As economic inequalities increase, the role of the *kyai* in providing a linkage between elite and peasantry becomes all the more critical. But educational change forced on the *pesantren* makes that role increasingly problematical. The *pesantren* has enjoyed an unusually long life for a traditional school, but it may finally be threatened with disappearance.

Notes

[1] In fact a very few Indonesian students, mostly Christian or Eurasian, had. been permitted to attend Dutch schools in the Indies as early as 1799, but, in general, a policy of educating the native population was considered unwise by the colonial administration in that it would lead to unrest and dissatisfaction with the Cultivation System or forced planting of export crops. A colonial regulation of 1849 actually forbade the entry of Indonesians into European schools on the grounds that the social status quo would be upset. By the end of the nineteenth century, the need for Dutch-speaking clerical personnel had led to the opening of a few schools restricted to sons of the traditional Javanese nobility which had become the backbone of the colonial civil service and through whom the Dutch ruled. The so-called Liberal Policy prevailing in the Netherlands, which led to more of a concern for welfare in the colonies, sanctioned the provisions of subsidies to private schools, including Muslim ones, and the establishment of "village schools." Little financial support was made available to the latter, however, in the belief that villagers would place more value on schools which they financed themselves. In a period of increasing rural debt, this belief proved ill-founded (see Penders 1968).

[2] Tibawi (1972:191) writes:

> The relationship between master and disciple was (in medieval Islamic education), in the nature of things, personal, not institutional. A scholar went to study a given subject or even a certain book with a famous teacher, not to a particular place of learning. Even after the establishment of the state of the *madrasah* as a fixed and systematic institute of higher learning, it was largely the reputation of the principal teacher at a given institute that determined its academic standing. Scholars wandered freely from one country to another to sit at the feet of famous teachers, and the custom became an established tradition of higher learning.

[3] Abdurrachman Wahid (1980:119) rightly points out that a *kyai* frequently started out by teaching village children from the lower economic strata, and it was from this base that he built up the reputation of his *pesantren*. This does not negate the fact, however, that *pesantren* education was primarily for the elite.

[4] Many Muslims in Indonesia reject the traditionalist-reformist di-

chotomy as no longer valid, and the use of the label "traditionalist" in particular as pejorative. I use it here following the definition of tradition in the *Shorter Oxford English Dictionary* (Little, et al., 1956: 2342): "A long established and generally accepted custom or method of procedure, having almost the force of a law."

[5] Terminology can be confusing. *Madrasah* was used in the medieval Middle East to denote a school of Islamic law. It later came to mean any Islamic school, and by the turn of the century, a school with classroom-style instruction even though the curriculum was wholly religious. The model for Indonesian *pesantrens* was a specific *madrasah*, Darul Ulum, in Mecca which served the Malay-speaking community including Indonesia. Today, virtually every *pesantren* has a *madrasah* based on this model within its boundaries. The term *madrasah* also refers, however, to religious schools with some secular curriculum administered by the Ministry of Religion.

[6] These were the *sorogan* and *banbongan* methods involving the *kyai* and his students reading specific texts rather than following a curriculum arranged by subject matter.

[7] On *watak mandiri* see Wahid (1980:115) on the distaste for bureaucracies. Also compare Castles (1966:31), who writes: "(The *kyai*) urges boys not to make 'public service' their objective and becomes angry if they still want to be *pegawai* (government officials). The reason he gives is that the *pegawai* is not free. In the Dutch time, officials, through taking orders from the Dutch all the time, eventually came to think like them."

[8] In fact there is a very strict hierarchy within the *pesantren*, but it is based less on economic distinctions than on knowledge and "closeness to the *kyai*."

[9] Would-be *hajis* accumulated land less for the prospect of speculative gain than in the expectation of larger cash returns for harvests.

[10] *Djago*: literally, a fighting cock, but used in Java to denote an expert in the Javanese martial arts and mystic science of invulnerability.

[11] Sartono (Kartodirdjo 1972:89–90) notes that at the end of the nineteenth century these Sufi orders seemed to be composed of young men and took on the form of secret societies. Exactly when these orders began to attract primarily old people is not clear, but by the 1940s the secret society *tarekat* seems to have largely disappeared. Today, not only are most initiates old, but they are overwhelmingly old women.

[12] The ideology, *Pancasila*, or the "five principles" was conceived by Indonesia's first president, Sukarno, in 1945 as a means of bridging

ideological differences within the nationalist elite. Under President Suharto, *Pancasila* has been elevated to the status of a state ideology. *Pancasila* courses are now required in all schools, special training courses in *Pancasila* are obligatory for government employees, and *Pancasila*, by law, must be formally accepted as the ideological basis of all social and political organizations in Indonesia. The five principles are: 1) belief in God; 2) humanitarianism; 3) nationalism; 4) democracy; and 5) social justice.

[13] Nahdlatul Ulama had firm control of the Ministry from 1953 to 1971. While this went against the grain of their long-standing distaste for bureaucracy, the Ministry was considered an exception to the rule since it provided patronage and employment for thousands of the party faithful, and since its funds could be used for religious purposes. It was the Ministry-administered or aided Islamic elementary schools, *madrasah ibtidaiyah*, from which most *santris* graduated.

[14] Since most *pesantrens* require basic literacy in Arabic, and more recently in Indonesian, and since they traditionally attracted adolescent or post-adolescent children, virtually all *santri* have completed primary school, either in the secular or Islamic school system, before entering the *pesantren*. Since Kediri is a traditionalist stronghold, both the concentration of *pesantrens* and the percentage of students in them are probably among the highest in Java.

[15] See Raharjo (1975) who cites the decline in enrollment in *pesantrens* around the Bandung area of West Java in 1972.

[16] These estimates are based on statistics of the Kantor Urusan Agam in Kediri. It should be emphasized, however, that statistics on *pesantrens* are notably unreliable. The general trend indicated by the statistics was, however, confirmed by *pesantren* leaders.

References

Anderson, Benedict R. 0'G. "The Idea of Power in a Javanese Culture." In *Culture and Politics in Indonesia,* ed. by Claire Holt, with Benedict R. O'G. Anderson and James Siegel, 1–69. Ithaca, N. Y.: Cornell University Press, 1972a.

———. *Java in a Time of Revolution.* Ithaca, N. Y.: Cornell University Press, 1972b

Asjari, Samudja. "Kedudukan Kjai dalam pondok pesantren." M.A. thesis, Gadjah Mada University, 1967.

Castles, Lance. "Notes on the Islamic School at Gontor." *Indonesia,* 1.1(1966):30–45.

Dhofir, Zamakhsyariyah. "The Peasantren Tradition." Ph. D. dissertation, Australian National University, 1980.

Geertz, Clifford. "The Javanese Kijaji: The Changing Role of a Cultural Broker." *Comparative Studies in Society and History,* 2.2(1960):228–49.

———. *The Social History of a Javanese Town.* Cambridge, Massachusetts: M.I.T. Press, 1965.

Horikoshi, Hiroko. "A Traditional Leader in a time of Change: The 'Kijaji' and 'Ulama' in West Java." Ph. D. dissertation, University of Illinois, 1976.

Kafrawi, H. *Pembaharuan Sistim Pendidikan Pondok Pesantren.* Jakarta: P.T. Cemara Indah, 1978.

Kartodirdjo, Sartono. "Agrarian Radicalism in Java." In *Culture and Politics in Indonesia,* ed. by Claire Holt, with Benedict R. O'G. Anderson and James Siegel, 71–125. Ithaca, N. Y.: Cornell University Press, 1972.

Little, William, H. E. W. Fowler, and J. Coulson, comp. *The Shorter Oxford English Dictionary,* 3rd ed. revised and ed. by C. T. Onions. Oxford: Clarendon Press, 1956.

Penders, C. L. M. "Colonial Education Policy and Practice in Indonesia, 1900–1942." Ph.D. dissertation, Australian National University, 1968.

Pigeaud, Theodore and H. J. de Graaf. *Islamic States in Java, 1500–1700.* The Hague: Nijhof, 1976.

Raharjo, Dawam. "The Kayai, the Pesantren, and the Village: A Preliminary Sketch." *Prisma,* 1.1(1975):32–43.

Scott, James C., and Benedict Kerkvliet. "How Traditional Rural Patrons
Lose Legitimacy: A Theory With Special Reference to Southeast Asia."
In *Friends, Followers, and Factions*, ed. by Steffen W. Schmidt, Laura
Guasti, Carl H. Lande, and James C. Scott, 439–58. Berkeley and Los
Angeles: University of California Press, 1977.

Sutherland, Heather. *The Making of an Indonesian Bureaucracy.* Singapore: Heineman, 1979.

Tibawi, Abdul Latief. *Arabic and Islamic Themes.* London: Luzac, 1972.

Wahid, Abdurrachman. *Bunga Rampai Pesantren.* Jakarta: C.V. Dharma
Bhakti, 1980.

Wiradi, Gunawan. *Rural Development and Rural Institutions.* Bogor:
Agroeconomic Survey (*Rural Dynamics* Series No. 6), 1978.

BETWEEN WORLDS: THEATER AND SCHOOL IN A PHILIPPINE VILLAGE, 1880–1940[1]

Resil B. Mojares

Introduction

There are few historical studies of cultural institutions in the rural Philippines. Here I shall consider the operation of two institutions, a local theater tradition and the modern public school, in a particular Philippine village. The village is barrio Valladolid in Carcar, southern Cebu, central Philippines, in the last years of the nineteenth and the first four decades of the twentieth century.

This period witnessed the rise and decline of a theater tradition and the advent of modern public education. It is an important period in other, larger ways. It saw the breakdown of the relative autonomy of villages in many parts of the country and their closer integration into the networks of the nation-state and a global economy. From communities largely turned *inward*, Philippine barrios became communities increasingly turned *outward*—toward the world of the nation-state, the market economy, and the evolving national culture.

In this movement, the school (in particular, the public school) is an important institution. It is the one single institution in the barrio that clearly symbolizes the "modern" world into which villagers are to be initiated. It should, then, be of some interest to ask how well the barrio school represents or serves as "broker" for this world, and how it functions as a moral or symbolic focus for the life of the village.

In Valladolid at the turn of the century such a focus was provided by a popular theater tradition called *linambay*, a form more widely known in the Philippines as *komedya* or *moro-moro*. Its power was not autonomous, as it was linked to larger ideological and ceremonial systems, the fiesta complex (the annual celebration of the feastday of the village patron saint) as well as the practice of the Roman Catholic religion. Nevertheless, there was no single, village-based institution that exercised as much moral and educative force. The Valladolid *linambay* flourished from the 1890s to the 1920s, but had begun to disintegrate by the start of the Pacific War.

The school in Valladolid was a marginal presence during these earlier years, but it grew in importance as the twentieth century wore on and the American public school system expanded. It progressed from an itinerant open-air "school" or *escuela* at the turn of the century, to a structure of

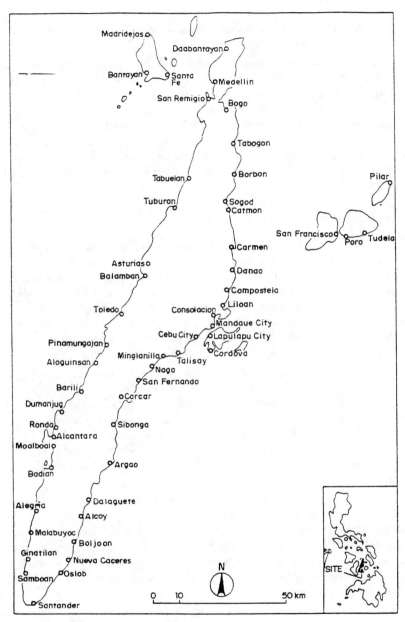

The Province of Cebu

light materials in 1913, and then to a semi-permanent building of wood and concrete with a fixed site in 1919.

The movement from stage to schoolhouse, from *linambay* to *escuela*, is expressed in the internal history of the village. I shall take a look at these cultural institutions or systems from two analytic viewpoints. The first derives from the view that both systems function as "brokers of worlds." They mediate and ritualize participation in a given mode of social existence, in terms both symbolic and real. The second derives from the view that local individuals participate in these systems as an "investment" to gain or firm up social status or earn a niche in the changing economy of rural dwellers.

The *Linambay* as Moral System

The turn of the century was a "time between times" in Cebu and Philippine history. The nineteenth century witnessed an increasing shift to cash-crop cultivation—sugar, abaca, tobacco—in response to world market demand, new colonial policies, and the intrusions of the various agencies of a capitalist economy. With the increased value of land and its products, significant shifts in demographic and landholding patterns occurred. Such shifts modified the relations between regional centers and the hinterland as well as the social structure and cultural configurations of rural communities.

Cebu City became one of the primary hubs of economic activity in the Philippine archipelago during the nineteenth century. From the port of Cebu radiated new economic and cultural impulses. Merchants and entrepreneurs—mostly Chinese mestizo (*mestizo sangley*)—fanned out to the countryside to acquire lands through various forms of purchase, lease, or seizure. While this increase in agricultural exploitation resulted in some prosperity, it also sharpened social tensions as increasing numbers of rural families became marginal to society.

The revolution against Spain (1898) and the war against the Americans (1899–1902) heightened this climate of tension. In Cebu, both events disturbed local society less in military terms than in those of a severe economic dislocation and the disturbance of the sociopsychological balance as latent class conflict surfaced in many places. Other forces at work— plagues, storms, and drought—made the first decade of the century a particularly trying one.

This was the general climate in which turn-of-the-century Valladolid existed, as well as the background for the rise of the village theater tradition. There was, however, a specificity to the experience of the barrio. While a crisis situation existed, Valladolid fared better than many communities. An agricultural community situated on alluvial lowland where the Minag-a River flows into Bohol Strait, Valladolid (with a population in 1903 of 2,689) lies in the earliest developed part of Cebu Island. Just two miles southwest is the *poblacion* (municipal center) of Carcar, one of the most prosperous towns of the province, and twenty-five miles north is the capital city of Cebu. While its location exposed it to all kinds of unsettling influences from the larger world, it also meant that by the turn of the century it had already built up a fund of coping mechanisms derived from a history that stretched back to the late sixteenth century when it was first visited by Spanish missionaries and colonial agents.[2]

The village had a relatively deep and diversified resource base. Together with cash crops like sugar and coconut, it subsisted on corn cultivation and fishing. Valladolid was not a mere satellite village, but the center of an informal resource network, as its leading residents also owned lands in neighboring towns and barrios. What also enabled Valladolid to absorb the tremors of the turn of the century was that it had evolved, by the close of the nineteenth century, a fairly coherent social structure which allowed it to "redistribute pain" in years of stress.

There was no large-scale dispossession of local families during the nineteenth-century encroachment of urban merchants and speculators into the area. Two families (*kabanay*, descent groups) composed of mid-nineteenth century mestizo immigrants from the Cebu port area—Regis and Gantuangco—came to control close to half of the land of the barrio, in addition to lands in adjoining areas. Older residents of Valladolid, however, managed to hold on to sizeable farm holdings. In 1915, Valladolid, with around 500 households, encompassed 938 land parcels claimed by 492 landowners, most of them residents of the barrio. The cadastral profile indicates that the relative concentration of land in the hands of a few families was joined to a diffuse landholding pattern and a low rate of landlessness.[3]

The Regises and Gantuangcos, the major landowners of the area, resided in the village and established multiple affinal and ritual ties with local families. Though themselves affinally-related, they did not form a centrally-managed estate or hacienda—like the Hacienda Osmeña of the powerful Osmeña family in the neighboring barrios of Kanasuhan and Bas— but maintained scattered holdings whose titles were held by as many as twenty individual members or households of the two families. A measure of diffusion, therefore, accompanied the concentration of economic and social power in the village. This provided the groundwork for the social integration the village had achieved by the close of the nineteenth century.

The *linambay* tradition of Valladolid reveals this integration. At the turn of the century, it was the only ceremonial complex that had a corporate, village-wide character. Valladolid did not have an alternative center around which the community could be organized. The barrio did not have its own marketplace or cockpit. The local church and schoolhouse were important reference points for the moral life of the village but they did not exercise the same expressive and centralizing power as did the *linambay*.

The barrio had a *kapilya* (small church), a *tabique* structure (nipa roofing and bamboo frames reinforced with lime) that was converted in 1919 into a more permanent construction of stone, wood, and zinc. As Valladolid was a mere *visita* (sub-parish unit), the church had no resident priest, and mass was celebrated only on Sundays and special holidays by a visiting priest. On other days it was visited only by individual worshippers or small groups on special devotions. The barrio also had an *escuela* (school) established as early as 1893.[4] It functioned, however, only as a place where some of the barrio children learned basic literacy skills and the Catholic catechism. It started as an itinerant school under a local teacher, open only to boys, holding sessions in a private home or in the open air. It was later housed, in 1913, in an impermanent shed of native materials and then, in 1919, in a more permanent building of wood and concrete. At the height of the *linambay* tradition, it did not function as a center of communal activity and was a marginal presence in the community. It was the *linambay* which was the preeminent focus of the moral life of the village.

The *linambay* is an elaborate costume play descended from European metrical romances (see Mendoza 1976 and Tiongson 1982) and perhaps, in part, also from older native forms of ritual dance. Also known as the *moro-moro* or *komedya*, it became a dominant theater form in Christianized parts of the Philippines by the eighteenth century. The play, involving a cast of as many as a hundred people, ran serially for several nights (ranging from five to ten) for a total of some thirty or forty hours of performance. In addition, rehearsals lasted some three months of consecutive weekends. The *linambay* depicts a plot built around the Christian-Moorish wars in Europe. In Valladolid, this historico-religious motif merely provided the initial impulse for the play as it quickly moved to the more congenial grounds of ceremonial romance, adventure, and supernatural wonders, where native and foreign elements were mixed in an uninhibited fashion. The action ranged through several kingdoms—España, Turquia, or inventions like Natolio and, even, Nebraska—and involved an array of hierarchically arranged characters— kings, princesses, dukes, soldiers, messengers, and maids-in-waiting.

THE BARRIO OF VALLADOLID

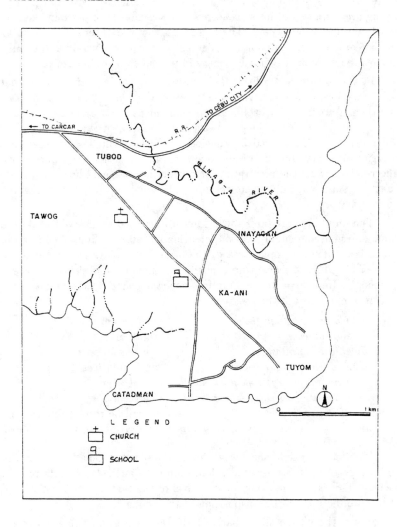

Held usually on the occasion of the village fiesta, the play was performed on a large, open-air wooden platform with a partly enclosed backstage area and a two-level frontstage. The main level was the primary acting area and served for such scenes as those that took place in the royal court, garden, or open field. The higher, narrower level served for scenes in the balcony, tower, or mountain. The use of the stage curtain and changes in cloth backdrops of painted scenery indicated changes of scenes.

In the nature of traditional literature, there is a limited set of patterns and formulas underlying the seeming diversity. Plot, verbal style, and themes are formulaic, set counters that the bard has arranged and rearranged. At the center of the play is the image of a satisfying, hierarchically-ordered society threatened by the forces of chaos—infidels, supernatural beings, and creatures of the dark forest. In its action, the play moves unerringly toward the restoration or affirmation of social harmony as villains are subdued, infidels converted, and monsters turned into ungainly buffoons.

The *linambay* gravitates toward inward-oriented themes of social decorum, cohesion, and subordination, creating an image of human community which is assumed to replicate a divine order. The plays express ideal notions of kingship, of a lord who consults his ministers and deals justly with his people. He is expected to manifest *noblesse oblige*. In the undated text of *Euriana*, a lord tells his vassals:

Cutub niini nga fecha	(From this day on
sa pagca amajan niño aco isipa	think of me as your father
dili niño hicalimtan	Do not forget this
hasta sa iñong catapusan	until your last days.
Cay ang maayo nga mga basallo	For good vassals
nga maga sunod sa pag buut co	who will obey my wish
aco ra ang mahibalo	I shall be responsible to them
pag hatag sa malipayon nga premio	and give them happy reward.)

The *linambay* symbolically reinforces the sense of social subordination and integration. It is the ritual celebration of a particular kind of peasant society. This is seen not only on the level of the text but in the character of the production and the disposition of the audience.

It was the village elite—particularly the Regises and Gantuangcos—who took the leading roles in the production in Valladolid. As a rule, they wrote the plays, owned the scripts, paid for the most expensive costumes, and mobilized the supply of goods and services. They directed the plays, chose the players, and played the most important roles—kings, princes, and princesses. Yet, the *linambay* was not strictly an elite production. The decision to stage the *linambay* was made by the barrio chapel association (*Kapunongan ni San Roque*) which, while made up of the more prominent landowners, was a body with village-wide representation. Furthermore, a sizeable portion of the village actively participated in the tradition. Small farmers contributed to the fiesta fund, sent food for the cast, spent for the costumes of sons and daughters who played secondary roles (such as generals and maids-in-waiting), or volunteered services in the building of the machinery and the stage. Even the schoolchildren in the village were conscripted to weave the coconut leaves for roofing the large *linambay* stage.

The existing social hierarchy, however, was reflected in the play itself and the organization of production. The leading residents were producers, directors, scriptwriters, and primary actors. Members of a secondary elite— middle-sized landowners, constituting around sixty households at the turn of the century—generally performed secondary functions. The rest of the village played the common roles in the cast, called *extras* or *todos*, and constituted the bulk of the audience.

This stratification was also evident in the disposition of the audience. The Regises and Gantuangcos watched the play from the *palcos*, specially-built elevated sheds close to the stage. Here they had a vantage point and could watch the play at their leisure or take time out to gossip, sleep, or eat. There were from four to seven of these *palcos* at a given performance. The rest of the audience, that could run to two thousand, staked out places on the ground where they could squat or stand as they viewed the play.

While, in many respects, the *linambay* was an elite activity, it was also a communal enterprise, involving the mobilization of a sizeable portion of the population and resources of the village. The *linambay* expressed an elite vision of the world and yet common villagers took this vision as their own. This duality is a key feature of the *linambay*; it tells us something as well about the character of the village.

It can be argued that this duality masks a real divergence in the motives and perceptions of the two key participants in the tradition—the local elite and "the rest of the village." Village landlords can be seen as having organized and funded the *linambay* as an investment to gain the goodwill of dependents and validate their own elite status. Likewise, small peasants participated in the *linambay* production as an investment in the form of deference in order to earn favor with those who controlled the resources on which their subsistence depended.

This view goes some way in explaining the structure of social motives in the production. Yet, it also simplifies by dissolving a rich range of behavior and perceptions into a dichotomy of rational cost-benefit calculations. The *linambay* tradition, to begin with, was not a monopoly of the village elite. A large cast allowed a large number of common villagers to have speaking parts. The play was not built around two or three personalities, but prominence was distributed among twenty to thirty performers with substantial roles. There was no strict one-to-one correspondence between social and fictional roles, for, by virtue of special skills, a small peasant might play the role of king and a member of the elite might cavort on the stage as a clown (*gracioso*).

Village society expressed a similar configuration. Valladolid was not made up of "two elite families and the rest of the village." Regises and Gantuangcos had married into local families. The most prosperous among the secondary elite considered the Regises and Gantuangcos less as patrons than *primus inter pares*. The majority of the rest of the village households were independent farm operators, petty farm owners who doubled as tenants, and farmer-fishermen. There was then, in large measure, occupational homogeneity, weak class divisions, and a developed corporate consciousness. This provided the social matrix for that overlapping of elite and non-elite interests expressed in the *linambay* tradition.

The function of the *linambay* was perceived in various ways by villagers themselves. It afforded the people with diversion and entertainment and it "pleased" the village patron saint—San Roque (St. Roch), the community's spiritual protector to whom the play was dedicated as *halad* or offering. It also taught villagers the "history" and manners of other countries, and it transmitted such values as religious faith, familial devotion, and decorous conduct. Interpretations vary according to the level of abstraction at which the play's value is considered. It is, however, in the analysis of the *linambay* as social ritual that it reveals its internal structure as well as the structure of the community itself.

The *linambay* functioned in the manner of Kenneth Burke's (1957) "strategies for the encompassing of situations" or Clifford Geertz's "models of/models for" social relations (Geertz 1973). It defined a world and structured moral participation in this world.

The Valladolid *linambay* succeeded because the need for it existed, and there were conditions and resources that enabled the community to satisfy the need. To begin with, the fragmented settlement pattern of the village, the social and economic anxieties of the turn of the century, and the potential for social tension in the unequal distribution of wealth created a need for social conservation. The *linambay* satisfied this need not only because it functioned, like the fiesta of which it was a part, as a redistributive institution but because it symbolized the most positive aspects of the social structure of Valladolid.

In all its interworking levels, the *linambay* was a ritual affirmation of the peasant community with its ethos of hierarchic ordering, social subordination, and patron-client reciprocity. Here the village elite produced a play in which they played the roles of enlightened rulers, courageous nobles, and beautiful princesses, in action affirming the image of a Christian kingdom that triumphs over such subversive threats as wayward adventurers, armies of infidels, and anarchic demons of the wilderness. This system of symbols is supported by a substructure of production roles, processes, and features which reaffirm the moral configuration of the play and ultimately of society itself. It can be said that the *linambay* expressed what was, essentially, an elite vision of the world. Yet, the *linambay* was not a piece of "court literature" but a true village tradition. It expressed, over a period of time and for large numbers of the village population, what villagers took to be the corporate image of Valladolid. Further, it can be said that the image expressed in the *linambay* does not correspond with reality. There were latent contradictions in the structure of the village as well as instances of open intra- and interfamilial differences and factional political conflict. Yet, the *linambay* succeeded because conditions in the village supported, or tended to support, the structure of the *linambay*. We have outlined these conditions: the existence of traditional, resident landlords linked to the rest of the village by multiple affinal and ritual ties; a diffuse landholding pattern; a relatively broad resource base; and a population fairly well-settled, in generational terms, in the area.

At the height of the *linambay* tradition—roughly from 1890 to 1930, during which time the play was staged practically every year—Valladolid was a relatively well-functioning, coherent society despite the tensions of this period. The tradition, however, did not last, as a number of forces eroded the ground on which it was built. There was increased demographic pressure on the land: the barrio population rose from 2,689 in 1903 to 3,337 in 1939. There was ecological deterioration, further fragmentation of landholdings through partible inheritance, and increased incorporation of the village in an external economy that subjected villagers to price fluctuations and taxation. All these forces led to growing economic impoverishment and erosion of the village's moral base.[5] These same forces had a centrifugal effect, pushing villagers out of their home community. Children of elite families moved to the *poblacion* or the city and their ties to the village began to weaken. Increased occupational differentiation undermined patterns of traditional patronage. The expansion of town-level electoral politics in the

1920s created an arena for prestige-building that was an alternative to the *linambay*. New forms of entertainment—like the *zarzuela* (a modern musical play) and the cinema—oriented villagers to the culture of town and city. For many, links to external centers of influence and power became more important than intra-village relations. The structure on which the *linambay* was based began to collapse.

In the 1930s the *linambay* underwent a number of transformations. Performances became less frequent and plays became shorter and less elaborate. The nine nights of staging became four, three, or even one; the cast of a hundred was reduced to twenty or ten players; such expensive features as the *tramoyas*—papier-maché monsters and other stage machineries—were eliminated; and the feasts for performers during rehearsals gave way to spartan rations of corn meal and a stew of beans and dried fish in coconut milk. The high themes of nobility, courtesy, and courage were diluted; stage movements turned from the stylized to the naturalistic; and the heightened lines of verse became common prose.

The central barrio tradition of the *linambay* broke down into minuscule, makeshift theatrical traditions in neighborhoods and *sitios* (sub-barrio units). These little traditions were sustained by smaller social groups, like neighborhood chapel associations. In the narrower spaces of the *sitio* the *linambay* lived on for a time in destitute, watered-down versions of the old, elaborate *linambay*. This spatial splintering of the tradition did not herald the rise of a new form or a counter-tradition. The austere *sitio* productions were the reflex movements, unintended caricatures, of a dying institution.

The Pacific War brought the Valladolid *linambay* to an end but, in truth, the tradition had begun to die at least a decade before the war came. In essential terms, what happened was that the *linambay* as social ritual lost its force, its power to compel belief, and became irrelevant. The moral world it symbolized no longer corresponded with the changing social reality of Valladolid.

The Counter-System of School

The *linambay* tradition can tell us something also about alternative "ideologies" or symbol-systems. In the rural Philippines, formal education is one such system, or axis for such a system. The folk theater tradition and the modern public school are not completely analogous or comparable institutions. A comparison of the two, however, particularly as brokers of "worlds," is instructive for an understanding of the processes of education and cultural change.

In rural Cebu, the first agent of "modern" education was the local sage who possessed knowledge of Catholic doctrine and literacy in romanized letters. Called *maestro*, his services were contracted by parents to teach the *abecedario*—primer or *cartilla* of the Roman alphabet—and *catecismo*—Catholic catechism—to an individual child or group of children in such informal settings as a private residence or a houseyard. This informal arrangement continued to exist even after the Catholic Church established parochial schools in the various *poblaciones* of Cebu.

At the start of the nineteenth century, there were already parish schools in the *poblaciones*. A few of the more prosperous barrios or *visitas* probably had schools as well. The number of these *visita* schools in the province is not known but they must have numbered less than ten at the close of the nineteenth century.

After the school reforms of 1863 placed education under the state, there was an expansion of public primary education. School attendance in the town of Carcar rose from 421 children in 1868 to 1,916 in 1879.[6] By 1893, schools are reported for Valladolid and Ocaña in Carcar, making them the first barrios to have schools outside the Cebu port area (Grifol 1894:337–39).[7]

It appears, however, that the early Valladolid *escuela* (school) simply took over the older, intra-village arrangement of contracting a private tutor for children. This older system was formalized, elaborated (though it continued to exist on its own), and placed under the regulatory authority of the church and the state. Until 1913 the Valladolid *escuela* existed as an informal, itinerant institution without a permanent site or building.

For children of the big landowning families in the area there was, moreover, access not only to more formal schools but also to secondary and higher education in Cebu City where, in the 1890s, institutions like the Colegio-Seminario de San Carlos and Colegio de la Immaculada Concepcion were in operation.

One can assume that many Valladolid children must have had at least a few years of formal schooling in the *escuela* either in the barrio or the *poblacion*. It must be remembered, however, that in addition to the narrow content of education (consisting of nothing more than basic literacy, numeracy, and Catholic doctrine), class attendance in the towns fluctuated according to the seasons of agricultural work, and the average pupil stayed in school for only three years. In barrios like Valladolid, school was conducted in makeshift fashion, either in the open air or in rented houses. H. E. Bard, Cebu school superintendent, spoke in 1903 of his observation of barrio schools in Cebu:

Usually very little is required of the teacher, and the teacher in turn, requires little of his pupils. A teacher may engage in almost any other work, either in or out of school hours. I know of one case where the teacher was engaged in dressing a pig at one side of the table while his pupils were studying their catechism at the other side. It is a common thing to find a teacher sitting quietly by, smoking his cigar, or mending his net, or repairing other fishing tackle, or doing some other similar work. But more frequently he will be found at the *tribunal* (municipal hall) or at some other common meeting place. A little nipa or even a mango tree will answer for a schoolhouse. (Bard 1903:874–75)

More important, village life provided little incentive for formal education. Taxes were paid through the village headmen (*cabezas*), the parish secretary (*fiscal*) filled the books to register baptisms, deaths or marriages, and there were scribes and translators to take care of legal documents such as those that pertained to land. No newspapers circulated in the barrios and even wealthy *ilustrado* ("enlightened") families in the *poblacion* had in their homes only a few Spanish romances, dictionaries, and tracts.

Even the *linambay*, which was script-based and had plots from European histories and romance-collections, did not really require literacy as it was essentially an oral, traditional art which used formulas of verbal style, theme, and plot. The versified lines were easily memorizable and could be extemporized and a prompter (*apuntador*) dictated lines aloud to the players during the performance. The ability to read was of some importance for major roles, particular in parts called *arranque* (long passages which had to be delivered without stops), but then these roles were usually filled by members of elite families. Elite families wrote and owned the scripts, but an illiterate bard could produce his own play by using an amanuensis and by inventing plots from the bits and pieces of a native oral tradition already filling up with the matter of European romance.

Behind the lack of enthusiasm for sustained formal schooling was the fact that there were few impulses that pushed villagers outwards to a world where the knowledge and skills proffered by schools were required. The brokering functions performed by educated village landlords were deemed adequate and legitimate. There were still few occasions, and few reasons, for common villagers to deal with the outside world directly and in their own terms.

Moreover, in the nineteenth century, the public schools were governed by a conservative colonial philosophy which cultivated values of decorum and subservience and oriented pupils to an idyllic world of farm and village.

This philosophy is best revealed in the various versions of the form called *manual de urbanidad* ("book of conduct"), used both at home and in school, which stressed as an ideal the decorous behavior of the good Christian and the good colonial.[8] The American deputy superintendent of schools in Cebu remarked in 1902 that Spanish education "never sought to draw out what there is in the native, but to put that into him which, like an embalming fluid in the corpse, would preserve him from corruption, indeed, but would never make him a master either of knowledge or of himself" (Staunton 1903:943).

The Spanish schools, then, did not effectively function as counter-systems vis-à-vis the informal educational system (such as the *linambay* represented) of the barrio. They were local-based, conservative institutions, managed largely by the parish priest, engaged in inculcating a modicum of literacy and cultivating parochial religious values. They either reinforced the moral system of the *linambay* or remained a peripheral influence on the lives of the villagers.

In the twentieth century, with the American occupation of the Philippines, radical changes were introduced into the educational system. The Americans promoted an ambitious system of popular education, reaching out to the barrios. This system stressed secular knowledge and civic responsibility, used English as the medium of instruction, and aimed at the enfranchisement of the underprivileged classes.

In 1900 the Americans established a Department of Public Instruction, with Americans constituting the administrative and teaching core. Rapid advances were made in institutional terms. From the end of the Spanish period to 1940, the number of schools in the country increased from 2,000 to 12,000, and enrollments rose from 200,000 to 2,000,000 (UNESCO, 1953:73, 84, 86, 93). In the first two decades of American rule, the number of schools in Cebu Province increased from 62 to 366. In the town of Carcar, for the same period, the number of schools rose from three to sixteen (Census 1918:IV, 46–47; Montero 1886:359).

The Americans aimed at extending primary education beyond the limits of the *poblaciones* to the barrios and *sitios* where more than eighty percent of the country's population lived. In 1903, the school superintendent of Cebu said that "many of the barrios in Cebu have barrio schools, if not supported from municipal funds, then by private contribution" (Bard 1903:875). By 1918 there were 219 barrio schools in Cebu Province, thirteen of them in Carcar (Census 1918:IV-2, 129–29).

With the stress on the democratization of access and the enfranchisement of the lower classes, the American public school system subverted traditional social arrangements and such village institutions as the *linambay*. In its fully developed form, the rural public school represents a distinct, alternative world-order: secular, egalitarian, and outward-oriented. It should then be of interest to consider how, in fact, this system has revised a social world and fostered new forms of coherence in rural life.

In sum, the impact of the public school system was discontinuous, contradictory, and less than what its more enthusiastic proponents had envisioned. The decision to establish a whole new national system based on the American plan created many problems. A large corps of teachers had to be trained, a new language propagated, and a nationwide infrastructure built up.

There were conflicting philosophies among policymakers with respect to the "appropriate" education for Filipinos (May 1980). One view, inspired by the Booker T. Washington model, stressed "industrial education" (then in vogue in the United States) as fit for a "backward, colored" race such as the Filipinos. This stressed practical training in the handicrafts and trades (such as weaving, carpentry, and embroidery), and later in agriculture itself, often with inadequate attention to how these skills and activities could be integrated into the local economy. The other view, Jeffersonian in inspiration, stressed literacy, training in civics and government, and criticized industrial education as promoting a subservient, exploitable labor pool for *caciques* (local bosses) and big business. David Barrows, Secretary of Public Instruction from 1903 to 1909, saw in the expansion of the class of "peasant proprietors" a specific goal towards which public education should be geared. However, as historian Glenn May (1980:104) has remarked: "Barrows appeared to overestimate the feasibility of effecting fundamental changes through educational reform."[9]

The highmindedness of American policy carried with it a racist paternalism that accorded little value to local institutions. This is illustrated in the perceptions of Americans like Samuel MacClintock, principal of the secondary school in Cebu. Writing in 1903, he praised the public schools as the agency doing the most "to win the people to our ideas," but then added that: "The ignorance of the native country teacher is unfathomable." Moreover, he said: "The native language is devoid of all culture, so it seems eminently proper that we should give these people a common language that contains the results of our progress for thousands of years" (MacClintock 1903).

The statistics on institutional expansion (number of schools, enrollments, teachers), while impressive, are somewhat misleading. On the eve of the Pacific War, the public school system was still largely a lower-grade system. In 1938 seventy percent of the total school enrollment was in the first primary grades (Hayden 1947:472). The significance of this fact was already noted in 1925 by the Monroe Commission which reported that eighty-two percent of pupils did not go beyond the fourth grade. The Commission concluded that "the mass of the Filipino people do not now stay in school long enough to develop for permanent use even the rudiments of an education."[10]

> Two years of the present instruction give children practically nothing of permanent value; three years serve the purpose of the school but little better. The Commission is of the opinion that four years is the basic minimum, and that this should be raised to five years certainly within the next decade. (BES 1925:133, 206)

Despite the democratic aims of the system, there were still large numbers of out-of-school children, and education beyond the primary grades largely remained the preserve of the wealthier classes. For instance, a 1925 survey of the class background of students in four Cebu high schools showed that close to ninety percent of the students came from what may be termed the upper and middle classes (BES 1925:326).

We have few historical, micro-level studies of Philippine rural schools. Available evidence, however, points to the fact that the school failed to be a truly effective cultural institution in the village. In large part this was due to the fact that the school was not a village-based institution but a small outpost of a highly centralized network that had at its center a national office from which came the stream of circulars, memoranda, appointments, and approved textbooks which guided and circumscribed instruction on the local level. There was, consequently, a frequent gap between the aims of the system and its operation on the village level.

American policy stressed as a goal of public education the emancipation of peasants from the stranglehold of *caciquismo*. It is extremely doubtful, however, that the public schools made truly significant headway in achieving this goal. To begin with, barrio schools were almost exclusively in the hands of native teachers, many of whom came from landowning families and had closer ties with the local elite than with small peasants of the area.[11] An anthropologist's characterization of contemporary rural teachers in a Philippine province is probably true of the Valladolid case as well: "They are precisely the kind of dependent, status-oriented group that promotes the traditional paternalism of the village" (Foley 1976:30).

There was little understanding of the structures of dependence in the village and less understanding of the new forms of dependence that the American colonial rule itself abetted. The old patron-client relations operated in the school system with equal force. Village patrons were often the leaders, brokers, and contributors in the establishment and maintenance of schools, and they played prominent roles in school-sponsored activities like agro-industrial fairs and community assemblies.

With their influence and learning, the elite had always been the brokers of "modern" education. In the Spanish period, schoolteachers usually came from the landed gentry and carried the honorific title of *Don*. They had to pass an examination conducted by a provincial commission on public instruction and their appointments were endorsed by the town head (*gobernadorcillo*) and members of the local elite (*commun de principales*).[12] In Valladolid, the earliest known move to have a formal school opened in the barrio was made in 1883 by Salvador Gantuangco, a leading landowner and *linambay* producer, who had studied at the Colegio-Seminario de San Carlos in Cebu City, qualified as a teacher, and was endorsed by the *gobernadorcillo* and *principales* of Carcar.[13]

The norms of traditional patronage in Valladolid persisted in the American period. At the turn of the century, classes were held in the groundfloor or yard of elite houses (such as those of Vicente Regis, Josefina Gantuangco, and Domingo Regis). Sometime in 1913, a structure of light materials (nipa roofing and walls of split-and-flattened bamboo, called *sasa*) was built on land made available by Rafael Regis (who, with Salvador Gantuangco, was the leading figure in the *linambay* productions of the early twentieth century). In 1919 the school was transferred to a site donated by Salvador Gantuangco where a semi-permanent building of concrete, wood, and galvanized iron was built. Subsequently, an extension site was donated by Domingo Regis. In this extended school the whole primary course of Grades I to IV was offered.[14]

Considering such facts, it is highly unlikely that in the first two decades of the century the public school represented a serious competing symbol system to the *linambay* tradition. In the mental map of villagers in the early twentieth century, the school was a peripheral institution.

There were attempts at adapting education to local conditions. An example is provided by a primary arithmetic textbook, published in the United States for Philippine schools, which proceeds from exercises in computation to lessons in crop-sharing and homesteading. In the textbook, it is suggested that teachers: (1) "Explain to the class what a tenant is, how crops are divided, why tenants do not always get the same share, etc.", and (2) "Explain to the pupils carefully the right which the Filipinos have to take up land, and urge them to carry the information to their parents."[15] By and large, however, there was much routinization of school work and little flexibility and initiative on the local level (BES 1925:47, 224–30).

Formal education, however, was to expand and become more consequential as the nation-state itself was strengthened and local communities were integrated more effectively into its network. By the 1920s the public school system in the Philippines had consolidated itself in institutional terms. The private education sector also expanded. In Carcar two secondary schools were established—Carcar Institute in 1918 and St. Catherine's School in 1923—and became centers for the diffusion of "modern" ideas in the district. As indicated by the recorded increases in the rate of literacy and the number of students in intermediate and secondary schools, it would appear that the school system had begun to make gains in bringing to villagers a wider awareness of the larger world.

All these form part of a larger process which, in turn, underlies the decline of the *linambay* tradition. As in the case of the *linambay*, the growing importance of the school system cannot be explained solely in institutional terms. A large part of the explanation resides in the social and economic changes which made formal education increasingly important to villagers.

From the 1920s on there was added intercourse between the village and the outside world with the expansion of bureaucracy, broadening of electoral politics, and improvements in transportation. The opening of the Cebu railway in 1908 and the expansion of bus transportation in the 1920s linked Carcar more closely to Cebu City. At the same time, population increase and growing economic stagnation pushed villagers outward in search of new employment in the town, Cebu City, and elsewhere. Some left the village permanently while others returned to it periodically as "makeshift migrants." At the same time, the old brokering functions of the village landlords were superseded or revised. Their power as brokers declined as some of them became impoverished or as the world with which they had to deal became increasingly differentiated. As social tensions increased with the decline of the village economy, the importance of dealing with the world directly became more apparent to villagers.

This changed moral world provided little support for the *linambay* tradition. It did, however, provide a rationale for the emerging world of the school. Whether the school became as meaningful and effective a construct for the villagers as the *linambay* in its time is an open question. In dealing with the problem, we need to consider not only the efficiency of the system itself but the efficacy of supportive or complementary conditions and institutions.

We can see the failure, as well as promise, of the school system in the issues raised over the vocational education program. A cogent criticism against the program was that, because of deficient implementation and the absence of a concerted advance towards industrialization, schools trained children for non-existent jobs.[16] Many educators recognized this and called for a stress on agricultural training. Camilo Osias (1921:6–7), a leading educator of the period, expressed the rationale thus: "This is one of the great problems of barrio school instruction—to educate the children *for* the farm and barrio life rather than *away from* the farm and barrio life." In this vein, educators lamented the interest of students and parents in clerical and white-collar jobs, a fixation they blamed on false values. The fear was raised that turning out graduates in these fields, which were already rapidly filling up, would produce a generation of "social parasites."

However, the promotion of agriculture in rural schools—which included such activities as agricultural clubs, hog-raising contests, prizes for cultivators of *maguey* (*Agave cantala*, grown for coarse twine) and "corn campaigns"—often paid little heed to actual conditions. Agricultural education aimed at enhancing efficiency and productivity. Cases from Valladolid could, however, be cited to show that the contrary resulted.

Maguey cultivation was promoted in Valladolid and gained ground in such coastal *sitios* as Tuyom and Catadman, particularly during the boom years of the First World War. Stress was placed on modernizing technology and increasing productivity, neglecting such considerations as the fact that the world market for *maguey* was highly unstable and that stripping machines could not be readily introduced into the Carcar area because *maguey* was cultivated by small planters in minuscule fields. Thus, the processes of stripping and drying the fiber remained primitive and, in the 1930s, *maguey* cultivation collapsed because of the declining demand and competition from superior fibers. The use of farm machines and fertilizers was encouraged in sugarcane farming, but it was not clearly recognized that such entailed costs and conditions small farmers could not meet. The biggest landowners in Carcar, like the Osmeña family, with their access to credit and bureaucratic assistance, were the ones who were able to mechanize, establishing capitalist estates, while the farmers of Valladolid were marooned in traditional technology and reduced to further dependency.

Schools promoted new ideas and methods without a full understanding of the material and structural limitations within which farmers worked. They disseminated knowledge of production techniques but cultivated little awareness of the widening economic contexts in which rural dwellers had to work. Among policymakers, there was little appreciation for the forces (population growth, market instabilities, growing landlessness, soil exhaustion, and others) that were pushing villagers outward.

In Cebu such factors as rural overcrowding and declining yields made off-farm employment increasingly important. The successive parceling of farms through inheritance produced less and less economically viable units, and farmers found it increasingly difficult to "capitalize" the new households of their children. In this context, there was greater consciousness of the value of "investing" in education to prepare children for employment in the town and city. For families whose farms could no longer support additional households, education appealed as an investment leading to off-farm employment.[17]

Education was not a casual investment. Schooling beyond the primary grade required a considerable cash outlay and meant the loss of a farmhand, as it required sending sons and daughters to the Carcar *poblacion* or Cebu City for extended periods. Moreover, the prospect of a meaningful job after graduation was very uncertain. That a very small percentage of the school population of the barrio had an education beyond the primary grades indicates that questions of cost and risk were frequently felt to outweigh prospective benefits.

A basic weakness, and one rarely articulated, is that the world "proposed" by the school (as Charles Keyes puts it in "The Proposed World of the School" in this volume) is not a readily habitable world. The education available to villagers is limited, and there is little meaningful employment for using the skills they do acquire. The domain of public life remains narrow, controlled by traditional leaders, and defined by continuing structures of patron-client relations. The bureaucracy remains an impersonal maze, governed less by rules of merit and open access than by pressures of personal and factional influence. The images of progress, of redistribution-of-wealth-through-education, find little correspondence in reality. "The road to progress goes through the doorway of the school"—so goes the educationalist's gospel. For most villagers, however, the road does not extend too far beyond it.

In the first flush of the American colonial enterprise, there was optimism that education would bring about a larger class of independent, landowning farmers; increase agricultural production; and strengthen popular participation in government. The experience of Valladolid shows the contrary movement: increased dependence and landlessness, declining productivity, and the continuing marginality of peasants to the political life of the nation. This does not, however, demonstrate the impotence of education, but only the lack of realism implicit in the educational system that was created. Administrators failed to appreciate fully the position of education within the colonial environment of the Philippines, or to acknowledge that it is not a free, autonomous agent but part of a larger network of interacting systems.[18]

For Valladolid, the tragedy was that, while the old moral world represented by the *linambay* had lost its coherence, the new world promised by the school had not quite taken a clear and satisfying shape. At its height the *linambay* was a symbolic focus for the subjective life of the village; it had a village-wide, centralizing power. Until 1940, the school remained a peripheral institution, fitful and discontinuous in its presence and in its celebration of such rituals as Parent-Teachers' Association (PTA) meetings, Garden Day, graduation ceremonies, and community assemblies. It was a door that opened out into a larger world, but a world that did not quite compel a sense of belonging or belief.

Conclusion

We have marked here a change in the cultural life of a Philippine village, analyzing such change around the axial points represented by a popular theater tradition and the modern public school.

The transition from theater to school was not an abrupt, sequential step. In terms of simple chronology, *escuela* and *linambay* coexisted during most of the period under consideration (1880–1940). We can see, however, that as the *escuela* moved from makeshift hut to a permanent building equipped with desks and blackboards, the *linambay* regressed from the fullness of a central barrio festivity to the destitution of *sitio* entertainments.

Though we have spoken of the two as competing systems, there was, in their actual operation, little direct hostility between them. The principal patrons of the *linambay* were also the principal patrons of the *escuela*. The schoolchildren contributed to the *linambay* by assisting in the building and decorating of the stage. Barrio schoolteachers themselves—like the schoolteacher-wife of Constancio Gantuangco (a leading *linambay* patron-playwright) who was a *linambay estatera* or lead actress—actively lent assistance to the production.

There was, nevertheless, a basic contradiction between the two systems. This was given public expression in 1919 in an acrimonious quarrel between Don Magno Regis, a maverick village landowner, and the rest of the village elite. Through the medium of a Cebu City newspaper, Don Magno criticized the *linambay* as a backward, wasteful practice that exhausted resources better spent on such modern innovations as artesian wells, roads, and schools.[19] Don Magno, in turn, was chided for indifference to village undertakings and a lack of *noblesse oblige*. The controversy escalated to a point where Don Magno transferred his house to the outskirts of the village, taking with him the image of the patron saint—San Roque—from the barrio chapel on the grounds it was his family's heirloom.

Outside of this instance of open conflict, the two systems coexisted peaceably. The lack of explicit tension is explained by factors we have already cited, such as the underdeveloped character of the barrio school and the carry-over of old forms of patronage from theater to school. Moreover, the shift in the center of gravity from theater to school corresponded to the gradual degradation of the village economy itself. It was not a sudden, dramatic change. Yet an important shift had taken place.

The *linambay* was an *inward-oriented* system drawing its power not only from its own aesthetic values but from a configuration of social and economic factors supportive of the "world" it expressed and mediated. The modern school, on the other hand, is an *outward-oriented* institution and one which similarly draws its effectiveness not only from narrowly institutional foundations, but from social and economic conditions that support and reinforce the values and imperatives of the world it brokers. In this same context, the villager's participation in either the *linambay* or the school was motivated and shaped by his perceptions as well as by his calculations of his position and chances in that world. In the movement from folk theater to modern school is thus expressed a whole social history.

We are not offering a conclusive judgment on the value and performance of the public school system as this study goes only as far as 1940.[20] Our primary interest here lies in clarifying the workings of a given symbol-system or cultural institution. An understanding of the factors and conditions which make such a system *work* should lead to an appreciation of the fact that what is ultimately crucial is not merely institutional but broadly social. J. S. Furnivall, one of the first scholars to consider the implications of the introduction of modern schools into Southeast Asian societies, wrote:

> Educationalists, in claiming that education should or must promote the good life, or change the social order, or soften the impact of western civilization, overlook the fact that education is not something given in the school or by way of formal instruction, but is the operation of the whole environment. (Furnivall 1956:403)

This does not, however, negate the function of the school as an important mediator and focus of that environment, nor does it cancel the possibility that, while it is bred of a given environment, it can also act on that environment. For all its seeming wholeness, the *linambay* was the captive of a dying order. The school need not be so.

Notes

[1] Part of this chapter is drawn from a study entitled *Theater in Society, Society in Theater: Social History of a Cebuano Village* (Quezon City: Ateneo de Manila University Press, 1985). I thank the Philippine Social Science Council, Inc., for providing initial funding for the project on which the study is based.

[2] The focal settlement of a large area of the sixteenth century, Valladolid (*Sialo, Daang Lungsod*) was first established as a parish by Augustinian missionaries on June 21, 1599. Around 1622 it was destroyed during a Muslim raid. The population shifted inland to the new settlement of Carcar (Kabkad) and Valladolid was relegated to the status of a satellite village. The single best introduction to the history of Cebu Province during the Spanish period is Fenner (1976).

[3] This analysis is drawn from a 1:2000 scale Bureau of Lands map of Valladolid, based on the cadastral survey of 1915, and an accompanying numerical list of claimants.

[4] Grifol (1894:337–39) lists Valladolid as one of the places in Cebu with a school in 1893. A document at the Philippine National Archives (PNA, Escuelas, Cebu, Bundle 1, August 13, 1883) indicates that no school existed in the barrio in 1883, although a decree of May 7, 1871 had authorized the establishment of a school there.

[5] Rapid population increase in Cebu took place from 1800 to around 1920 when population growth was 1.8% (as against the national percentage of 1.61%). From 1920 on, the population growth rate dropped to 1.06% (while the national average rose to 2.36%). For an agricultural and demographic profile of Cebu Island, see VanderMeer (1962).

[6] The figures are from Fox and Mercader (1962:46) and from a series of *relaciones* or reports of monthly school attendance submitted to Manila by the politico-military governor of Cebu. There are sixteen of these reports scattered for the period 1876–1881 in the Philippine National Archives (PNA, *Escuelas*, Cebu, 3 bundles, 1860–1882).

[7] Spanish educational statistics, like Grifol's reference to 114 "schools" in Cebu in 1893, can be misleading. Boys and girls in the Spanish system were segregated, with each group forming an *escuela*, thus accounting for the norm of two "schools" to a town. In the American coeducational system, such schools were counted as one.

[8] The best Visayan example of this class of works is *Lagda sa Pagca Maligdon sa Tauong Bisaya* (Binondo: Imprenta de M. Sanchez y Cia, 1865). Five known editions run from 1734 to 1893.

[9] For a statement of Barrows's views, see RPC (1903:III, 694–705) and RPC (1905:IV, 407–11).

[10] The Monroe Survey is the most important study of the Philippine educational system of this period. It was authored by Acts Nos. 3126 and 3196 of the Philippine Legislature, and carried out in 1925 by a commission headed by Dr. Paul Monroe of Columbia University. See BES (1925) and Hayden (1947:473–74).

[11] We have the names of fifteen persons who taught in Valladolid in the years before 1940: Salvador Gantuangco, Tomas Laña, Roman Alo, Juan de Veyra, Jose Alcordo, Brigida Alvarado, Felipe Alcuitas, Jose Cortes, Olimpia Enriquez, Alejandro Flores, Ramon Regis, Columba Villasorda, Magno Baritua, Rosita Montesclaros Cavan, and Julieta Villarosa Reynes. Oral data indicate the following profile: they came from landowning families, and those who came from outside the village later married into local families. Furthermore, six of the fifteen belonged to the Regis and Gantuangco families, either by blood or marriage.

[12] For an example, see PNA, *Escuelas*, Cebu, Bundle 1, "Expediente del maestro substituto de Carcar Dn. Guillermo Galicano" (June 12, 1872). Our knowledge of the nineteenth-century teachers whose names have survived—Don Salvador Gantuangco and Don Valeriano Gandionco—bears this elite pattern out. See PNA, *Escuelas*, Cebu, Bundle 1 (October 26, 1871, June 12, 1872, August 13, 1883) and Bundle 3 (June 23, 1887).

[13] PNA, *Escuelas*, Cebu, Bundle 1, "Expediente personal de Dn. Salvador Gantuangco" (August 13, 1883). It is not clear, however, whether Gantuangco actually succeeded in opening a school and teaching in Valladolid.

[14] Interviews with Sofronio Gantuangco and Teodulfo Regis, Valladolid (April 19, 1983) and Marcel M. Navarra, Valladolid (April 25, 1983).

[15] Mabel Bonsall and G. E. Mercer, *Primary Arithmetic: Part III* (rev. ed., New York, 1908), pp. 113–16. Cited in May (1980:193–95).

[16] This criticism was made by various sectors of the Philippine press as well as by the Monroe Survey Report of 1925 and the Prosser Report of 1930. The latter report was based on a commissioned study of vocational education in the Philippines done under Dr. C. E. Prosser. See Hayden (1947:520–31) and BES (1925:59–62, 278–83).

[17] In a 1925 survey of seniors in the Cebu High School, only one out of a class of 147 seniors gave farming as his intended career after graduation

(BES 1925:335). An excellent discussion of how the "investment ethic" works in Philippine peasant communities is in Fegan (1979).

[18] Such naiveté is expressed in the pronouncements of many educators and policymakers of the period. A classic statement of this view is to be found in Osias (1921, 1940).

[19] See the articles of Magno Regis and Porfirio Gantuangco in the following issues of these Cebu City periodicals: *The Freeman* (September 21, 1919), *Nueva Fuerza* (November 6, 1919; November 11, 1919; and November 18, 1919).

[20] Studies of the postwar performance of Philippine rural schools indicate the persistence of many of the problems cited here. They show that, on the basis of its stated goals, the educational system has not been vital and effective as an agent of social change. See Foley (1976) and Manalang (1977).

References

Bard, H. E. "Best Plans for Establishing and Conducting Barrio Schools." Paper presented at the Superintendents' Convention, Manila, March 23–27, 1903. In *RPC*, 1903:874–77.

Board of Educational Survey (BES). *A Survey of the Educational System of the Philippine Islands*. Manila: Bureau of Printing, 1925.

Burke, Kenneth. *The Philosophy of Literary Form: Studies in Symbolic Action*. New York: Vintage Books, 1957.

Census. *Census of the Philippine Islands, 1903*. Washington, D.C.: U.S. Bureau of the Census, 1905, vol. III.

———. *Census of the Philippine Islands, 1918*. Manila: Bureau of Printing, 1921, vol. IV.

———. *Census of the Philippines, 1939, Population: Province of Cebu*. Manila: Bureau of Printing, 1940.

Fegan, Brian. "Folk Capitalism: Economic Strategies of Peasants in a Philippine Wet-Rice Village." Ph.D. dissertation, Yale University, 1979.

Fenner, Bruce L. "Colonial Cebu: An Economic-Social History, 1521–1896." Ph.D. dissertation, Cornell University, 1976.

Foley, Douglas E. *Philippine Rural Education: An Anthropological Perspective*. DeKalb, Illinois: Northern Illinois University, Center for Southeast Asian Studies, Special Report No. 13, 1976.

Fox, Frederick, and Juan Mercader. "Some Notes on Education in Cebu Province, 1820–1898." *Philippine Studies*, 9.1(1961):20–46.

Furnivall, J. S. *Colonial Policy and Practice: A Comparative Study of Burma and Netherlands India*. New ed., New York: New York University Press, 1956.

Geertz, Clifford. *The Interpretation of Cultures*. New York: Basic Books, 1973.

Grifol, Daniel. *La Instruccion Primaria en Filipinas*. Manila: Tipo-Litografia de Chofre y Comp. a, 1894.

Hayden, Joseph Ralston. *The Philippines: A Study in National Development*. New York: Macmillan Company, 1947.

MacClintock, Samuel. "Around the Island of Cebu on Horseback." *American Journal of Sociology*, 8.4(1903):433–41.

Manalang, Priscila S. *A Philippine Rural School: Its Cultural Dimension*. Quezon City: University of the Philippines Press, 1977.

May, Glenn A. *Social Engineering in the Philippines: The Aims, Execution, and Impact of American Colonial Policy, 1900–1913.* Westport, CT: Greenwood Press, 1980.

Mendoza, Felicidad M. *The Comedia (Moro-Moro) Re-Discovered.* Makati: Society of St. Paul, 1976.

Montero, Jose. *El Archipelago Filipino y las Islas Marianas, Carolinas, y Palaos.* Madrid: Imprenta y Fundicion de Manuel Tello, 1886.

Osias, Camilo. *Barrio Life and Barrio Education.* New York: World Book Company, 1921.

——. *The Filipino Way of Life.* Boston: Ginn and Company, 1940.

RPC. *Report of the Philippine Commission.* Washington, D.C.: U.S. Government Printing Office, 1902–05. (This multi-volume series, here cited as RPC, ran from 1900 to 1915.)

Staunton, John A. "The American Teacher in the Community." Paper presented at the American Teachers' Institute, Cebu, June 16, 1902. In *RPC*, 1902:II, pp. 943–48.

Tiongson, Nicanor G. *Kasaysayan ng Komedya sa Pilipinas, 1766– 1982.* Manila: De La Salle University, Integrated Research Center, 1982.

UNESCO. *Fifty Years of Education for Freedom, 1901–1951.* Manila: National Printing Company, 1953. (Published by UNESCO-Philippine Educational Foundation.)

VanderMeer, Canute. "Corn on the Island of Cebu, the Philippines." Ph.D. dissertation, University of Michigan, 1962.

LANGUAGE AND LEARNING
IN A VISAYAN COMMUNITY[1]

Jean-Paul Dumont

A Problem with Education

"Education" is a word which cannot be uttered lightly, for it contains a highly emotional charge. It is not a mere concept but a whole cultural program. This is revealed less by the history of its contextualized successes and failures than by the very etymology of the word itself. To educate, from Latin e-ducere, is, in a sense to educe, that is to lead away, to disengage from. The same etymology pertains to the equivalent Spanish verb educar. Cebuano, a Visayan language[2] which has the greatest number of native speakers in the Philippines, has borrowed from its first colonial experience the verbal form idukar[3] (to educate) and such derivatives as idukadu (educated) and idukasyun (education).

In all these forms, a decidedly Western process can be recognized, whereby individuals are led away from an initial state of ignorance or, worse, of evil, by omission or by commission. This could be called a process of "denaturation" if one were to follow Lévi-Strauss' (1969:3–11) idea of passage from nature to culture. It is identifiable from the very beginning of the Spanish colonization with its insistence on the participation of soul-saving priests. In this regard, Humabon's hasty conversion in Cebu by Father Valderrama (Blair and Robertson 1903–09:xxxiii, 149) is a case in point. And, in fact, a modern historian (Zaide 1979:i, 314) assesses the achievements of the early Spanish missionaries in the Philippines in terms, at times unfortunate, which reinforce the idea of an "e-ducation:"

> To the lasting glory of the Church, it can be said that the pioneer Spanish missionaries were the first educators of the Filipinos. They founded the first schools and colleges in (the) Philippines, many of which still stand as veritable citadels of Catholic education in the Pacific world. It is true that the early Spanish missionaries were responsible to a certain extent for the destruction of the ancient Filipino writings. But viewed from a larger perspective, the burning of these old native writings was a blessing to the Filipinos, for it facilitated their assimilation of the Latin alphabet, the Spanish language, and the Occidental knowledge that the missionaries had brought to the Philippines.

Even though it is difficult to endorse the apologist's tone or to deny the nature of the described facts, the style of this statement is interesting for its assumption of erring natives prior to colonization.

On the other hand, while the word *idukasyun* places the accent upon the leading-away process to which individuals are submitted, it is possible to emphasize instead the leading-toward aspect of the movement, its informative rather than reformative guise. Indeed, the Cebuano language has at its disposal the strictly native *tudlu*. As a verb, it can be translated as "to teach," but it also conveys "to point out" as well as "to point at." It stresses directionality, which is easily understandable, because as a substantive it refers both to the fingers in general and to the index finger in particular. As opposed to the borrowing, *idukar*, which, as we have seen, educes in a process of denaturation, the native *tudlu* brings about and persuades and thus induces in a process of enculturation which I would call "in-ducation," could such a word pass for a neologism rather than emerge as a barbarism.[4]

We may wonder whether the tension which already begins to appear in the language between a movement away and a movement toward pervades the manner in which rural people in the Central Visayas apprehend and interpret the world in which they live, and, furthermore, transmit such apprehension and interpretation to their children. In this respect, it will be useful to focus attention on a specific community on an island which, from our present point of view, offers the additional advantage of being entirely rural.

Education and Local Culture on a Philippine Island

Siquijor, where my wife and I settled during 1980–81, is located between the islands of Negros, Cebu, Bohol, and Mindanao. It had been the smallest province-island in the Philippines when it acquired its provincial status in 1972. Small without being tiny with its 343.5 square kilometers, modest without being insignificant with its 70,000 inhabitants, Siquijor offers a remarkable ethnic and cultural homogeneity. Among the individuals who report a gainful occupation, over 75 per cent are involved in agriculture and/or fishing (see Philippines 1975:26–61). Over 80 percent of the *Siquihodnon*, as they call themselves, are at least nominally Roman Catholics and the rest are unequally distributed between Aglipayan and several Protestant confessions. An equivalent percentage of *Siquihodnon* still finds marriage partners on the island itself. The census of 1975 (see Philippines 1975:25) indicates that 99.56 percent of the *Siquihodnon* are native speakers of Cebuano while only 0.11 percent are native speakers of Tagalog. Such uniformity is strikingly reflected in the pool of last names which reveals immediately to the outsider a Siquijorian identity, since the

majority are putative or actual lexical derivations from the Cebuano vocabulary such as Baguio (typhoon), Paglinawan (peacefulness), Gabas (to
saw) or Aso (smoke).

The cultural homogeneity of Siquijor, immediately perceptible to the
most casual observer, may be vitiated if looked at from a different angle.
I introduced the linguistic contrast between the two lexical items *idukar*
and *tudlu* not as a vain scholastic exercise, but because it points to what
may at first appear as an irreconcilable chasm in the sociocultural reality
between native roots and colonial past, or, more accurately, colonial pasts.
Although many people on the island were likely to identify their occupation,
or someone else's, by the Spanish borrowing *maestro* or *maestra*[5], or more
frequently, by the English word "teacher," some also used the Cebuano substantive *magtutudlu* (derived from *tudlu*). Interestingly, I never heard this
last word used by a teacher, but rather by older *barangay*[6] informants who
were monolingual Cebuano speakers. They rarely used it in reference to
people whose main occupation was teaching, but rather to designate technical specialists, for instance a tailor or a carpenter who had an apprentice.
Similarly, one of my informants, who oriented me with patient perseverance
through the perilous intricacies of Cebuano grammar, was also referred to
as my *magtutudlu*. From this standpoint, there is indeed an apparent contradiction between the *magtutudlu*—the informal informant and instructor
of things native, and the *maestro*—the formal educator and instructor of
things foreign.[7] The roots of such a contradiction can be found in the sed-
imentation of successive historical layers, the repository of which is today's
culture.

Given the colonial history of the Philippines, it is not surprising that
a number of Cebuano words related to formal schooling are Spanish bor-
rowings. Such is the case, among others, of *kwadirnu* ("notebook" from
Sp. *cuaderno*), *lapis* ("pencil" from Sp. *lapiz*) or even *iskuylahan* ("school"
from Sp. *escuela*). As early as 1609, Antonio de Morga had noted that "at
the same time that the religious undertook to teach the natives the precepts of religion, they ... established schools for the reading and writing of
Spanish among the boys" (Blair and Robertson 1903–09:xvi, 152). Already
by 1843, Sinibaldo de Mas could write that "in proportion, there are more
persons who can read and write in these islands than in España and in
some (other) civilized countries" (Blair and Robertson 1903–09:xlv, 246).

Even though the educational decree of 1863 could not be implemented
before the very last decades of the Spanish regime, it established for the
first time a public school system in the Philippines. For instance, in the
municipality of Lazi in Siquijor, the first *maestro*, a Don Juan Yber, was not

nominated before 1879[8], while the first *maestra*, a Doña Guillerma Farling was certified only at the end of 1881.[9] By 1888, both were respectively in charge of 502 schoolboys and 791 schoolgirls.[10] Taking the lowest possible estimate for the population of that municipality in the 1880s and early 1890s, the presence of these two educators represents, at best, a ratio of one teacher for more than 2,500 inhabitants. In Lazi there were 5,217 inhabitants in 1878 (*Guia Official de Filipinas* 1878:293), 7,142 in 1884–85 (Romero de Madrijeros 1884–85:ii, 291) and 8,038 in 1892 (*Guia Official de Filipinas* 1892:497).

The educational situation had indeed deteriorated since 1870 when there were sixty-one teachers of both sexes for 153,734 inhabitants[11] (Cavada y Mendez de Vigo 1876:ii, 149), thus giving a ratio of one teacher per 2,520 inhabitants. Matters improved in Lazi only in the mid–1890s, when the aforementioned Don Yber and Doña Farling were reinforced by two teaching-aides, Don Juan Lumacad and Doña Paula Balmadres.[12] Yet the census of 1903 (U.S. Bureau of the Census 1905:78) indicates that less than 45 percent of all people at least ten years of age could read, while only half of those could claim any ability to write.

Carson (1978:6) summarizes the situation inherited by the second colonial power:

Arriving as a new governing power after 1898, the Americans found no one tongue that could command more than a limited following. When a public-school system was established in 1901 on the U.S. pattern of the day, the language problem was met by the policy of teaching in English. In the beginning this was accomplished by the importation of English-speaking teachers. When the Republic of the Philippines was inaugurated on July 6, 1946 the school system was taken over bodily and English retained as the language of instruction.

However, Renato Constantino (1966:436) sheds a different light on the situation:

From its inception, the educational system of the Philippines was a means of pacifying a people who were defending their newly won freedom from an invader who had posed as an ally. The education of the Filipino under American sovereignty was an instrument of colonial policy. The Filipino had to be educated as a good colonial.

And the same author (Constantino 1966:438) adds:

The first and perhaps the master stroke in the plan to use education as an instrument of colonial policy was the decision to use

English as the medium of instruction. English became the wedge that separated the Filipinos from their past and later was to separate educated Filipinos from the masses of their countrymen.

Unfortunately the "language problem" did not end when the Filipinos gained their independence. As early as the inauguration of the Commonwealth in 1935, the issue had arisen of which national language was to be selected from the pool of native languages in the Philippines. Tagalog, the language of Manila and its surroundings, became in 1946 one of the official languages of the Philippines, and is currently taught in schools. But, as pointed out by Agoncillo and Guerrero (1977:619):

> The bitter controversy that arose from the national language issue led the authorities of the Department of Education to propose a solution by using Pilipino, instead of Tagalog, as the national language. The reason is based not on any scientific explanation but on purely practical grounds, namely, to neutralize the bull-headed opposition of the professional anti-Tagalog by not mentioning the word Tagalog which, to the oppositionists, smacks of superiority. So Tagalog is now being used only as a *basis* but is not *the* national language, although to all appearances Pilipino, or the national language, is patently Tagalog.

Not only is Pilipino taught in schools nowadays, but following the educational decree of 1972[13], Pilipino has become the mandatory medium of instruction for several subjects since the school year 1978–79.

In the context of Siquijor, the struggle against illiteracy has produced spectacular results. The census of 1975 (Philippines 1975:80) counted 698 "professors and teachers" on the island; that is roughly one per one hundred inhabitants. Although the achievements are indeed remarkable, they should not be misinterpreted as having reached the idyllic perfection that official statistics would lead one to anticipate. While in Siquijor, I noted that teachers systematically reported a one hundred percent rate of attendance with genuine, if erroneous, enthusiasm. However, this was not—indeed could not be—the case. I frequently met children in the *barangay* who were supposed to be at school. Some farming and fishing activities were incompatible with the regular attendance demanded of pupils. Children of both sexes farmed, boys fished, and girls often tended younger siblings while their parents were involved in some other activity. The economic value of children is well-documented (see for instance Arnold *et al.* 1975, and Bulatao 1975), but it is a primary source of conflict between formal schooling and on-site training, in other words between education and enculturation. Free education is still costly to peasants for two main reasons. A child at school produces nothing; on-site practical training in productive activities is more important for the child's likely future as a peasant than is formal schooling.

In this respect, there is a significant contrast in attitudes toward schools between the *barangay* residents and the inhabitants of the *publasiyun*[14]. The *barangay* people are fishing and/or farming peasants who live in a scattered habitat. The *publasiyun* is a settlement clustered around the *munisipyu* (town hall), the *simbahan* (church), the *mirkadu* (market), and ultimately the *bulangan* (cockpit)[15]. Although by no means exclusively, it is *par excellence* the domain of the local bourgeoisie: the *balikbayan*[16] who has returned to the Philippines, the *pinsiyunadu*[17] whose income derives from his veteran's benefit or from some retirement program, the doctors and lawyers, the store owners, the jeepney operators, the copra dealers, and the legion of civil servants to which the teachers belong.

Even though school teachers are not, by far, the wealthiest town dwellers, they can count on regular paychecks from which to save and invest. For example, I once encountered two teachers, one of whom wanted to buy my motorcycle while the other wished to acquire its sidecar in order to start a *pedikab*[18] operation. Another teacher dealt in copra and peanuts, and yet another had acquired a general store under the name of his wife. All teachers seemed able to afford to invest in a variety of commercial ventures.

If all the townspeople are not economically well off, most are at least better off than the *barangay* peasants. Many members of the town elite are more or less successful entrepreneurs who extend their economic, political, even religious patronage to their *barangay* clients. They all have an available monetary surplus which they can dissipate at the mahjong table and at the cockpit, or transform into capital, which in turn will fructify thanks to the labor of the *barangay* people. This is achieved in various ways, such as securing the fisherman's means of production (boats, nets, and lines), acquiring land cultivated by *saup* (sharecroppers), or loaning cash for mortgages or pawned property[19].

Thus, living above the bare subsistence level to which most *barangay* peasants are confined, the townspeople have the means as well as the will to educate their children. School attendance among townspeople is regular indeed, because it is perceived by children and parents alike as a way to better social status and maintain or even increase economic advantages. Town children can readily nourish ambitions for higher education, while the *barangay* children cannot realistically do so and are, from an economic standpoint, probably better off maximizing their technical competence in traditional *barangay* activities. For the townspeople, there is no such distinction. They can release their children without hesitation to the educative hands of specialists, the teachers who belong to their peer group. Inasmuch as teachers are or have become townspeople, school attendance by town children is merely a part of—not apart from—their enculturation process.

In this light, we can now see why the *barangay* people experience formal education in contradiction with their way of life, while the townspeople perceive it as a continuation of theirs. Both groups gravitate, as it were, toward different spheres. Their value systems are necessarily different, and this is reflected in their scholastic attitudes. Although primary schools are located in town as well as in the different *barangay*, they are often staffed by teachers who commute from the *publasiyun*, sometimes from another municipality, and who are correctly perceived as townspeople. Even if teachers are themselves children of the *barangay*, they have "made it" in the system and, to a certain extent, do not belong in the *barangay* anymore; they have become townspeople and as such have acquired a different orientation.

Townspeople may indeed travel to urban centers such as Cebu and even Manila; they may also consider emigrating to the United States. Their value orientation is definitely western; they know that a solid education with a college degree is a key, if not the best guarantee, to success. For them, fluency in English is a must, while Pilipino is an administrative imposition which they tend to resent. For a few, Pilipino is a new obstacle in their children's path to success, erected as a consequence of a new kind of internal colonialism. For others it is perceived as it is meant to be—a future national language. But for the majority it is passively resisted.

The *barangay* people, on the other hand, have few illusions about their children's fate. They know that the possibility of becoming even a modest entrepreneur is unlikely. They must survive in the *barangay*. If they cannot make ends meet there, they too will have to emigrate, but it will be to sell their labor somewhere on the southern frontier in Mindanao. To a large extent they have internalized their poverty as well as their powerlessness. They and their children have a limited use for schools which they tend to see as important and prestigious but relatively inaccessible and irrelevant. The immediate demands of their productive activities leave them little opportunity to climb the merit scale or ascend the social ladder. Cebuano is the native language of the *barangay* dwellers. Since they will spend their lives among Cebuano speakers, English, although prestigious in town, is of little use to them, and they will never learn enough of it for it to become useful. Pilipino, which they neither read nor write, neither speak nor hear outside a classroom context,[20] is even more foreign than

English, and becomes lost in utter irrelevance. Education in the formal sense is considered a luxury, while the really important technical know-how of fishing and farming is slowly transmitted by family tradition. Under these conditions, the attendance of children at school is understandably rather nonchalant.

The Ambiguous Teacher

There is a strong distinction between the local values and realities of the *barangay* and those of the town elite. The *barangay* remains on the side of tradition while the town opens up, partially at least, to the outside world. For the former, enculturation and education are two processes which are not entirely compatible; for the latter, education is part of the process of enculturation. And yet, although *idukar* and *tudlu*—to e-ducate and to in-form—contrast, they also constitute a polarity within which a dynamic tension is at play in daily practice. Such a tension between contradictory tendencies pervades the cultural life of the *Siquihodnon* to whom we now return.

In order to explore the subtle oscillations of this tension between the two extremes, it will be useful to look at the position of the teacher in society. The *barangay* inhabitants do not necessarily perceive townspeople as equally rich and learned individuals, but they have interiorized the hierarchical relationship which separates them from the town dwellers. In the upper stratum, lawyers and doctors—and of course it is not perchance that these two professions are also the two most prestigious occupations in the United States—are indeed educated, but the years of formal education needed to join their ranks place them far beyond the *barangay* horizon. Successful store-owners are also indeed rich, but since they were born and/or married that way, they too fall beyond the reach of the *barangay*. However, the situation is rather different for teachers.

Teachers have *kinaadman* (general culture) rather than a specific, but at the same time, limited, technical *ka-alam* (know-how)—words share the same root *alam. They are *may hibangkaagan* (learned) and *manggihibaluun* (knowledgeable) and, still compared to peasants, they are also *datu* (rich). For all these reasons, they inspire *tahud* (respect). Furthermore, their knowledge-induced wealth is definitely within the *barangay* horizon. On the one hand, the prestige associated with the status of educator is noticeably reinforced by the uniform they wear, a mark of achievement which gives extra visibility to any teacher, especially when s/he appears in a *barangay*. On the other hand, for a peasant's child to become a teacher is still an acceptable and realistic goal within reach, no matter how difficult that goal may be to achieve.

My principal informant, now in his mid-forties, explained to me that he had excelled in the early grades. Motivated by a strong desire to leave poverty behind him, he had wanted to become a teacher. Unfortunately, his family's poverty prevented him from going to high school because he had to fish and farm on his father's land instead. He hoped that his youthful ambitions would be fulfilled by his children. The untimely demise of his wife leaving him with a dozen children, as well as his subsequent proletarization, placed a serious check on that too. This tends to indicate that between the "away" and the "toward," a tension exists. Furthermore, each individual has some room to maneuver conceptually at least, even though, in practice, the constraints are stronger than may be expected.

Interestingly, this man's niece is likely to do better than he did, not just because she is talented and motivated, as he was, but for more important reasons. Both her parents are alive; she has unmarried sisters who can free her from having to take care of her younger siblings; her mother is a small-scale *labasira* (female fish vendor) who supplements the father's modest income as a fisherman; she has fewer sisters than brothers whose income, modest as it is, can nevertheless help toward her educational struggle; the whole family has been able so far to back her efforts and, in particular, to buy her the school uniform without which children feel too *ulaw* (embarassed) to attend school.

As the case of my *barangay* informant illustrates, teachers occupy an ambiguous position; their status mediates between the traditions to which the *barangay* clings and the modernity to which the town pretends. They are often of *barangay* extraction although ill at ease, if not slightly at odds, with their sociocultural inheritance. This was explained to me by several teachers who, in their own terms, had wanted "to enlarge their horizon." When they return to teach in the *barangay* schools, they often settle and reside in town. They are rich and educated like the townspeople, but their formative years have been spent in the *barangay*. In other words, they find themselves caught between *barangay* and town, between tradition and modernity, between Cebuano and national and foreign languages.

Furthermore, along with perhaps nursing and religion, teaching is one of the very few avenues of escape from the *barangay*, and it is more readily open to women than to men. Since the prevalent type of post-marital residence is virilocal, a girl's future depends upon her marriage unless she succeeds in a teaching career, which gives her relative freedom. No wonder, then, that girls rather than boys are pushed into teaching. Nothing reflects better the ambiguity of their status than the inordinate number of unmarried female teachers. One might say that teachers, particularly those who were raised in the *barangay*, often have gained the security of steady income and social achievement at the disconcerting expense of their cultural identity.

The Quandary of Language

This situation is compounded by a linguistic problem. Although the medium of instruction for the first years of primary schools is vernacular, that is, Cebuano in the case of Siquijor, it changes later to English, in which most textbooks are still written, and, to Pilipino. But most teachers find themselves in the impossible position of having to use linguistic media with which they feel ill at ease. Their English is stilted and bookish because it is genuinely a foreign language, and, whenever they can, they revert to Cebuano. Their Pilipino is in worse shape, because, except for a rare voyage outside the Visayas, they have no opportunity to practice it. In addition, non-Cebuano speakers who come from other regions of the Philippines are more likely to use English than Pilipino during their stay in Siquijor. This was vividly illustrated for me when several scientists from Manila who had come to Lazi to investigate local geoseismic activities gave what they called, in English, a "press conference" which was, in fact, a town meeting to quell popular worries about a rumored earthquake (see Dumont 1980). The first official delivered his speech in Pilipino which only a handful of people could understand. It had to be translated into English before someone could finally retranslate it into Cebuano.

The tragedy of the broader linguistic quandary, illustrated in the above examples of fractured speech, is manifested in the experience of schoolchildren. They must confront a situation in which they are taught neither proper English nor Pilipino, while their own language is left by the wayside after the first years of schooling. Pupils do not learn only what the *maestro* explicitly teaches. They tend also to mimic his or her style. If the teachers are hesitant in their linguistic orientation, so are the schoolchildren, who perceive an element of prestige in foreign languages that they will never speak with ease. They find also an element of inadequacy in their own language, the nuances, intricacies, and sheer beauty of which they may never be taught. Because of this mostly superficial exposure to English and Pilipino, some of each language manages to filter into the speech of the average *Siquihodnon*, thus giving rise to an incredible *pot-pourri*. The ambiguities of the teachers' cultural orientations are undoubtedly also transmitted to the children. The teachers are pushed and pulled between a native language, convenient but without prestige, and foreign languages, prestigious but unfamiliar. Under their tutelage, pupils have been all too quick to learn linguistic hesitations. It is for this reason that daily conversations may give to the outside observer an impression of extreme imprecision, as if linguistic assurance were totally lacking.

Some sense of this can be illustrated in the following example from a taped interview in the *barangay*. The speaker had been asked who had accompanied him on an ill-fated fishing trip several years ago. He replied:

"*Nalimut na ku, kuan,* that's his name, I forget already, *kuan. Mau tu akung kauban. Nagkuan pa ang asawa niya duul sa kuan, sa palengke.*"

Translated and rephrased in standard English, it reads:

"I have forgotten, uh, I have forgotten his name, uh. He was my companion. His wife what-do-you-call-it (lives) close to the uh, to the market."

The answer is manifestly interesting not so much for its minimal content, but for the variety displayed in its form. The Cebuano word *kuan* is a pause word which marks hesitation and indicates that the speaker searches for the words. It is also a replacement for any lexical item that the speaker cannot recall from memory. As I discovered to my dismay, it is indeed possible to be told: "*Gikuan ku ang kuan ba ni Kuan,*" i.e., approximately, "I did what-do-you-call-it to what's-his-name's whachamacallit" and meaning "I bought Berto's net." Only the context can indicate that the speaker does not wish to say, "I sold Dodong's fish" or "I fixed Nonoy's roof," both possible translations. If the flexibility is extreme, so is the communicative blur that it entails.

In addition, the word *kuan* tends to be used to indicate the language code is about to change. This is not automatic, but it is likely to occur because the speaker, failing to find the word he wants to utter in the code he is presently using, hopes for better luck in another language. Consequently in the taped interview above, the word *kuan* occurred not only as a substitute in the verbal form *nagkuan*, but also as a marker of a switch from Cebuano to English, again before the switch back to Cebuano, and finally before the use of the Tagalog word *palengke* instead of the Cebuano *mirkadu*. Although I have obviously chosen this example for the sake of my argument, these changes back and forth, particularly between English and Cebuano, do occur frequently in everyday conversations.

And yet, not everyone hops with equal ease from language to language. The *barangay* dwellers who have less familiarity with foreign languages, and are less educated, are also more restricted in their use of code changes. They tend to limit such changes to short sentences or isolated words. The town elite, on the other hand, who are better educated and consequently more familiar with English, and who, in addition, have a larger Pilipino vocabulary, are better equipped to utter longer discourses in one language before feeling the need for a change of linguistic code. The code-switching in town is conditioned by the context: the townspeople talk in Cebuano to their employees, to the *barangay* people—their clients, and in English to important outside visitors. With their peers they have the flexibility of passing from Cebuano to English and back depending upon the social context in which they find themselves and the topic of conversation.

But such contextual shifting is more than gratuitous maneuverability. I observed that individuals manipulated, at times carefully, these switches. Among *barangay* teenagers, dropping a Pilipino word here and there or an English phrase drawn from school experience was clearly a way of showing off and impressing one's peers. It is indeed a way of separating oneself from one's peers by boasting or pretending to boast of one's education. And yet because of the peer pressure of the *barkada* (a gang of coevals who hang around together), such displays never went unnoticed. This permissible deviance was often sanctioned by laughter as if to prevent the pretense from getting out of hand.

Among the town bourgeoisie, the choice of language was also an acknowledgement of the social status of others. If a member of the local elite could routinely address his employees or his *barangay* clients in a Cebuano which was, for the occasion, purified of any English, and if the same person could also speak a fluent English within his or her *barkada*, it is clear beyond any doubt that it was meant to recognize as well as to manipulate the speaker's and hearer's relative status. One could therefore pretend to initiate a symbolic social ascent by addressing someone better educated in English rather than Cebuano. But the same individual could thereby run the risk of being put down. The addressee, instead of ackowledging peerage by replying in English, might deny it, in an occasional display of passive-aggressive nastiness, by answering in Cebuano. As I discovered with some measure of distress, in my eagerness to practice my Cebuano, it was perceived as an insult for me to address in that language people who had some competence in English, although it was equally offensive for me to address in English those who had none.

Because in town as well as in the *barangay* everybody knows where s/he stands in relation to almost everybody else, the stage is set for communication to occur smoothly and flawlessly. But at the very same time it also sets the stage for such linguistic manipulations to occur in conflictual exchanges where one can display to others one's education and reassert or attempt to improve one's place in the local social order.

In the linguistic plurality of the Siquijorian reality, language transcends its communicative function to become performative in the extreme. To borrow from Saussure's (1962) vocabulary, it could be said that the *langue* perverts the *parole*, since what is said in the small talk of routine conversations appears to be less important than the language in which it is said. Performance is thus a displayed competence which is made not only manifest but public, and which expresses social and cultural articulations in interpersonal communication. To that extent, the code is indeed the message. Linguistic competence thus becomes power as it acquires symbolic efficiency, which can be further attested by an example drawn from the religious domain.

In the *barangay*, women are organized under the banner of the *Virgen sa Rosario*[21] to recite the Rosary every day at a different house. The prayers are chanted in Cebuano. On the other hand, when an individual dies, prayers have to be said in the home of the deceased for nine consecutive days. Often a prayer leader is called in to recite the Rosary in Latin—a very strange text indeed because the leader's memory is not necessarily faithful to the original. Latin, I was told, allows the prayers to be *kusug kaayu*, "very forceful." In other words Latin, which has all but disappeared from Roman Catholic rituals since Vatican II, is believed to offer a supplement of efficiency precisely because it is understood neither by the prayer leader nor by any of the participants in the ritual. Here again the code is omnipotent.

The Dynamics of a Contradiction

In retrospect this sheds light on the problems with which we began. The contradiction noted between two opposites, the "toward" and the "away," information and education, on-site training and formal schooling, tradition and modernity, *barangay* and *publasiyun*, can now be recognized with more accuracy, less as static than as dynamic. Within these congruent polarities there is no dialectic resolution whereby the conflicts are reduced and end in synthesis. But individuals are drawn into the contradictions, perpetually condemned to make and identify existential choices.

The problem however is that one's schooling determines to a large extent, although not exclusively, the facility (or lack thereof) with which individuals are capable of manipulating in their utterances one language or the other. The range of oscillation within which individuals can choose is itself not achieved but rather ascribed by their degree of schooling, which is in turn determined by socioeconomic as well as ideological factors. What is ultimately at stake is a moving tension between the enculturation into the traditions to which Cebuano belongs and into which the *barangay* folk tend willy-nilly to persevere, and on the other hand, the acculturation to exterior forces to which English and Pilipino belong and to which the townspeople tend to aspire.

The teachers are historically the agents of that acculturation. Furthermore they both grant and deny the possibility of linguistic manipulations, since increased language use is acquired in their schools. Finally, teachers are betwixt and between, mediators between *barangay* and *publasiyun*, and they themselves, in the tensions that their own persons, statuses, and roles encapsulate, are the living icons of such a liminality. No wonder then that they inspire *tahud*, a respect bordering on awe, in the uncompleted mediation they initiate for each individual child in the persisting tension between an "away" and a "toward."

Notes

[1] Field research in the Philippines in 1979 was made possible by a Summer Grant from the Graduate School Research Fund of the University of Washington (Seattle) and in 1980–81 by a Fulbright-Hayes Research Fellowship administered by the Philippine-American Education Foundation (Manila) while I was affiliated with the Department of Sociology and Anthropology, Silliman University (Dumaguete) and with the Cebuano Studies Center, University of San Carlos (Cebu). The earliest version of this chapter was written in the summer of 1982 under a post-doctoral grant from the Joint Committee on Southeast Asia of the American Council of Learned Societies and the Social Science Research Council. To all these institutions, I express my gratitude. I am also grateful to the participants and organizers of the conference on "Cultural Change and Rural Education in Southeast Asia," for the stimulating atmosphere they provided in Penang, Malaysia, in July of 1983. Finally, I wish to thank E. Valentine Daniel, Elinor Dumont, Carol M. Eastman, Lawrence Epstein, and Hans Houshower for their critical comments.

[2] According to Wolff (1972:I,vii): "Cebuano is spoken in the central portions of the Philippines: on the islands of Cebu and Bohol, on the eastern half of Negros, western half of Leyte, along the northern coast of Mindanao, and on smaller islands in the vicinity of these areas."

[3] In transcribing Cebuano words, I follow Wolff's (1972) spelling.

[4] The word "induction," deriving from "to induct," has altogether different connotations.

[5] I have kept the Spanish spelling for these two words.

[6] After the declaration of Martial Law in 1972, the term *barrio*, reminiscent of the colonial past, was replaced by *barangay*. This older native term had originally a different geo-political meaning. Today, it is defined as "the smallest political subdivision in the country" (Philippines 1975:xii).

[7] Despite the accuracy and usefulness of this opposition, prudence is in order, for the word *maestro* can also be used in a different sense beyond the educational context to designate craftsmen particularly skilled in activities which can be perfectly traditional. For instance, a carpenter, especially one who, in English, would be considered a master carpenter, can be, and frequently is, addressed and referred to as *maestro*.

[8] Philippine National Archives (Manila). *Varias Provincias, Bohol,* 12 unclassified bundles (of these 12 catalogued bundles, only 6 exist to-

day). *Bimonthly Report of the Governor of Bohol to the Governor General of the Philippines*, October 15, 1879.

9 *Idem,* January 15, 1881.

10 *Idem,* July 31, 1888 and September 30, 1888.

11 Siquijor was administratively attached to the District of Bohol between 1854 and 1890.

12 Philippine National Archives (Manila). *Varias Provincias, Negros,* 9 unclassified bundles. *Pueblo de Lacy. Mes de Febrero. Presupuestos de fondos locales de gasto de 1896–97. Nomina de los haberes de los Maestros y Ayudantes de ambos sexos correspondientes al presente mes,* February 28, 1896.

13 Presidential Decree No. 6-A, dated September 29, 1972.

14 A municipality is made up of several *barangay* and one *publasiyun* (from the Spanish *población*) which, following the local English usage, I translate by "town."

15 Although legally, the cockpit is supposed to be outside of the nucleated settlement.

16 A *balikbayan* is literally a "returnee to the country." This term is a borrowing from Tagalog. *Balik* means "to come back" in both Tagalog and Cebuano. *Bayan* means "country," "nation," "homeland" in Tagalog and its Cebuano equivalent would be *nasud.*

17 The *pinsiyunadu* (from Spanish *pensionado*) are individuals who receive a pension, either from some retirement program or as Veterans of the United States Armed Forces in the Far East which, in 1941, were under the command of General Douglas MacArthur.

18 A *pedikab* is a motorcycle with a sidecar which is equipped for carrying passengers. It is operated by a driver who pays a daily rent to the owner more often than it is driven by the owner.

19 There is indeed a strong correlation between *barangay* and rural proletariat on the one hand and *publasiyun* and local bourgeoisie on the other hand. Yet the geographical distribution of wealth and poverty is too fluid to turn such correlation into an equation.

20 Comic books, movies, and television are the major mass media which have been instrumental in promoting effectively Pilipino throughout the Philippines. This however has not yet occurred in Siquijor. Although occasionally a newspaper (in English and Pilipino) found its way to the town of Lazi, people there tended to read, if they read at all, *Reader's Digest* (in English) or the weekly magazine *Bisaya* (in Cebuano). Comic books (in Pilipino) were rare but not unknown.

Furthermore, I never saw anyone in the *barangay* read any text, not even a comic book, in Pilipino. Siquijor was and remains out of the way and for all practical purposes off limits to the distribution of the written word in any language. In addition, there was no movie house on the island, and hardly any television set since there was no electricity. When, in July 1983, I returned for a brief visit on the island, a privately-owned Betamax, run on a private generator, was used in Lazi to show movies publicly for a fee. The electrification of the island, consisting of a main line linking the six municipalities, was slowly under way, and its inauguration was scheduled for September 11 to coincide with President Marcos's birthday. It is doubtful, however, that such a deadline could have been met. As I was told privately: "If we cannot reach it, the First Lady's birthday will do!" This left some leeway, for Mrs. Marcos was born on July 2nd. On my latest visit to Siquijor in September of 1986, the *barangay* residents would see, some with stoic indifference, most with manifest envy, the lights of the town glitter in the distance.

21 *Virgen sa Rosario* is a prayer association (see Dumont 1986). I have kept the spelling for this name as it appears on its banners.

References

Agoncillo, T. A., and M. C. Guerrero. *History of the Filipino People.* 5th ed. Quezon City: R. P. Garcia Publishing Co., 1977.

Arnold, F., *et al. The Value of Children: A Cross-National Study.* Vol. 1. Honolulu: East-West Population Institute, 1975.

Blair, E. H., and J. A. Robertson, eds. *The Philippine Islands, 1493–1803.* 54 Volumes. Cleveland: The Arthur H. Clark Co., 1903–09.

Bulatao, R. A. *The Value of Children: A Cross-National Study.* Vol. 2. Honolulu: East-West Population Institute, 1975.

Carson, A. L. *The Story of Philippine Education.* Quezon City: New Day Publishers, 1978.

Cavada y Mendez de Vigo, A. de la. *Historia geográfica, geológica y estadística de Filipinas. Con datos geográficos y estadísticos de las islas de Luzon, Visayas, Mindanao y Joló; y los que corresponden a las islas Batanes, Calamianes, Balabac, Mindoro, Masbate, Ticao y Burias, situadas al N. SO. y S. de Luzon.* 2 vols. Manila: Imp. de Ramírez y Giraudier, 1876.

Constantino, R. "The Mis-Education of the Filipino." In *History of the Filipino People,* ed. by T.A. Agoncillo and M.C. Guerrero, 435–41. 5th ed. Quezon City: R. P. Garcia Publishing Co., 1966.

Dumont, J.-P. "Rumor and Tremor in a Visayan Community: Some Anthropological Reflections on Symbolic Power." *Silliman Journal,* 27.4(1980):258–64.

——, "Praying in the Barangay: The Indigenization of Christianity in a Visayan Community." Paper presented at a conference on "The Indigenization of Christianity in Southeast Asia," sponsored by the Joint Committee of the Social Science Research Council and American Council of Learned Societies on Southeast Asia, Cebu City, the Philippines, 1986.

Guía oficial de Filipinas. Anuario histórico-estadístico-administrativo. 1879. Manila: Imprenta de Amigos del Pais, 1878.

Guía oficial de Filipinas. 1892. Manila: Tipo-Lit. de Chofré y Ca, 1892.

Lévi-Strauss, C. *The Elementary Structures of Kinship.* Tr. by J. H. Bell & J. R. von Sturmer, trans. Boston: Beacon Press, 1969.

Philippines, National Census and Statistics Office. *1975 Integrated Census of the Population and Its Economic Activities. Population. Siquijor.* Manila: National Economic and Development Authority, 1975.

Romero de Madridejos, B. *Pastorales y demás disposiciones circuladas a los párrocos de esta diócesis de Cebú (y tambien á los de la de Jaro antes de su separación) por los señores obispos ó sus vicarios generales para el buen gobierno de la diócesis y tambien las disposiciones remitidas por el gobierno y comunicadas a los párrocos y algunas notas de interés histórico, que para gobierno y observancia del clero manda imprimir para los archivos de cada parroquia de su diócesis el Ilmo. y Rmo. Sr. P. Fr. Benito Romero de Madridejos.* 2 vols. Manila: Establecimiento Tipográfico del Colegio de Santo Tomás, 1884–85.

Saussure, F. de. *Cours de linguistique générale.* 3rd ed. Paris: Payot, 1962.

U.S. Bureau of the Census. *Census of the Philippine Islands. 1903.* Washington: Government Printing Office, 1905.

Wolff, J. U. *A Dictionary of Cebuano Visayan.* 2 vols. Ithaca, N.Y.: Cornell University, Southeast Asia Program and Manila: Linguistic Society of the Philippines, 1972.

Zaide, G. F. *The Pageant of Philippine History.* 2 Vols. Manila: Philippine Education Company, 1979.

THE PROPOSED WORLD OF THE SCHOOL: THAI VILLAGERS' ENTRY INTO A BUREAUCRATIC STATE SYSTEM

Charles F. Keyes

Introduction

In Thailand, all children except those whose families can afford to send them to private school, enter public school at age seven. Since the promulgation of the Primary Education Act of 1921, children have been required to attend school, and since the 1930s the law has been implemented in most communities throughout the kingdom. For village children, schooling marks a significant shift in the accustomed routines of life—routines shaped by the tempo of family life, the agricultural cycle, and play with friends. In this chapter, I shall consider how schooling opens up a new world for children in rural Thailand. After first considering the relationship of the state-sponsored school to the Buddhist monastic or *wat* school which it supplanted, I will examine the role of the school in one community in northeastern Thailand, a region that remains the most intensely agrarian and contains the highest concentration of rural poor of any part of the country.

Modernization theorists—and most notably Alex Inkeles (Inkeles 1969, 1974; Inkeles and Smith 1974)—have argued that the type of school system such as that instituted in rural Thailand in the 1930s is an effective tool for the creation of new, non-traditional persons equipped to contribute to the economic development of their society. To some extent the evidence I present supports such a thesis, for at least a few Thai villagers have gained certain types of knowledge from their schooling—notably literacy, numeracy, and a sense of time as a product that can be used efficiently—that serve as the basis for new, more productive economic action. Acquisition of these types of knowledge have been generally effective in preparing villagers to undertake transactions in a market economy. The role that the village school has played in instilling a "development" orientation in villagers pales markedly, however, beside that which it has played in preparing villagers to accept a subordinate position in the centralized bureaucratic world of the Thai nation-state.

As village children have little experience of any world beyond that of the village when they enter school, the world referred to in the messages communicated through schooling is a "proposed world." A "proposed world" is one known not through the experience of actual social relationships, but rather through a set of coherent messages, presented through what I term a "work of culture," that open up the possibility of relationships that may be established in the future.[1] In the Thai case, schooling serves to prepare students for types of relationships—most notably those with government officials—that they are most likely to have, if ever, only after they have left school and assumed adult roles in society.

This proposed world is opened up not only through formal instruction using a specified set of textbooks. When Thai children go to school, they enter a spatial culture that itself serves as a model of the state. The interactions that students have with teachers, as well as those teachers have with villagers more generally, also anticipate in form and significance the relationships that villagers have with representatives of the state. While having as a secondary objective the preparing of children to participate in a market economy, formal instruction serves primarily to inculcate knowledge— especially knowledge of standard Thai language and the essential elements of national culture—will make it possible to act appropriately within the world of the Thai state. Insofar as the system of state-sponsored popular education has been successfully implemented—and it has become increasingly so—villagers in Thailand have come to accept the domination of the Thai state as an unquestioned given in their social life.

Education for a Buddhist World

The school that exists today in rural communities throughout Thailand is an alien institution of quite recent vintage. Nonetheless, it has links with the premodern Theravada Buddhist schools found in nearly all villages that contained a *wat* (temple-monastery), that is, in most of those villages which had existed for any length of time. Education designed to inculcate literacy and thus provide access to the *dhamma*, the teachings of the Buddha, was first introduced among those Tai-speaking[2] peoples who had converted to Theravada Buddhism beginning in about the thirteenth century. By perhaps the fifteenth century, *wat*-schools existed in most communities of Tai-speaking peoples located in the area of what was eventually to become Thailand.

Many, perhaps most, boys in villages in premodern Siam, as Thailand was known before 1939, attended *wat*-schools for a period ranging from a few months to several years. Instruction was structured primarily as preparation for entry into the Sangha; since only males could be ordained as novices or monks, girls did not attend these schools.[3]

Boys first learned to master a script so that they could read religious texts. While scripts varied in different parts of the country, the language most commonly taught was Pali rather than a vernacular one. Being able to read texts in Pali, although not necessary to understand what was read, was essential for memorization of the chants used in rituals. While a *wat* education was designed primarily to provide access to Buddhist teachings, it also enabled a few men to read other types of hand-written texts. From the manuscripts found in a *wat* library, a literate man in a premodern village in Thailand might acquire a knowledge of non-Buddhist ritual, astrological and medical practices, legends and myths, poetry or customary law.

Wherever literacy exists, it serves to permit the "fixing" (cf. Ricoeur 1971:331–32, 537f; also in Ricoeur 1981:195–99, 203f) of knowledge in a way not possible by means of an oral tradition. Such "fixing" entails an objectification of knowledge such that its presentation is not dependent on particular speakers being constrained by their abilities to recall what they have memorized. The same texts can be read in very different places at very different times. A text has no significance until it is read (and reading can include hearing a text read by someone else as well as reading it oneself) and the reading of a text entails a choice that a text is worth reading. Such a choice is made not on the intrinsic character of the text itself, but by some authority which marks a text as having relevance to meaningful action in the world.

In premodern Tai communities in Siam, Buddhist monks were the ultimate authority as to what texts were worth reading, and thus what knowledge was worth knowing. Because Buddhist monks in these communities themselves accepted the authority of their preceptors who had identified a core body of texts considered central to the tradition, and because these texts were common to all Theravadin countries, Tai appropriated a vision of the world as projected by these texts that was, in a fundamental sense, the same as that appropriated by Theravada Buddhists elsewhere. Those who "read" the same texts incorporate the same past into their different presents.[4]

Not all the texts read in local Tai communities were, however, the same as those read in other Theravada Buddhist communities. This was especially true of texts written in a vernacular as contrasted with those written in Pali. Moreover, authoritative selection and use of texts never rested solely with monks. In every community, there were also lay specialists who made use of a distinctive body of texts to perform functions considered essential for social life. What texts a man might master in order to lead congregations in offering alms to the Sangha, in securing the vital essence (*khwan*) that ensured the continuance of life, in concocting medicinal preparations, in calculating astrological influences, or in reciting or performing legends differed among the Lao or among the Yuan (northern Thai) as compared to the Siamese, although all shared the same basic Buddhist culture.

Much of the knowledge acquired by villagers through reading of texts, to which they gained access from instruction offered in monastic schools in premodern Siam, was similar to what might be acquired through an oral tradition. The textual tradition associated with Theravada Buddhism added, however, an additional dimension to this knowledge. Buddhist texts projected a view of the world rationalized according to logically-interrelated Buddhist concepts. The world of "sentient existence" (*samsara*) is characterized by "suffering" (*dukkha*), "impermanence" (*anicca*), and "insubstantiality" (*anatta*) owing to the inexorable working of the law of *kamma*, that is, of the effects of action whose nature is morally positive or negative. Salvation for this world is to be gained through the cultivation of "morality" (*sila*), "mindfulness" (*samadhi*) and "wisdom" (*pañña*). All notions of cause and effect—those relating to nature and the body, for example—are related systematically in the texts of all Tai Buddhists to an ultimate framework derived from Buddhist premises. By comparison, the knowledge of preliterate peoples, such as the tribal peoples living on the peripheries of the Tai world, had an *ad hoc* quality.

Written texts not only permit a more rationalized and systematic view of the world than the oral forms used to reproduce knowledge in a preliterate society, but they also represent a distinctive type of *cultural capital*, to use Pierre Bourdieu's (1977) term. Such capital can be accumulated and controlled by those holding particular social statuses in a way not possible in an oral tradition. Bourdieu says that:

> Literacy enables a society to move beyond immediate human limits—in particular those of individual memory—and frees it from the constraints implied by mnemonic devices such as poetry, the preservation technique par excellence in non-literate societies; it enables a society to accumulate culture hitherto preserved in embodied form [i.e., by individual persons], and correlatively enables particular groups to practice *primitive accumulation of cultural capital*, the partial or total monopolizing of the society's symbolic resources in religion, philosophy, art, and science, by monopolizing the instruments for appropriation of those resources (writing, reading, and other decoding techniques) henceforward preserved not in memories but in texts. (Bourdieu 1977:187; emphasis in original)

Literacy is always associated with a social division of knowledge that, in turn, contributes as much to the structuring of the realm of social relations as does the social division in the ownership of the means of production.[5]

In all Theravada Buddhist societies, monks assumed a preeminent social position commensurate with their monopolization of knowledge associated with written texts. This position was indicated by the laity in their use of a highly deferential language and display of deferential behavior when interacting with Buddhist monks and by the material support that even relatively poor villagers were willing to provide the Sangha from the small surpluses they generated in their productive activities. Their high status notwithstanding, Buddhist monks did not constitute a privileged class comparable to the Catholic clergy in Europe or Latin America. Monks in all Theravada Buddhist societies were almost invariably from the same background as those in the communities in which their monasteries were located. Even though monks from aristocratic backgrounds controlled the major temple-monasteries in towns and cities, such monks did not exercise any defined authority over rural monks. The most respected monks were preceptor-teachers and meditation masters, and such monks were at least as often from peasant backgrounds as from urban elite ones. Because rural monks, who constituted the vast majority of the Sangha in premodern Theravadin societies, were neither members of an aristocracy nor agents of one, they did not use their positions to impose an elite's view of the world on the peasantry.

Monks also did not form a permanent class segment of rural society in premodern Siam, because most monks did not remain in the monkhood for life. It was the custom for most males to enter the Sangha for a temporary period—at least one "lenten" period of three months. A man who had been a member of the Sangha was considered to have been morally tempered and thus to be a better lay person and not, as in the case of Catholic priests or monks who renounced their vows, to be religiously flawed. Even those who remained in the Sangha for life rarely used their positions for personal gain, as their actions were markedly constrained by the discipline to which they adhered. Throughout premodern Siam, but unlike in Sri Lanka and some parts of Burma, monks did not own the temple-monasteries where they resided; nor did they own or control monastic estates. A monk who abused his position could find himself at the mercy of the laity on whom he depended for his food, shelter, clothing, and medicines.

Former members of the Sangha constituted another group within rural society who held high status as a consequence of the knowledge they controlled through being literate. A man who had been ordained, whether as a novice or as a monk, was ever after designated by a title indicating the level of attainment he had reached in the monkhood. Literate ex-clergy commanded respect from their fellow villagers and assumed leadership roles in communal affairs, or became specialists in certain practices such as astrology, curing, or legend-singing. Like monks, ex-clergy did not constitute a privileged class since any male could join them by attending a monastic school and being ordained as a novice or a monk. In many villages, former members of the Sangha could account for as many as two-thirds or more of their adult men.

Women in premodern Siamese society were excluded from access to text-based knowledge. The cultural capital which women controlled— their practical knowledge of domestic affairs, farming, weaving, or even marketing, as well as the specialized knowledge that a few women gained of the spirit world—received far less public prestige than knowledge acquired through a study of texts. On the other hand, the "nurturing" of the Sangha undertaken by women was highly valued, for it was through provision of foodstuffs on a regular basis by women that members of the Sangha were able to devote themselves to study. From an outsider's perspective, the status of illiterate women vis-à-vis literate men, and especially literate monks, might be considered disadvantageous; however, from the perspective of women and men alike in premodern Siam, the relationship was mutually supportive (cf. Keyes 1984; 1986a).

In premodern Siam, men who were illiterate and who had therefore acquired insufficient knowledge of texts to assume one of the specialized roles in their communities were often more disadvantaged than women. Although it might be possible for an illiterate man to gain social respect by becoming a clever trader in buffaloes or cattle, most came from families too poor to accumulate the wealth necessary to sponsor an ordination. Thus, illiteracy among males tended to be associated with low economic status within a community.

It is worth noting that few used the literacy they acquired in monastic schools to improve their economic status. While the poor might remain illiterate, those who became literate usually did not become substantially richer as a consequence. Literacy was not an essential skill for traditional marketing. There was little currency in circulation in rural Siam, even as late as the 1920s, and it was not necessary to be literate to use what currency did pass through peasant hands. Villagers required no bookkeeping skills to engage in business, since trade was carried on mainly through local exchanges or purchases from peddlers rather than through centralized markets. Even village headmen seem to have kept no records to comply with tax and corvée demands levied on villagers by local lords or representatives of the king.

The education acquired by villagers in monastic schools in premodern Siam did, however, contribute indirectly to the legitimation of the authority of the king and the officials or local lords who served under him. Villagers considered a king or lord legitimate if he "possessed merit" (*mi bun*)— a quality that was demonstrated primarily through conspicuous support of the Sangha. Villagers came to understand the notion of "possessing merit" in part as a consequence of knowledge acquired from texts, and most especially those texts containing narrative accounts of the actions of a Buddhist prince or king. From monastic education, as well as from rituals performed in their local temple-monasteries, villagers also acquired a view of the cosmos as hierarchically structured, and within this cosmological structure kings and lords were an inherent part of the social order.

In the latter decades of the nineteenth century, the social order reproduced in great part by the traditional system of monastic education in premodern Siam began to be seriously challenged. Western powers "opened" the country, leading to a marked reshaping of the local economy as it was incorporated into a global system. Of perhaps even greater significance, King Chulalongkorn (1868–1910) and his chief advisors began, in the 1890s, a process that would transform the traditional state of Siam into the modern-nation state of Thailand. As part of this process, a new system of education was created that became the primary means whereby the transformation was successfully accomplished.

State-Sponsored Popular Education

In November 1898 King Chulalongkorn promulgated a "Decree on the Organization of Provincial Education."[6] The decree retained the traditional monastic schools, with monks as teachers, but gave these schools a new function, namely that of instructing students in a "modern" curriculum devised by a state agency. This curriculum included the teaching of standard Thai, which had been made the national language, arithmetic, and elementary science. Moreover, the government decreed that the results of instruction in the reorganized monastic schools were to be tested in standardized examinations.

The hybrid school—part religious, part state-sponsored—created by the 1898 decree proved to be only a transitional type.[7] By the reign of King Vajiravudh, who came to the throne in 1910, the government became dissatisfied with schools being staffed by monks who were ill-trained and not committed to education as a vocation. While King Vajiravudh retained Chulalongkorn's ideal that modern education should be tempered by instruction in Buddhist morality, he and his advisors envisioned a system of popular education in which teachers would be trained by and responsible solely to the state. This system was outlined in the "Primary Education Act" of 1921, an act that made state-sponsored education compulsory for all citizens.

One of the most important social implications of this Act was that it made school attendance mandatory for girls as well as boys. The requirement was not an empty one; between 1921 and 1925 the percentage of female students throughout the country jumped from seven to thirty-eight (Vella 1978:159). The government also instituted measures designed to centralize and standardize education (cf. Vella 1978:165); the success of these measures depended on replacing monks with trained persons who had taken up teaching as a vocation.[8] The government established teaching-training institutions throughout the country, and, by the late 1920s, secular teachers were graduating in increasing numbers.

Progress in implementing the 1921 Act was slow, primarily because the governments of King Vajiravudh (1910–1924) and King Prajadhipok (1924–1935) allocated rather modest amounts of money for education. The situation changed significantly after the revolution of 1932 which led to the establishment of a constitutional monarchy and a shift of power from the royalty to a bureaucratic and military elite. The "Promoters" who staged the revolution saw popular education as "the best preparation for full democracy" (Landon 1939:98) in the country. Governments in the 1930s allocated much higher percentages of their budgets for education than had the preceding royal governments. Between 1933 and 1936, appropriations for education were raised from 3.7 million *baht* to almost 12 million *baht* (Landon 1939:98).

During the 1930s, the process of replacing monks with government-trained lay teachers was accelerated. Moreover, the government established new schools in many communities where *wat* schools had not previously existed. By the outbreak of World War II, as Thompson and Adloff (1948:37) observe, "centralization of educational facilities by the government [was] far more complete in Siam than in neighboring countries." Nowhere else in Southeast Asia, except in the Philippines, had a state-created school system become so well-established in rural communities as it had in the villages of Siam by the late 1930s.

There is no evidence to suggest that villagers (or townspeople, for that matter) anywhere in Siam actively resisted the establishment of state primary schools. Nor did they resist religious schools being supplanted by sec-

ular ones as has been the case in some areas in Malaysia and Indonesia. Yet
the Buddhist Sangha had a number of reasons to encourage such resistance.
While *wat* schools continued to exist, they were, in fact, unequivocally subordinated to secular schools. Moreover, the government made completion of
compulsory primary education a prerequisite for entering the novitiate[9]—a
requirement which dampened boys' interest in becoming novices, for once
they had already acquired literacy in a secular school they had less incentive
to enter monastic schools (cf. Holmes 1974:91–92). In turn, fewer novices
went on to become monks. The Thai Sangha saw its social role as well as
its size reduced as a result of the success of the state secular educational
system.

Far from leading villagers in an effort to retain or restore the traditional *wat* school in opposition to secular schools, most monks, in fact,
participated actively in promoting the new school system. In the early
part of the twentieth century, the government had coopted Sangha leaders
into assisting in the creation of a new system of mass education. From
the 1920s on, when government policy sought to replace monk-teachers by
lay-teachers, the Sangha leadership remained supportive because the government included (Buddhist) moral instruction as part of the curriculum.
Monks continue, even today, to be called on to provide this instruction,
albeit for a very small number of hours in each teaching-week.

Even when monks were teaching only ethics in the new type of schools,
the fact that most village schools continued to be housed in *wat* buildings
perpetuated the link in villagers' minds between state-supported secular
schools and premodern monastic schools. Despite the fact that it had a
fundamentally different mission, the local school was often viewed as an
extension of the *wat* by village monks and laypeople alike. Monks have often
agreed to help sponsor money-raising projects for schools located in *wats*,
thus rendering such fund raisers a form of traditional merit-making. Hanks
reports that in the Central Thai village of Bang Chan in about 1950, for
example, the local abbot encouraged villagers to make resources available
to build a new school building to replace the one that had blown down. The
abbot told villagers "that making merit by building schools equals the merit
of building temples" (Hanks 1960:23). In 1963, monks in the northeastern
Thai village of Ban Nǫng Tųn, where I carried out research, joined in
sponsoring a "temple fair," the purpose of which was to raise money for
a new school; again local monks stated that donations to the school fund
at the fair would yield merit, thereby giving them a religious significance.
These cases, which are quite typical, especially in villages where schools
have continued to use *wat* buildings, reflect the extent to which the Sangha

has gone in helping to transfer legitimation from monastic schools to state-sponsored secular schools.

While villagers were neither incited by monks nor themselves motivated to defend traditional monastic schools against secular schools, they have not accorded the new schools a positive reception. Writing about villagers in Bang Chan in central Thailand in the 1950s, Hanks (1960:27) observes that: "The new educational program has appealed little to the rice farmers and, despite twenty years of exposure, the community continues unenthusiastic." In her novel, *Little Things* (1971), Prajuab Thirabutana noted a similar lack of enthusiasm for a similar period for northeastern Thailand. Well into the 1950s, Thai villagers received the new secular schools with "indifference" (Hanks 1960); that is, they saw the knowledge gained from attending a state-sponsored school as having little relevance to the world in which they lived (also compare Aree Sanhachanee 1970:107 and Holmes 1974:46, 97).

As alien as the school might have seemed and as indifferent as villagers might have been about secular education, the fact remains that, for at least forty to fifty years, most villagers throughout Thailand have spent the requisite four years (recently six years) attending school. Absenteeism in Thailand has been remarkably low. While villagers may have considered formal education irrelevant to the world of the village, they have, nonetheless, acquired a new perspective on that world as a consequence of what they have learned in school. From the mid-1950s on, that world has, moreover, been changed radically as the state, represented by local officials and the market, embodied in the middlemen with whom villagers deal, have increasingly impinged on villagers' lives (cf., the chapter by Chayan Vaddhanaphuti in this volume). Villagers' horizons have expanded to include the entire political-economy of the Thai state—an expansion wrought primarily through the education acquired in state-sponsored schools.

The Spatial Culture of a Thai Village School

I should now like to consider how a world with an expanded horizon has been opened up by the state-sponsored school in one Thai rural community, that of Ban Nǫng Tụn in Mahasarakham province, northeastern Thailand, a community in which I first began fieldwork over twenty years ago.[10] In constructing my picture, I will draw on both my own researches in Ban Nǫng Tụn and on other studies made in northeastern Thai villages over the past twenty-five years.[11] While I consider only northeastern Thailand, much of what I say applies also to villages throughout Thailand (see, in this connection, the chapter by Chayan Vaddhanaphuti in this volume).

The Ban Nǫng Tụn school was founded in 1935 and, thus, dates from the 1932–1937 period when most schools were established in rural communities in up-country Thailand. Between 1935 and 1965 it was situated in the *salawat*, the assembly hall on the grounds of the *wat*. Children who attended school in Ban Nǫng Tụn during this thirty-year period first entered the *wat*, whose boundaries were marked by a line of reliquaries (*that*) containing the ashes of deceased members of the community. Within the *wat*, there were two other major structures in addition to the *salawat*—the *kuthi*, where members of the Sangha resided and on whose porch some religious rituals were held, and the *bot*, an ordination hall that in Ban Nǫng Tụn was used primarily as a place to store temporarily the cremated remains of the deceased. On religious holidays, the *salawat* was preempted for ritual events even if the day happened to be one which was not an official school holiday.

In entering the *wat* to go to school, a child was first oriented in space by the reliquary shrines that stood as a link between the present community of the living and the past community of the dead. Within the *wat* grounds, the child would recognize himself or herself as being within a ritual space that included both the structures where rituals were held and the critical ritual actors, the members of the Sangha. Within this ritual space, the school occupied a subordinate position.

The school did, nonetheless, have its own spatial culture, one that reflected a political rather than a religious order. In my fieldnotes of July 1963, I set down a description of the Ban Nǫng Tụn school as it then existed:

> The school is located in the *salawat* (an assembly hall on the grounds of the Buddhist monastery), a building open on all four sides. ... Desks for the students consist of low benches about a foot above the floor. These are also about a foot wide and about three feet long. Behind each of these, three, and sometimes four, students will kneel on the floor. The students come in with their papers, erasers, and rulers wrapped in a *phakhoma* (male waistcloth) or a piece of rough cotton. These are placed underneath the low desks when the children are in class. The four grades are divided by woven bamboo partitions that can be removed (as can most of the rest of the school equipment) when the *salawat* is used for other purposes (as it is on ritual occasions). In the front of each "classroom" is a chair, a desk (roughly hewn) and a fold-away blackboard that are used by the teachers.
>
> There are various posters, announcements, pictures, and so on placed on the posts of the building. The most important of

these is an assemblage of the following placed on the center post: a picture of the king below which are the national colors, and below that a "shrine" with a glass statue of the Buddha and vases of artificial flowers on it. There are also a number of placards that always begin with the phrase, "*phutta orot*," "Buddha says," followed by several words in Pali ... and a Thai translation of a moral aphorism such as "As a person speaks, so he shall do." There are also several little wooden blue boards on which a part of a poem, again usually with a moral message, is written. There are two biological diagrams, one showing the internal organs and one about the teeth. There is also a small map of Thailand together with several pictures of important buildings and *wats* in Thailand.

As one enters the school one sees the blackboard on which is written: "Statistics concerning numbers of students in Wat Ban Nǫng Tyn school." The statistics include the number of students in each class and are supposed to include the daily statistics on the number of students who are sick, tardy, or truant. Also included are the names of each teacher and the grades they are teaching. There is also another blackboard on which important announcements are written, such as: "Today is examination day" or "Today is honoring-the-teachers (*wai khru*) day." There is another board to which pictures from magazines are occasionally pinned.

The spatial culture evidenced in this description, and in comparable descriptions in other accounts of northeastern village schools (see Gurevich 1972:123–25; Compton 1972:166–67; also cf. Khamman Khonkhai 1982:23) serves to represent the state in microcosm and to prepare the child for entry as a subordinated and rather ignorant villager into a world where certain types of relationships are structured with reference to the existence of the state. Conspicuous in the Ban Nǫng Tyn school, as in every village school, are the linked images of the Buddha, the king (sometimes the king and queen or the king and other members of the royal family), and the national flag or colors. These juxtaposed images point to the three pillars of national identity that have been promoted by the state since the time of King Vajiravudh (see Vella 1978)—the Buddhist religion (*satsana*), the kingship (*phra maha kasat*), and the Thai nation (*chat*). As the child leaves the school and begins to move into an adult world, he or (albeit less often) she will confront these linked images every time he or she enters a government building or office. They will also be displayed on all national holidays.

The posters and charts that have been attached to the walls of village schools anticipate a bureaucratic domain of social action. Only in schools and in bureaucratic offices does one find multi-colored posters that carry messages that are intended to instruct or exhort; only in bureaucratic offices and schools will one find charts summarizing some aspect of social life in statistical tables. School children rarely read the charts that are in the schools any more than a villager would read the charts on the blackboards or walls of the district office. They are meant primarily for other officials who have been especially trained to read and construct such texts. The very presence of these charts does, nonetheless, indicate for the children, as for villagers in bureaucratic offices, that one is in the presence of those for whom such texts are relevant.

Although the students in the Ban Nong Tun school, as I observed it in July 1963, had less adequate desks than did children in many other northeastern Thai schools of the time or than Ban Nong Tun children would have but a short time later, the relationship between the desks of the children and the desks of teachers in Ban Nong Tun is one found in all schools, today as well as in the past. Teachers' desks are always situated in such a way as to indicate clearly the superiority of teachers over students. Teachers sit on chairs behind high desks, while children sit on the floor or on low chairs behind low desks. In entering the school and taking his or her place at the desk, the village child places himself or herself in a position subordinate to the teacher. While a village child would also subordinate himself or herself before a monk-teacher as well, in the state school context, the teacher is not simply the dispenser of knowledge; he or she is also a representative of the state.

So long as state schools were located in *wat* grounds, the spatial culture of the school could never unambiguously orient villagers toward a world shaped by the state. It is hardly surprising, thus, that Thai governments tolerated housing state schools in *wat* buildings only as a temporary expedient. Not until quite recently, however, has the government made a concerted effort to establish state schools separated from *wats* in all communities. In northeastern Thailand the separation of state schools from *wats* proceeded rather slowly until about the early 1960s. Since then, the government has used a carrot-and-stick approach in promoting the building of new schools on public land that does not belong to *wats*. The carrot has consisted of monetary subsidies for most of the materials needed for building a school. The stick has been wielded by headmasters who have placed strong pressures on village leaders to set aside land for a school, to encourage villagers to contribute their labor to erecting the new school, and to persuade villagers to donate additional monies that can be added to the government subsidies. In Ban Nọng Tụn, a new school was built in 1965 through this combination of mobilization of village labor and resources and of subsidization by the government.

The new building, which I saw for the first time in 1967, was a marked improvement over the old school: the structure was much more solid and much larger, although classrooms were still divided by bamboo partitions. In the late 1970s, additional government monies were made available and the school was even more radically transformed. In my fieldnotes in July 1980 I contrasted the new school with the one I had seen seventeen years previously:

> The school grounds now contain three buildings, the middle one being the "new" school (built after we left in 1964). The first building was completed last year at a cost of 300,000 *baht* (about $14,500), the money having been provided by the government. The last building, an open-sided structure, was built by voluntary labor and contributions from villagers and others. ... The school has been, it would appear, well-supported. This year the school received 7,000 *baht* worth of materials from the government. ... The school also has a 220 foot deep pump well built in March 1978 by the Department of Mines and Mineral Resources at the request of the teachers.

What is especially striking about the process leading to the establishment of a separate school in Ban Nọng Tụn and to its upgrading is the marked increase in the amount of government support provided. As a function both of this support and of the requirement that the school structure conform to government plans, the Ban Nọng Tụn school had become clearly identified by all in the village—adults as well as children—as an agency of the state.

In the new school, elements of a spatial culture orienting students toward the state that were present to some degree when the school was located in the *wat* have been elaborated. There are more charts, more posters, more pictures of the king than before. But these elements are no longer surrounded by the trappings of traditional Buddhist culture; they unambiguously assert the preeminence of the state. The child who enters the fenced compound of the school now moves immediately into a space that orients him or her toward the state.

In the new school grounds, other uses of space are also disjunctive with traditional village life. Teachers are strongly encouraged by their superiors to make use of the school grounds to instruct students about health, or to train them in modern techniques of food production. In addition to the well, the new school in Ban Nǫng Tụn now boasts the toilet which has become a ubiquitous edifice on every school grounds. Although the toilet is, in fact, reserved solely for teachers and high-status visitors, it stands, nonetheless, as a symbol of the concern with health that the government seeks to inculcate in villagers. The well has more than symbolic significance, for in an area of the country where most ponds and shallow wells dry up during the dry season, villagers have become increasingly dependent on pump wells.

A portion of the Ban Nǫng Tụn school grounds has also been set aside for planting improved varieties of seeds.[12] While teachers coopt students to help plant and cultivate these gardens, it is still uncertain whether villagers have used the methods employed in these experimental plots in their own gardening efforts. School gardens, today a conspicuous aspect of the spatial culture of schools, are a relatively recent development, a function, in part, of the fact that so long as schools were located in *wats*, teachers could not make use of the surrounding land as they wished. In the past decade or so, the government has also asked that teachers devote more attention to these gardens than they did in the past. Insofar as the gardens exist and prove productive, or, in other words, that their yields are significant, they serve as possible models of productive action that might be emulated by villagers.

The spatial culture of rural Thai schools has thus been divorced from earlier religious meanings. While it has developed certain aspects that relate to economic productivity, the dominant elements by far are those that orient villagers toward the state. These elements of the spatial culture serve to reinforce the dominant messages contained in the formal instruction provided students and the implicit messages carried in the behavior of teachers toward students as well as toward other villagers.

Teachers and the Authority of Educational Culture

In the 1930s, when the government decided to move more aggressively to sever the links between the traditional *wat* schools and the modern secular schools, a significant number of lay people began to enter teacher-training institutions. There they were trained in government-prescribed programs of teacher education before being posted to village schools to replace the existing monk-teachers. The lay teacher (*khru*), who in the past two decades was as likely to be a woman as a man, became a new and distinctive actor on the village scene, and one who more than any other person in that local world, including village headmen, served to orient villagers toward the state. While teachers might be viewed as a type of "cultural broker," to us a concept once popular in anthropological writings (see Geertz 1960; Press 1969; Silverman 1965; and Wolf 1956, 1966), their role, in fact, has leaned less toward brokering knowledge relevant to the villagers' world than to establishing the authority of a particular form of knowledge.

Until even the early 1960s, many village schools, especially those in remote areas like northeastern Thailand, lacked sufficient teachers and were often staffed by teachers who were underqualified. Ban Nǫng Tựn offers an example that was far from atypical of rural northeastern schools in the 1950s and 1960s. Between 1959 and 1963 there were four teachers at the Ban Nǫng Tựn school—the requisite number if there were to be a teacher for each class—for only three out of the five years. Because of retirements and job transfers, seven different teachers served at the school during this period. Of these seven, two had no certification at all and two held only the pre-primary teacher certificate and should, thus, not have been qualified to teach in primary school (for further details, see Keyes 1966:152–55).

While teacher salaries improved in the early 1960s when compared with salaries that "scarcely exceed the income of a peasant" reported for the 1930s (Landon 1939:103), they still remained low in absolute terms. In Ban Nǫng Tựn in 1963–1964 teachers' salaries ranged from 625 to 750 *baht* ($31.25–$37.50) per month. Such incomes appear markedly better than those of ordinary villagers, for in 1963 the median household cash income in Ban Nǫng Tựn was 866 *baht* ($43.30) per *year*. Given, however, that teachers had to use cash not only to pay for many of the goods a farmer produced for his family's consumption but also for such items as better clothing and travel, in addition to contributing to teachers' aid and welfare funds, the actual monies at his or her disposal were hardly enough to maintain a standard of living above that of a middle-income farmer.

Even though salaries were increased in the late 1960s, the net income teachers took home remained low. Gurevich reports for a village in Khǫn Kaen province, where teachers had better qualifications than those in Ban Nǫng Tựn, that in 1970 net incomes averaged only 539 *baht* ($26.95) per month as compared with an average gross salary of 959 *baht* ($47.95) per month (statistics based on Gurevich 1972:216, Table 12). In his novel, "Village Teacher" (*Khru Ban Nǫk*), Khamman Khonkhai (1982, see, esp., pp. 160ff), tells how teachers in the 1970s had much of their income taken away in deductions or for loan payments for such items as motorcycles which they felt they must own if they were to maintain a standard of living commensurate with their status. It is hardly surprising, therefore, that many teachers have found it necessary to augment their salaries with secondary sources of income. In a 1969 study, Gurevich found that over fifty percent of teachers in the province of Khǫn Kaen had secondary incomes (Gurevich 1972:213); conversations with teachers suggest that the percentage would be at least as high today.

Until recently, the types of secondary incomes most village school teachers have been able to generate have been drawn from the rural economy. Many teachers own farms, while others run shops or rice mills or village-based trucking firms. Through these activities teachers have become involved in relationships with villagers in guises other than those associated with being a teacher. Such relationships appear, however, to be less common among younger teachers. Gurevich, who made a study of village teachers in rural Khǫn Kaen province in 1970, found that younger teachers—those who had been recruited from about the early 1960s on— "have little commitment to the land and to traditional village economic activities, as it affects their livelihood. They hardly venture outside the administrative structure to find other sources of income, using the system to advance themselves and increase their incomes" (Gurevich 1972:221). Gurevich points out that one of the major reasons for the change lies in the fact that the new generation of teachers has attained higher educational levels than had the older generation and is therefore eligible for increased salaries and benefits within the state educational system.

The longer a teacher studies, the more likely it is that he or she will orient himself or herself toward a non-rural world. Even Piya, the hero of Khamman Khonkhai's novel (1982) about a rural school teacher in a northeastern Thai village, despite his great commitment to the village way of life, found it difficult to engage in farming. His long period of education had made the experience of helping his parents in farming activities seem quite remote.

Some among the newer generation of teachers have found it possible to augment their family incomes by marrying teachers. By 1970 at least twenty percent of village teachers were women (Keyes 1966:151; Compton 1972:181). The recruitment of women to the role of khru has resulted in one of the most striking contrasts between the modern village school and the traditional monastic school. Most women school teachers marry other teachers or bureaucrats; rarely do they marry a villager, despite the fact that most have come from village backgrounds. On the other hand, male teachers are sought after by village girls as husbands and by parents as sons-in-law. The attractions of an alliance with a village girl increase the longer a young male teacher remains in a village school. Once such an alliance is made, even teachers of the new generation often find themselves drawn willy-nilly into the rural economy.

Village school teachers almost invariably come from rural backgrounds, and most come from villages near the community in which they teach. A study made in about 1970 found that out of a sample of 58 rural teachers in northeastern Thailand, 66 percent had been born in the same province in which they taught and 48 percent had been born in the same district. All had been born in the same region (Compton 1972:169). Teachers from rural backgrounds are rarely chosen for urban teaching jobs because neither they nor their families have the power to influence those who determine the postings. As Khamman Khonkhai records in his novel (1982:ch. 2), bribes are sometimes employed by those with resources and connections to persuade educational officials to select a particular teacher for a choice position. A child who makes his or her way out of the village as a student pursuing more advanced education will typically return to a local school as a teacher.

While village school teachers are almost always villagers themselves by origin, and while many teachers have a stake in the rural economy, they are still "outsiders" in the village world, both in their own eyes and in the eyes of the villagers in whose community they teach. Such alienation from the village world derives from the fact that the local school is a state, not a community, institution. It is the state that determines the qualifications a teacher must possess before being certified to teach. As Bourdieu (1977:187) has argued, certification "makes it possible to relate all qualification-holders (and also, negatively, all unqualified individuals) to a single standard, thereby setting up a *single market* for all cultural capacities and guaranteeing the convertibility of cultural capital into money, at a determinate cost in labor and time" (emphasis in original; also see Bourdieu and Boltanski 1977 and Bourdieu and Passeron 1977). As the Thai government has set the standard for certification, the "qualified" teacher thus embodies the state's dominance of the "cultural capital" that can be acquired by those who attend school.

In the Thai system, teachers are not only certified by the state; they are also state employees. Teachers are not accountable to local school boards, and village education committees serve primarily as mechanisms whereby headmasters can seek to mobilize village support for school projects (cf. Keyes 1966:147). While teachers belong to Teachers' Associations, these have been created by government fiat and are in no sense unions.

Although village teachers are insulated to some degree by their postings in rural communities from the constant supervision of bureaucratic superiors—who are unable or disinclined to visit any particular school very often—they nonetheless must seek to impress their superiors if they are to be promoted, given raises, or transferred to better schools. Most evaluations of teachers are based on the results of examinations; good teachers are expected to have students who pass the exams. Such an expectation leads to an emphasis on cramming for exams under the guidance of teachers.

The subservient position of the village teacher in relation to those holding higher positions in the bureaucracy is perhaps most evident on the rare occasion when a superior pays a visit to a school. If the visit is anticipated (and it is rarely unannounced), the headmaster will have mobilized all the teachers and students to put everything in order. While superiors cannot observe the substance of teaching, they can observe the context in which it takes place. Thus, considerable efforts are put into cleaning classrooms, posting new charts, and even planting flowers. When the District or Provincial Educational Supervisor or some other official comes to the village, the headmaster and teachers receive him (rarely her) with lavish hospitality. Such hospitality usually runs to a meal with lots of chicken or even pork or beef and with liquor or beer (which in Thailand is more expensive than liquor). The costs can be quite high and are borne by the teachers (see Gurevich 1972:203; Khamman Khonkhai 1982:123–24). The head of a Supervisory Unit in Khǫn Kaen province summarized well how teachers are expected to show subservience to their superiors:

> Teachers have been accustomed to the old way of working— receiving orders or acting on the strict suggestions of their supervisors. ... They have been ... allowed to be only good followers. They still fear the high authority of their administrator who holds the key to their promotion in position and salary. (quoted in Gurevich 1972:207)

Despite occasional efforts to institute "reform," this conclusion remains as applicable to teachers in the 1980s as it was in the 1960s when it was written.

While village teachers are lowly subordinates to the bureaucratic officials responsible for administering public education, they are "lordly" in their relationship with ordinary villagers. This quality of "lordliness" finds expression in the Thai phrase *caonai*, meaning literally "lord and master," used today as a designation by villagers throughout Thailand for those whose positions as "servants of the crown" (*kharatchakan*) empower them to exercise the authority of the state in some matter or another (cf. Rubin 1973a and 1973b; Holmes 1974:79–80). Villagers feel inferior to teachers because they "do not have rank or honor" (Gurevich 1972:227), while teachers clearly do. Adult villagers tend to view the "lordliness" of teachers not in a totally negative way, for a teacher can choose to use his or her higher status to benefit those villagers he or she favors. Moreover, the degree to which a teacher can assert his or her authority is constrained by a number of factors. For one, villagers are conscious of the fact that the teacher comes from a rural background. Secondly, teachers have to depend on the members of the local community to cooperate if certain activities associated with the school are to be undertaken. Finally, the teacher is, after all, only a lowly member of the bureaucracy in which the quality of "lordliness" is vested.

However much a teacher may express his or her lordliness in a *noblesse oblige* form, the fact remains that the teacher is a part of the authority system of the state. As such, he or she is oriented to a world quite different from that in which villagers normally act. The alienation of teachers from the village world is associated with a pattern of teachers choosing to reside in communities where there are other teachers, even if this means commuting to the village where one teaches.[13] Even when teachers are local residents, their relationships with other villagers tend to be rather distant and less influential—with the exception of affairs relating to the school—than might be expected given their status (cf. Gurevich 1972:ch. VI).

While the teacher is viewed with some ambivalence by other adult villagers, he or she is typically viewed as an unquestioned authority by students. In a previous study based on my researches in Ban Nọng Tụn, I described the relationship between teachers and students as follows:

> The relationship between teacher and student in Thailand is one which places great emphasis on the pupil absorbing without question the knowledge which the teacher dispenses. This relationship is epitomized in the "saluting of the teacher" (*wai khru* in Thai) ceremony which is held annually near the beginning of each school year. In this ceremony the students symbolically demonstrate their deference to and dependence upon the teacher. According to custom and belief throughout the kingdom, only when this ceremony has been completed can the teacher then impart the knowledge which he possesses. (Keyes 1966:158)

The actual teaching process serves to underscore strongly the authoritarian stance of the teacher towards the students. Village pupils are expected to learn through rote memorization and are not encouraged to place questions before their teachers. The nature of the teacher-student relationship is perhaps most evident when teachers correct the work of their students. In Ban Nọng Tụn in 1963 and 1964 I observed the teachers sitting in the front of a classroom while each student, one by one, brought his or her copybook up for inspection. The teacher read over the student's work, and if no mistakes were found, then tossed the copybook to the floor from where the student reclaimed it. If the teacher found errors, he or she grabbed the student by the earlobe, holding tightly while explaining what the correct form should have been. Such behavior of teachers toward students has been described for other villages (see Gurevich 1972:144–45) and is far from atypical even today.

It is true, as a number of observers have noted, that the authoritarian manner adopted by the modern school teacher toward his or her students perpetuates a pattern that also existed in the past between monk-teachers and their pupils. There is, however, an important difference in the significance of the pattern for the two types of teachers. When a monk-teacher asserted his authority, the students were subordinated to a representative of the religion; when a modern teacher asserts his or her authority, the students are subordinated to a representative of the state. As I concluded in my previous study: "Given such a character to teacher-student relationships, the teacher is in a crucial position for communicating to future adult villagers conceptions of their place in the nation" (Keyes 1966:559).

Formal Instruction and the Opening of a New World

Perhaps the first thing a village child learns on becoming a student at the local school is to order his or her life according to a structuring of time that is quite different from that which he or she has known before. Prior to entering school, the child probably has little consciousness of time as such; life has heretofore moved according to the basic rhythms of family, agricultural, and ritual life. Now, instead of rising at dawn with the family and following the flow of the day thereafter, one takes care to be at school *in time* for the raising of the flag that precedes the beginning of formal instruction at 9:00 a.m. While some village school children, like their counterparts in other societies, do not make it to school *on time*, what is noteworthy is the fact that most do. Throughout the day, the child receives instruction in different subjects punctuated by breaks that, again, are ordered with reference to clock time (for a listing of the teaching schedule employed in the four grades of primary school in 1970, see Gurevich 1970:134).

The chronological ordering of the school day is situated within a school calendar that differs from the calendrical reckoning employed in villages for agricultural and ritual purposes. Whereas ritual events are held primarily with reference to a lunar calendar, the school follows an official calendar based on a five-day work week and a two-day weekend. It is not uncommon

TABLE 1: SCHOOL CALENDAR, BAN NQNG TỤN, MỤANG DIS-
TRICT, MAHASARAKHAM PROVINCE, NORTHEASTERN THAI-
LAND, 1963–1964

Date	Occasion	Village Observance
May 1	Official school opening	none
May 7	*Witsakhabucha* (religious festival commemorating birth and death of the Buddha)	none
June 6	*Wai Khru* ("Saluting the Teachers")	none
July 7	*Khao Phansa* (religious festival marking the beginning of Buddhist lent)	ritual
July 19	School closed to permit students to engage in farm work	villagers planting & transplanting
Sept 3	School reopening	none
Oct 3	*Qk Phansa* (religious festival marking the end of Buddhist lent)	ritual
Oct 7	*Wan Dek* ("Childrens' Day")	none
Oct 23	Chulalongkorn Day (commemorating King Chulalongkorn [1868-1910])	none
Nov 22	Sport's Day	none
Nov 27	Public Health Day	none
Dec 5	King's Birthday	none
Dec 10	Constitution Day	none
Jan 1	New Year's Day (modern calendar)	none
Feb 8	*Makhabucha* (religious festival)	none
Mar 29	End of term; beginning of summer holiday)	none

Note: Some dates given here actually fell on a Saturday or Sunday when
school was closed anyway. However, since these holidays are marked
in the school calendar when they do not fall on a weekend, they are
included in the table. Some official holidays (Chakri Day, traditional
New Year or *Songkran*, and the Queen's birthday) fell at times when
the school was in recess. Of these, only the traditional New Year was
observed by villagers.

Source: Keyes (1966:162)

that a school day will conflict with a religious holiday. In Ban Nǫng Tụn I observed that when the school was located in the *wat*, the religious calendar was accorded precedence over the school calendar; however, since the school has been separated from the *wat*, school is held on religious holidays except when these holidays have been designated as official holidays as well. I suspect that the same pattern could be discovered in most other villages as well.

The school calendar (see Table 1) makes students aware of days that have national significance. I found that few Ban Nǫng Tụn villagers in 1963–64 observed any national holidays, save for two religious ones, but school children were aware of them because the school closed on these days, and teachers explained their significance. The long recess in the rainy season—typically in July or August (cf. Khamman Khonkhai 1982:30, 98)—is the one major concession to village patterns—in this case those stemming from agricultural pursuits—built into the school calendar. During this period, the labor of children (and sometimes also of the teachers) is needed for the transplanting of rice.[14] School was also closed in April, typically the hottest month of the year.

The temporal order into which a child moves when he or she enters school is linked with a methodical communication of knowledge. Prior to entering school, few village children would have been conscious of any "distanciation," to use Ricoeur's (1981, esp. pp. 132–34) term, of knowledge of the world from experience in the world. There is a givenness to such knowledge; it is so self-evident that it appears to require no reflection. On entering school, the child experiences what Schutz has called a "shock": this shock "compels us to break through the limits of this finite province of meaning and shift the accent of reality to another one" (Schutz 1970:254). The compulsion lies in the presentation of knowledge in an alienated form, the textbook.

The textbook serves as the primary medium for the communication of knowledge in the rural school in Thailand even when, as in Ban Nǫng Tụn as I observed in 1963–1964, most children do not possess texts. In such cases, teachers copy out from the textbooks the lesson of the day on a blackboard and direct students in turn to copy the lesson into their copybook. The result is that the student acquires a textbook while at the same time "appropriating" (Ricoeur 1976:43–44, 91–94; 1981, esp. pp. 182–93) the knowledge contained therein, at least to the degree necessary to pass the examinations (cf. Gurevich 1972:144). In the last decade or so, the government has provided subsidies to enable students to own textbooks, and I noted that in Ban Nǫng Tụn in 1980 all children possessed the requisite texts. The emphasis on copying has not, however, declined; rather, today, copying can be carried on at home as well as in the classroom.

The function of the teacher is not to disseminate his or her interpretation of the texts, much less to encourage students to undertake their own interpretations, but to facilitate the mastery of the knowledge contained in the texts. Lesson plans are not drawn up by teachers on their own initiative, but are provided to teachers in a standard format by educational authorities. While there have been some shifts in emphasis, the structure of the curriculum today is little different from what I found it to be in the early 1960s (see Table 2), and that, in turn, reflected curriculum decisions that dated back to at least the 1930s.

The primary objective of the national system of education in Thailand has been, and continues to be, to prepare children throughout the country to enter into a "Thai" national world, a world structured with reference to the Thai state. Such an objective was enshrined in the first constitution of modern Thailand, the Constitution of 1932 (see Manich Jumsai 1958:52). In the early 1950s, Hanks (1960:25–26) found that teachers in the central Thai village of Bang Chan "recognize and accept their role in remaking the nation." In their instruction, he reports, they made use of texts containing such "newly written aphorisms ... as 'Buy Thai goods; love Thailand and love to be a Thai; live a Thai life, speak Thai, and esteem Thai culture'." To be able to enter this world, the essential first step has always been the inculcation in children of a knowledge of the standard Thai language, especially in its written form.

Standard Thai is an "official" or "public" language acquired only through school. When people speak standard Thai, they are often aware that the "prior texts"[15] are in fact written texts—school books, official documents, newspapers and the like. Even more salient, when people use standard Thai there is often implicit acceptance of the authority of the Thai state. This acceptance is evident in the precise use of particular pronouns and polite ending forms that situate the speakers within the status system validated by the state. As Bourdieu (1977:21) observes, "the constitutive power which is granted to ordinary language lies not in the language itself but in the group which authorizes it and invests it with authority. Official language, particularly the system of concepts by means of which the members of a given group provide themselves with representation of their social relations ..., sanctions and imposes what it states, tacitly laying down the dividing line between the thinkable and the unthinkable, thereby contributing towards the maintenance of the symbolic order from which it draws its authority."

TABLE 2: FORMAL CURRICULUM AND ALLOCATION OF TIME PER SUBJECT: BAN NQNG TỤN SCHOOL, MỤANG DISTRICT, MAHASARAKHAM PROVINCE, NORTHEASTERN THAILAND, 1963–1964

Subject	Number hours/week taught			
	Grade 1	Grade 2	Grade 3	Grade 4
Thai Language	$6\frac{1}{2}$	$6\frac{1}{2}$	$7\frac{1}{2}$	$7\frac{1}{2}$
Social Studies (civics, geography, history)	$6\frac{1}{2}$	$6\frac{1}{2}$	$6\frac{1}{2}$	$6\frac{1}{2}$
Health and hygiene	6	6	6	6
Singing and drawing	$4\frac{1}{2}$	$4\frac{1}{2}$	4	4
Arithmetic	$3\frac{1}{2}$	$3\frac{1}{2}$	3	3
Elementary Science	3	3	3	3
Morality and religious instruction	X	X	X	X
Sports	X	X	X	X
Scoutcraft and Jr. Red Cross	X	X	X	X
Manual Training	X	X	X	X
Total number of hours	30+	30+	30+	30+

Note: "X" indicates extracurricular activity, that is, an activity that is scheduled outside of normal school hours.

Source: Keyes (1966:164).

In the first two years of schooling in the Thai system, instruction in all subjects, not only in language per se, is related to the goal of inculcating in children the rudiments of standard Thai (see Keyes 1966:163, 165). In a northeastern Thai village like Ban Nọng Tụn, this task is rendered more difficult than it would be in a central Thai community because the northeastern Thai child speaks Lao at home, a language quite different from standard Thai in its phonology (including tones) as well as in its grammatical forms and vocabulary. The northeastern Thai child does not, however, find standard Thai quite so alien as does a child from southern Thailand whose domestic language is a dialect of Malay, or a child from the hills of northern Thailand who also speaks at home a language totally unrelated to any Tai language.

The fact that children who enter school do not already know standard Thai poses a dilemma for teachers. They have to decide how much use to make of a local language in order to make their instruction understood. In 1963–1964 I found that teachers in Ban Nọng Tụn instructed in Lao except when teaching Thai language as a subject (Keyes 1966:160, 165). Gurevich (1972:152–53) reported that a rather similar situation existed in a village in Khọn Kaen province where he carried out research in 1970. It should be recalled in this connection that most village school teachers in northeastern Thailand, unlike their counterparts in Malay-speaking areas of southern Thailand (see Uthai Dulyakasem in this volume), come from the same ethnolinguistic background as their students.

Despite some compromising by teachers of the requirement to instruct in standard Thai, the four years of schooling (and now six) that most children have received still appear sufficient to provide them with a basic competence to use standard Thai for speaking and reading. If, however, this competence is not used, it is likely to be lost in a few years. Writing about effective literacy in Thailand generally, Watson (1980:212) has said: "of those who have gone to elementary school it is estimated that 34% revert to illiteracy within a few years of leaving school through lack of reinforcement." In 1980 in Ban Nọng Tụn, I found many adult women under the age of forty uncomfortable in speaking standard Thai despite the fact that all but one in this age group had completed the four grades of primary education. Adult men in the same age group were much more competent in standard Thai, a function of the fact that they had many more occasions to use it both as a spoken and written language.

The loss of effective competence in standard Thai following completion of four years of schooling was one of the major reasons why compulsory education was raised from four to six years. The government has also attempted, in recent years, to maintain postschool literacy by establishing periodical reading centers in many villages throughout the country (Watson 1980:213).[16] Such a center was established in Ban Nǫng Tụn in 1980, but initially it contained very little material for villagers to read. By 1984, however, it had been relatively well-supplied with newspapers, magazines, and some books. Those using the center, I observed, were young and predominantly male.

One of the major values of literacy in village eyes is that it permits the literate villager to gain access to bureaucratic documents (as, for example, forms for registering land claims and transactions, marriages, ordinations, or deaths; permits for operating a vehicle or to hold a ceremony) that are increasingly a concomitant of many aspects of village as well as urban life. For the most part, village women defer to their husbands or adult sons in handling these documents. The uses of literacy are not confined, however, to relationships that villagers have with state agencies. Literacy has made it possible for many villagers to improve their effectiveness in market transactions, and to gain access to the knowledge of how to employ new forms of technology (fertilizers, machinery), since such knowledge often appears in the form of written instructions (cf. Holmes 1974:100, 102). I also found in my visits back to the village in the early 1980s that many Ban Nǫng Tụn villagers, including women, followed written rather than oral instructions regarding the use of medicines and some other types of products (beauty treatments, for example) that they purchased at shops in the village or in nearby towns. This represented a significant change from what I had observed in 1963–64 when most such communication was carried on orally. While the acquisition of literacy in standard Thai has functioned primarily to draw villagers into a world dominated by the Thai state, it has also served to give villagers greater access to the market economy and to products associated with that economy.

Next in importance to instruction in standard Thai in the village school is instruction that aims at projecting a national world within which the student will come to assume the status of a citizen. The lessons in language as well as those in social studies concern the interrelatedness of the monarchy, the nation, and the religion—the three pillars of the Thai nation. Students are also instructed in national history, a history that links the present nation with the reigns of past kings of the reigning Chakri dynasty, and underplays or ignores the divergent pasts of the different peoples now living within Thailand. It is in school that children throughout Thailand are first exposed to a national Thai culture through instruction in songs with nationalist themes, through participation in ceremonies celebrating national heroes as well as honoring the present king and queen, and through explanation of such national symbols as the flag, the national colors, and pictures of the king and other members of the royal family.[17]

While not all this teaching will "take," the high degree of redundancy of themes ensures that the basic idea of being a Thai citizen and a subject of the Thai king will be deeply rooted in most children by the time they finish the fourth grade, as I observed on the basis of my first fieldwork in Ban Nong Tyn:

> Throughout his school days, the student continuously has his attention directed to the associated symbols of monarchy and religion, monarchy and school, monarchy and nation. By the time he completes *prathom* [primary grade] four (or serves out his seven years), the student has developed a sense of relationship to and identification with the Thai king which is likely to remain and to be reinforced in other contexts for the rest of his life. Respect and reverence for and curiosity about the king (and interest in the rest of the royal family, especially the queen) certainly are not based only on school experience, but the school helps to shape the ideas which the Isan villager has about the Thai monarchy.

> More important than simply a respect for the King is the idealization or even sacralization of the kingship. ... King and Buddha are placed on equal planes for "worship" ... by the students and teachers. The educational program firmly establishes the monarchy as an important element in the villagers' world view. The recognition of the particular Thai King and the idealization of the Thai kingship are the main elements which underlie the villager's sense of citizenship. (Keyes 1966:180)

The extremely positive image of the Thai monarchy projected in instruction in primary schools from about the mid-1950s on[18] has served to predispose villagers to see themselves as loyal subjects of the king even when dissatisfied with many of the things the government has done in his name. It is hardly surprising, thus, that many villagers were easily recruited in the late 1970s into the royalist mass movement, the "village scouts" (*luk sua chao ban*) (see, in this connection, Muecke 1980). Even to this day, the criticism of the monarchy heard among some activists and intellectuals rarely finds its way into villages.

Since 1951, education has been explicitly linked to the national policy of promoting economic development (cf. Watson 1982:137). Such a policy notwithstanding, the aim of using mass education as a means to stimulate improvements in agricultural production has clearly been much less effectively implemented than has the goal of inculcating in the populace a sense of being citizens within a Thai nation-state. Holmes (1974:142) concluded, on the basis of research carried out in 1972 in a village in Khǫn Kaen province, that "villagers, whatever the planner might wish were the case, do not look to schooling to make them more intelligent or skillful *farm* dwellers" (emphasis in original). Villagers in the Khǫn Kaen community in which he worked, Holmes (1974:86) reported, do not believe that farm techniques can be taught in school; rather they are acquired as a concomitant of growing up in a village. The sentiments of farmers in this village, and they are typical, echo those of a Burmese villager who, in the 1930s, was overheard to say: "Any one can be taught to read and write, but one must be born and bred a cultivator" (Furnivall 1943:5). Despite the intention of the governments which have ruled Thailand since the early 1950s, most villagers throughout Thailand still see education as economically valuable only if it leads to a job in the bureaucracy (cf. Hanks 1960 and Holmes 1974:102–103, 147).

While this view cannot be gainsaid, the relevance of formal schooling for economic endeavors undertaken by villagers is not negligible. Literacy has, as already noted, made it possible for at least some villagers to gain access to new types of information useful for their agricultural pursuits. Farmers can read instructions on fertilizer packages, brochures explaining new methods of agriculture, and equipment manuals. Numeracy, also a skill learned in school, has also proven useful to many farmers, especially in connection with the sale of their products to middlemen. It is also important in this regard to note that some villagers have themselves become middlemen as well as village shopkeepers; for these local entrepreneurs, the ability to keep records of transactions has proven essential. In northeastern Thailand, as elsewhere in rural Thailand, few villagers ever became middlemen before the advent of compulsory primary education.

While it is difficult to assess how much formal education has contributed to the remarkable decline in birth rates which has been achieved in Thailand since the late 1960s, I believe that it has been an important factor. Most birth control practiced in villages, as I observed in Ban Nǫng Tụn, is undertaken by women on their own initiative without being told precisely by a health officer or their husbands how to practice it. All birth control methods available to villagers are more effective if the woman is literate. Moreover, they entail a type of reasoning about natural cause and effect which is more characteristic of formal education than of traditional culture.

Finally, while it probably is the case that few villagers have acquired a "modern" scientific outlook from their schooling, some may have developed a more self-conscious approach to their economic activities as a result of some aspects of their learning experiences in school. The ordering of events in school with explicit reference to time can perhaps be seen as the source of the notion that time can be "used" rather than adapted to. This notion has often been reinforced in the minds of those villagers who have been away to urban centers to work, where they have had to structure their work to a time schedule. This new orientation to time is symbolized, I believe, by the fact that such villagers typically bring back watches when they return to the village. In Ban Nọng Tụn I was struck by the fact that several villagers—most notably the non-agricultural entrepreneurs— sought to "use" their productive time efficiently, while most other villagers continued to follow more traditional rhythms.

The methodical "use" of time is sometimes associated with the self-conscious "use" of space, another lesson that may be learned at school. While nearly every household in Ban Nọng Tụn of 1963–1964 had a household garden in which various fruits and vegetables were produced for home consumption, I do not recall that any had the type of carefully planned gardens which I noted at a number of households in 1980 and 1983. In these new gardens there was not only a greater variety of fruits and vegetables, but the gardener also often employed manure, something that had never been done in 1963–1964. The village school garden, which itself had markedly improved in the two decades, may not have been the only model for the new type of garden cultivated by some villagers, but it is certainly one that is immediately available. Moreover, while in school, children gain first-hand experience through working in school gardens as part of the instructional program.[19] Thus, while few villagers may credit their school experience with having any relevance to their productive life, they may have appropriated from that experience more than they are conscious of.

Conclusions

The local state school has many attributes that mark it as an alien institution within the world of villagers throughout Thailand, and especially in the village world in those regions, like northeastern Thailand, where the people are ethnically dissimilar to the dominant people of the country. Nevertheless, the process whereby this institution came to be established in the village has meant that, for many years now, the school has played a major role in shaping the cultural orientation that villagers have toward the world. In Thailand, as throughout most of Southeast Asia, the state school has been instituted at the expense of traditional schools. In Thailand,

the manner in which the state school all but totally replaced the traditional Buddhist monastic school engendered almost no conflict, in marked
contrast to Malaysia and, especially, Indonesia where tensions between Islamic schools and state schools persist to the present. Neither did the state
schools in Thailand require a revolution to institute them as was the case
in Vietnam. Further, in Thailand, the demise of the Buddhist monastic
school and its successor, the hybrid school in which monks served as teachers of state-determined curricula, came much more quickly than it did in the
other Buddhist countries of Southeast Asia—Burma, Laos, and Cambodia.
Whereas in Thailand the hybrid school had effectively ceased to exist by
the mid-1930s, it persisted in Laos and Cambodia until the revolutionary
changes of 1975. "Even today," Steinberg (1982:101) has written recently
of Burma, "when secular primary education has virtually blanketed Burma,
there are still many monastic schools" (also see Nash 1961 and 1965).

While the state school has been ensconced in most Thai villages since at
least the mid-1930s, it was initially not a very effective cultural institution.
As more teachers were trained, and better-trained teachers were posted to
village schools, more and more students received the type of instruction
that made it possible for them to pass the requisite examinations. Based
on records kept in the Ban Nọng Tụn school, I was able to calculate that of
the students entering school between 1937 and 1944 and remaining in the
school until the requisite age or until completing the fourth grade, only 20.2
percent succeeded in passing all four grades. In marked contrast, of those
children who entered between 1945 and 1955 and stayed the course, 90.6
percent passed all four grades. Since 1956 it has been the rare exception
when a student does not complete all four grades, although a few always
have to repeat a grade. The percentage of villagers above the age of sixteen
who had had some schooling increased from 81.2 percent in 1963 to 95.8
percent in 1980. While in 1963, most villagers twenty-six years of age and
older had not completed the four grades, in 1980 more than 90 percent of
those 43 years and younger had done so. In 1980, moreover, an increasing
number of villagers, especially in the youngest cohort (16–20) had studied
beyond *prathom* (primary grade) four. This statistic does not reflect the
fact that the school had been recently upgraded to a six-year school because
those in this cohort had not been required to study for six years. Rather,
it reflects the commitment on the part of a number of village families to
send their children to schools outside of the village in order to obtain more
education than that offered in the village school.[20]

When parents do send their children for education beyond that offered
in the village school, the intent is, as Holmes (1974) found in his study of

another community in northeastern Thailand, that the child will find work in an occupation other than farming. A few who obtain middle school and high school educations and even tertiary educations, although they may not go into farming, may return to villages to live and work. In the past the "educated" villager was invariably a school teacher; today, with competition for white-collar jobs, especially those in government service and in such enterprises as banks, being such that only the most qualified are successful, some "educated" villagers return to their home communities rather than taking blue-collar or proletarian urban jobs. The implications of "educated" and job-frustrated people living in rural communities in Thailand have yet to be explored.

For most villagers, formal education does, however, point them away from their home communities. This is true even of the basic four year schooling. A knowledge of standard Thai, including a spoken as well as written knowledge, makes it possible for villagers to assume roles in the capitalist sector of the economy, a sector in which standard Thai is the dominant language.[21] Since the 1950s, and especially during the last twenty-five years, there has been large-scale migration of northeastern Thai villagers to Bangkok and to other urban centers in search of temporary work. While males have constituted the majority of temporary migrants, many females have also joined the migrant stream. In Ban Nọng Tụn, I found that in 1963, 49 percent of all men over the age of 20 and only 0.7 percent (1 case) of women had been to Bangkok to work; in 1980 I found that 39 percent of men and 17 percent of women in the over-twenty age group had engaged in temporary migration.[22] Elsewhere the percentages for women have been even higher (cf. Lightfoot 1984; Fuller, et al. 1983). Most migrants have taken low-paying laboring jobs—in construction, in domestic work, and, for women, in prostitution[23]—as they lack any skills, beyond a rudimentary knowledge of standard Thai, that would qualify them for higher-paying jobs. For those who aspire to better jobs, the requisite skills must be acquired in some sort of training beyond the education offered by the local school.

While primary schooling has functioned primarily to orient villagers to a world beyond the village—a world that for the most part they enter as disadvantaged subordinates—it has also reshaped the world of the village itself. Perhaps the most profound change has come about as a result of the separation of secular from monastic schooling. In social terms, this separation has been associated with the emergence of a new rural literati, the village teachers (khru), distinguished from the traditional intellectual elite, the monks. Whereas the monks did not form, as I have argued, a class segment within rural society, teachers appear to constitute at least an incipient class. In addition to the perquisites of office, such as an assured monthly income and some government-provided benefits, credit with merchants, and familiar relations with some officials, many teachers also hold economically dominant positions as rice millers, large land owners, truck owners, and shopkeepers in the rural economy. Furthermore, they often vie with local leaders for control over certain communal affairs. Despite this, teachers do not command the high respect accorded monks by villagers. Moreover, given their lowly status in the civil service, many teachers are inclined to see themselves as members of a disadvantaged group. It is not surprising, thus, that some village teachers (or ex-teachers) have been attracted to radical politics, including the Communist-led insurrection (cf. Montri 1985).

As school teachers have become significant actors in the village world, Buddhist monks have become less so. Village men are less attracted to entering the monkhood since the secular school has preempted the educational functions once carried out by the *wat*. There has, as a result, been a marked decrease in the number of clergy available for religious functions. Increasingly, also, men who perform such traditional roles as folk medicinal practitioner, soul-securing specialist, or folk song or opera performer are more likely to have acquired the necessary literacy through formal schooling than through having been a member of the clergy.

Since the establishment of government schools, literacy is no longer the prerogative of males only. Girls in villages today have equal access to literacy; the fact that there are female teachers in nearly every village school serves to underscore the notion that literacy is also open to women. It remains true, nonetheless, that there are marked sexual divisions in the uses of literacy. Since women are barred from entering the Buddhist Sangha, they are very unlikely to use their school-acquired literacy for religious purposes or even for the related ends of becoming a specialist in one of the traditional roles such as folk medicine practitioner requiring literacy. Moreover, since women have fewer contacts with government officials than do men, they are also less likely to use their literacy for dealing with the state's laws and regulations. Women, like men, have assumed new economic roles that have been facilitated, at least in part, by their education, but they have done so less often than have men. Women today—including those women who have worked in Bangkok and have returned to their villages, and, most especially, women school teachers—do not appear to be playing any larger role in village affairs than they did in the past. Indeed, the fact that women undergo the same schooling as men has made the sexual division of labor in rural society, in some ways, more apparent than it was traditionally.

The government has recently implemented a national policy to upgrade primary education to provide six, rather than four, years of education for the general citizenry. More schooling means more state-determined education; villagers throughout Thailand lack any means whereby they might make the schools in their communities responsive to local concerns. The proposed world of the village school thus continues to prepare children to accept the political and economic inequalities of the state-oriented world of modern Thailand.

Notes

[1] I take the notion of "proposed world" from Paul Ricoeur (1981:142): "For what must be interpreted in a text is a *proposed world* which I could inhabit and wherein I could project *one of my own most possibilities*" (emphasis added). I seek to interpret the world in which those in whose social action I am interested might project themselves. My interpretation is predicated, thus, on engaging the "text"—in this case the work of culture emergent in schooling—with reference to the actual world of relationships I anticipate, on the basis of my observations outside of the school, that village children might enter into when they become adults.

[2] The form "Tai" is used to refer to any people who speak a language belonging to the Tai (Daic) family. The form "Thai" is reserved for designating peoples who are citizens of modern Thailand.

[3] Tambiah (1968:95) has said that "occasionally a girl might be included" in the premodern school found in the northeastern village of Ban Phra Muan, Udǫn province in which he carried out fieldwork. This statement appears to apply to a time (ca. 1916– 1932) when the *wat* schools were beginning to assume the functions of a modern educational institution. Some women in premodern urban settings did become literate, but rural women were, almost without exception, illiterate until after compulsory primary education was instituted.

[4] On the cultural process of incorporation of the past into the present, see Becker (1979) and Bloch (1974).

[5] Indeed, I would argue that social division of the ownership of the means of production is also associated with a differential accumulation of knowledge, and that this knowledge cannot be dismissed as "superstructure."

[6] David Wyatt's *The Politics of Reform in Thailand* (1969) provides a detailed and insightful analysis of political debates and conflicts surrounding the modern educational system during the reign of King Chulalongkorn. Also compare Wyatt (1975).

[7] No full study has yet been made of the hybrid schools of the period from 1898 to 1932. Such a study would contribute not only to an understanding of the process of change in Thai education, but also of the transformation of the role of Buddhist monks. A comparison could also be profitably made with similar hybrid schools in Burma, Laos, and Cambodia.

[8] There are some very few exceptions allowed. One of the more interesting is the school at Wat Si Soda in Chiang Mai where boys from tribal background are provided the opportunity to gain a primary education. Many of these boys are ordained as novices for at least part of the period while they are at the school.

[9] The secular school has not completely displaced the educational role of the *wat*. To this day, a villager can gain an education while a member of the clergy, and use it for secular (and non-agricultural) purposes at a later stage in his life. See Wyatt (1966), Holmes (1974:90–93), and Tambiah (1976:288–312) for examples of how rural people have used monastic education as a means to achieve social mobility.

[10] I first spent eighteen months in Ban Nǫng Tǔn in 1963–1964 and returned for brief visits several times in the late 1960s and in the 1970s. In 1980 I spent two months doing a systematic restudy of some aspects of social and economic life in the village, and followed up on this research during another month's visit in 1983. I also made a brief visit to the village in 1984. I have discussed education in Ban Nǫng Tǔn in my dissertation (Keyes 1966) and in a more recent report (Keyes 1982) based on my 1980 research. I am grateful to the Foreign Area Fellowship Program and the Southeast Asia Fellowship program of the Ford Foundation, the University of Washington, and the United States Agency for International Development for support of my field research. I am indebted to my wife, Jane, for her invaluable assistance in my researches in 1963–1964 and again in 1983, to Dr. Paitoon Mikusol who assisted me in 1980 and 1984, and to Suriya Smutkupt who helped me in 1980 and 1983. I want to acknowledge a special debt to Ngao and Nuan Khamwicha who have been not only my chief informants in Ban Nǫng Tǔn, but also our *phinǫng* with whom we have lived in the village.

[11] The best study of traditional education in northeastern Thai rural society is Tambiah's (1968) "Literacy in a Buddhist Village in North-East Thailand" (also see Tambiah 1970). Prajuab Thirabutana (1971), in her novel, *Little Things*, portrays the attitudes of some northeastern villagers—in this case those living in Ubon province—toward education in a period just prior to World War II. For more on the same period, see Prajuab's (1958) autobiography, *A Simple One*, and Khamphun Bunthawi's (1976) novel, *Luk Isan* [Son of the Northeast]. Gurevich (1972 and 1975) and Holmes (1974) both carried out studies on rural education in villages in Khǫn Kaen province in the early 1070s, and Compton (1972) made a more general study of the role of the teacher in

rural northeastern society for the same period. Khamman Khonkhai, in his novel, *Khru Ban Nǫk* [Village School Teacher], recently translated by Gehan Wijeyewardene under the title of *The Teachers of Mad Dog Swamp* (Khamman Khonkhai 1982) depicts well some aspects of rural education in northeastern Thailand in the late 1970s. Also see Khamman's (1979) *Cotmai cak nǫng ma wǫ* [Letters from Mad Dog Swamp].

[12] Khamman Khonkhai (1982) describes well the efforts of one village teacher to demonstrate the possibilities of a school experimental garden.

[13] In 1983 when I returned to the village, the headmistress had persuaded the government to provide money to build a house for a teacher on the grounds of the school. A single male teacher who had just been hired was living in the house. The headmistress pointed out to me that it was very exceptional for a rural school to have a house for a teacher at the school.

[14] Holmes (1974:95) reports that there was also a twenty-day recess in the harvest season (December-January) in rural Khǫn Kaen province.

[15] I am indebted to A. L. Becker for the concept of the "prior text."

[16] See Khamman Khonkhai (1982:174–75) for the story of the founding of such a center.

[17] See Keyes (1966:165–69) for a detailed discussion of the nationalist content of instruction.

[18] From 1932, when a revolution established a constitutional monarchy, until about the mid 1950s when King Bhumibol Adulyadej began to play a conspicuous public role, the role of the monarchy was deemphasized by the government. See, in this regard, Keyes (1986).

[19] See, in this connection, the description of a school garden in Khamman Khonkhai's (1982:86–91) novel.

[20] Since 1967, my wife and I have provided a modest annual scholarship fund for villagers to use for study beyond the primary grades available in the Ban Nǫng Tyn school. While it is difficult to determine how many of the students have gone on to study because of this incentive, it should be noted that it has probably made Ban Nǫng Tyn somewhat atypical for villages in the area.

[21] Chinese and English are also used in certain businesses, but rarely exclusively, so, it is in those businesses that people from village backgrounds are employed.

[22] I suspect my 1980 data understate the actual incidence of migration. Klausner (1972) found that significant numbers of women in a village in the northeastern Thai province of Ubon in which he carried out fieldwork were migrating to Bangkok as early as the late 1950s.

[23] The incidence of prostitution among migrant women from the Northeast, while not insignificant, is much less than the incidence among migrant women from northern Thailand (see Pasuk Phongpaichit 1981).

References

Aree Sanhachawee. "Evolution in Curriculum and Teaching." In *Education in Thailand: A Century of Experience*, 95–114. Bangkok: Department of Elementary and Adult Education, Ministry of Education, 1970.

Becker, A.L. "Text-Building, Epistemology, and Aesthetics in Javanese Shadow Theatre." In *The Imagination of Reality*, ed. by A.L. Becker and Aram A. Yengoyan, 211–43. Norwood, N. J.: Ablex Publishing Co., 1979.

Bloch, Maurice. "Symbols, Song, Dance and Features of Articulation: Is Religion an Extreme Form of Traditional Authority?" *European Journal of Sociology*, 15(1974):55–81.

Bourdieu, Pierre. *Outline of a Theory of Practice*, tr. by Richard Nice. Cambridge: Cambridge University Press, 1977.

Bourdieu, Pierre, and L. Boltanski. "Formal Qualifications and Occupational Hierarchies." In *Reorganizing Education*, ed. by E.J. King, 61–69. London and Beverly Hills: Sage Publications, 1977.

Bourdieu, Pierre, and Jean-Claude Passeron. *Reproduction in Education, Society and Culture*. London and Beverly Hills: Sage Publications, 1977.

Compton, James Lin. "Factors Related to the Role of the Primary School Teacher as Mediator-Facilitator in the Communication Process between the Rural Village Community and the Larger Social System in Northeast Thailand." Ph.D. dissertation, University of Michigan, 1972.

Fuller, Theodore D., Peerasit Kamnuansilpa, Paul Lightfoot, and Sawaeng Rathanamongkolmas. *Migration and Development in Modern Thailand*. Bangkok: The Social Science Association of Thailand, 1983.

Furnivall, J. S. *Educational Progress in Southeast Asia*. New York: Institute of Pacific Relations, 1943.

Geertz, Clifford. "The Javanese Kijaji: The Changing Role of a Cultural Broker." *Comparative Studies in Society and History*, 2(1960):228–49.

Gurevich, Robert. "Khru: A Study of Teachers in a Thai Village." Ph.D. dissertation, University of Pittsburgh, 1972.

——. "Teachers, Rural Development and the Civil Service in Thailand." *Asian Survey*, 15(1975):870–81.

Hanks, Lucien M. "Indifference to Modern Education in a Thai Farming Community." *Practical Anthropology*, 7(1960):18–29; first published in *Human Organization*, 17 (1958):9–14.

Holmes, Henry Cobb. "School Beyond the Village: A Study of Education and Society in Northeastern Thailand." Ed.D. dissertation, University of Massachusetts, 1974.

Inkeles, Alex. "Making Man Modern: On the Causes and Consequences of Individual Change in Six Developing Countries." *American Journal of Sociology*, 75(1969):208–225.

——. "The School as a Context for Modernization." In *Education and Individual Modernity in Developing Countries*, ed. by Alex Inkeles and Donald B. Holsinger, 7–23. Leiden: E. J. Brill, 1974.

Inkeles, Alex, and D. H. Smith. *Becoming Modern*. Cambridge: Harvard University Press, 1974.

Keyes, Charles F. "Peasant and Nation: A Thai-Lao Village in a Thai State." Ph.D. dissertation, Cornell University, 1966.

——. *Socioeconomic Change in Rainfed Agricultural Villages in Northeastern Thailand*. Seattle: Thailand Project, Department of Anthropology, University of Washington, 1982.

——. "Mother or Mistress but Never a Monk: Culture of Gender and Rural Women in Buddhist Thailand." *American Ethnologist*, 11.2(1984):223–41.

——. *Thailand: Buddhist Kingdom as Modern Nation-State*. Boulder, Colorado: Westview Press, 1986.

——. "Ambiguous Gender: Male Initiation in a Buddhist Society." In *Gender and Religion: On the Complexity of Symbols*, ed. by Caroline Bynum, Stevan Harrell, and Paula Richman, 66–96. Boston: Beacon Press, 1986.

Khamman Khonkhai (Khammaan Khonkhai). *Cotmai cak nǫng ma wǫ* [Letters from Mad Dog Swamp]. Bangkok: Bannakit, 1979.

——. *The Teachers of Mad Dog Swamp*, tr. by Gehan Wijeyewardene. St. Lucia: University of Queensland Press, 1982.

Khamphun Bunthawi. *Luk Isan* [Son of the Northeast]. Bangkok: Bannakit, 1976.

Klausner, William J. *Reflections in a Log Pond: Collected Writings*. Bangkok: Suksit Siam, 1972.

Landon, Kenneth Perry. *Siam in Transition*. Shanghai: Kelly and Walsh, 1939.

Lightfoot, Paul. "Circular Migration in Northeastern Thailand." In *Strategies and Structures in Thai Society*, ed. by Han ten Brummelhuis and Jeremy H. Kemp, 85–94. Amsterdam: Universiteit van Amsterdam,

Antropologisch-Sociologisch Centrum, Publikatieserie Vakgroep Zuiden Zuidoost-Azië, No. 31, 1984.

Manich Jumsai, Mǫm Luang. *Compulsory Education in Thailand.* Paris: UNESCO, UNESCO Studies on Compulsory Education, No. VIII, 1951.

Montri Cenawitkun. *Khru prachaban: botbat kantǫsu thang kanmyang* (Local Teachers: [Their] Role in Political Opposition). Bangkok: Thammasat University Press, 1985.

Muecke, Marjorie A. "The Village Scouts of Thailand." *Asian Survey,* 20(1980):407–27.

Nash, Manning. "Education in a New Nation: The Village School in Upper Burma." *International Journal of Comparative Sociology,* 2(1961):135–43.

——. "Village Schools in the Process of Social and Economic Modernization." *Social and Economic Studies,* 14(1965):131–43.

Pasuk Phongpaichit. *Rural Women of Thailand: From Peasant Girls to Bangkok Masseuses.* Geneva: International Labor Organisation, 1981.

Prajuab Tirabutana (Prajuab Thirabutana). *A Simple One: The Story of a Siamese Childhood.* Ithaca, N. Y.: Cornell University Southeast Asia Program, Data Paper, No. 30, 1958.

——. *Little Things.* Sydney: Collins, 1971.

Press, Irwin. "Ambiguity and Innovation: Implications for the Genesis of the Culture Broker." *American Anthropologist,* 71(1969):205–17.

Ricoeur, Paul. "The Model of the Text: Meaningful Action Considered as a Text." *Social Research,* 38(1971):529–62.

——. *Interpretation Theory: Discourses and the Surplus of Meaning.* Fort Worth, Texas: The Texas Christian University Press, 1976.

——. *Hermeneutics and the Human Sciences,* tr. and ed. by John B. Thompson. Cambridge: Cambridge University Press., 1981.

Rubin, Herbert J. "Will and Awe: Illustrations of Thai Villager Dependency upon Officials." *Journal of Asian Studies,* 32(1973):425–45.

——. "A Framework for the Analysis of Villager-Official Contact in Rural Thailand." *Southeast Asia,* 2(1973):233–64.

Schutz, Alfred. *On Phenomenology and Social Relations,* ed. with an introduction by Helmut R. Wagner. Chicago: University of Chicago Press, 1970.

Silverman, Sydel F. "Patronage and Community-Nation Relationships in Central Italy." *Ethnology,* 4(1965):172–89.

Spiro, Melford E. *Buddhism and Society: A Great Tradition and Its Burmese Vicissitudes.* New York: Harper and Row, 1970.

Steinberg, David I. *Burma: A Socialist Nation of Southeast Asia.* Boulder, Colorado: Westview Press, 1982.

Tambiah, Stanley J. "Literacy in a Buddhist Village in North-East Thailand." In *Literacy in Traditional Societies,* ed. by Jack Goody, 86–131. Cambridge: Cambridge University Press, 1968.

———. *Buddhism and the Spirit Cults in North-East Thailand.* Cambridge: Cambridge University Press, 1970.

———. *World Conqueror and World Renouncer: A Study of Buddhism and Polity in Thailand against a Historical Background.* Cambridge: Cambridge University Press, 1976.

Vella, Walter F., assisted by Dorothy Vella. *Chaiyo! King Vajiravudh and the Development of Thai Nationalism.* Honolulu: University of Hawaii Press, 1978.

Watson, Keith. *Educational Development in Thailand.* Hong Kong: Heinemann Asia, 1980.

Wolf, Eric R. "Aspects of Group Relations in a Complex Society." *American Anthropologist,* 58(1956):1065–78.

———. "Kinship, Friendship, and Patron-Client Relations in Complex Societies." In *The Social Anthropology of Complex Societies,* ed. by Michael Banton, 1–22. London: Tavistock Publications, Association of Social Anthropologists Monographs, 1966.

Wyatt, David K. "The Buddhist Monkhood as an Avenue of Social Mobility in Traditional Thai Society." *Sinlapakǫn* (Fine Arts) (Bangkok), 10(1966):41–52.

———. *The Politics of Reform in Thailand.* New Haven: Yale University Press, 1969.

———. "Education and Modernization of Thai Society." In *Change and Persistence in Thai Society: Essays in Honor of Lauriston Sharp,* ed. by G. William Skinner and A. Thomas Kirsch, 125–50. Ithaca, N.Y.: Cornell University Press, 1975.

EDUCATION AND ETHNIC NATIONALISM:
THE CASE OF THE MUSLIM-MALAYS
IN SOUTHERN THAILAND*

Uthai Dulyakasem

Introduction

Schools, the institutionalized form of education, are generally called upon to perform many roles in society, ranging from simple child care to the teaching of highly specialized cognitive and technical skills. Schools are also expected to socialize children into the prevailing societal norms, whatever those might be in a given context. Moreover, they are often expected to generate what might be called controlled social reform. But although these roles may be expected, educational planners and social scientists have been unable to reach any definite conclusion as to what degree of success is possible in schools' performance of these roles. The assumption that schools do produce their intended outcomes seems to be well accepted, but recognition that education also produces unintended outcomes leads us to wonder what factors account for such phenomena.

This chapter is an attempt to address this issue. It is argued that the outcomes produced by a particular school system cannot be predicted without knowing the specific sociopolitical conditions under which the system operates, but if these are known, then outcomes can be foreseen. We will examine the expansion of modern secular education by the central Thai nation-state into two peripheral Muslim districts of southern Thailand, along with the results of that expansion. The two districts are Teluban in Pattani province and La-ngu in Satun (Satul) province. Their socio-economic and political histories are markedly different, and, while modern education was introduced into the districts in much the same manner and under the same sets of assumptions and legal conditions, the outcomes in the two districts have not been the same.

The Case of La-Ngu

La-ngu is presently a district of Satun (Satul) province, located north-

---

* Dr. Uthai prefers "Siam" rather than "Thailand" as the designation for his country. The term "Thailand" has been used in the title of his chapter in order to correspond with usage elsewhere in the volume; "Siam" has been retained in the body of his chapter [ed.].

west of the provincial town of Satun. It has an area of about 397 square kilometers, and is bounded by Tungwa district to the north, Muang district and the Indian Ocean to the south, Kuan Kalong district to the east, and the Indian Ocean to the west. The district town is connected by road to the provincial town of Satun and to Tungwa district, distances of about 40 kilometers and 27 kilometers respectively. In 1979 the total population of La-ngu, according to an official census conducted in that year, was 34,149, and the population density of the district was 85 persons per square kilometer. The census shows that 85 percent of the population was Muslim and 15 percent Buddhist. There were 28 *majids* (mosques), one Buddhist monastery, and one Chinese temple in the district.

Political and Economic History of La-ngu

La-ngu is not Malay-speaking, even though it is a Muslim district. Its political and economic history is closely tied to the history of Satun province. At one time the present territory of the province formed just one of 128 *Mukims* (districts) in the state of Kedah (a *Mukim*, according to Newbold [1971:20], contains a mosque and forty-four families or more). Satun had no chief until 1913, when King Rama III appointed one Tenghu Bisnu to the position. Even then, this chief did not reside in Satun, and visited it only occasionally (Lungputeh 1957:6). After his death in 1815, Satun had no ruler for another eighteen years. In 1839 Kedah was divided into three principalities (Perlis, Kedah, and Satun), each independent from the other and headed by a Siamese-supported Malay ruler under the authority of a Siamese governor. In 1882 conflict between the ruler of Satun and his brother, Tengku Mohammed, forced the latter into exile. He settled in La-ngu, about fifteen hours by boat from the town of Satun, where he built a new "town" and set himself up as a chief (Lungputeh 1957:22). But La-ngu did not last long as a principality; it came to an end three years later when Mohammed was accused by the ruler of Satun of being a traitor.

In 1909, following the signing of an agreement between England and Siam, La-ngu was promoted to the status of a sub-district (*king amphoe*). Thus La-ngu became a political unit within the structure of a modern Siamese bureaucratic system. It was never a Malay sultanate nor did it ever have a raja as its chief. The head of the sub-district, the *palad king amphoe*, was a civil servant who received a regular salary from the Siamese government. La-ngu remained a sub-district for over twenty years, becoming a district, or *amphoe*, in 1930. The length of time it took to be promoted to the status of a district clearly indicates the political and economic insignificance of the district. The first head of the sub-district office was a Muslim-Malay, and most officials at that time could speak both Siamese and Malay, according to one informant. As time went on an increasing number of Siamese who were not locally born were appointed to official positions within the subdistrict.

There is no record of the ethnic composition of the population in early La-ngu. Fragmentary accounts and information from local residents indicate that the first settlers were Malay (the majority), Chinese, Siamese and Sam-sam, or Thai-speaking Muslims.[1] Chinese and Malays generally engaged in trade and fishing. Siamese, Sam-sam and some Malays engaged primarily in agricultural activities and charcoal production. After La-ngu became a sub-district, people from neighboring provinces moved there as wet-rice farmers, upland vegetable growers, and fishermen. The town of Kuala Bara, the site of the first settlement and about ten kilometers from the present district center, was once a busy seaport, exporting charcoal, black pepper, and other agricultural products to Sumatra and Penang. This business came to a near halt, however, after the Second World War.

Without the trade that had operated out of Kuala Bara, many Chinese and Malays moved away to Perlis (Malaysia) and Satun. Those who remained continued working on farms and in petty trade. Except for the trade at Kuala Bara, La-ngu had a subsistence economy. There was no clear cultural division of labor and no evident ethnic competition.

Prior to 1955 La-ngu had no roads to other districts. The only means of transportation were by water or by elephant, and in the monsoon season, even the waterways could not be used. The first dirt road connecting La-ngu to Satun was built in 1955 and covered with asphalt in 1973. A government savings bank was opened only in 1978, and even as late as 1980 there was still no commercial bank, no telephone service, and electricity only in the central area of the district. La-ngu is still rural today, and the pace of economic change there remains quite slow.

All Muslim informants in La-ngu considered themselves Siamese. They said they had no sentimental feelings about the past glory of the Pattani kingdom to the east. Nor did they show any emotional attachment to the Malay aristocracy, either in Satun or in Kedah. Some informants, who initially I thought were of Malay origin, insisted that they were Siamese-Muslims, and none of them could speak or understand the (Pattani) Malay language.

Linguistic Structure of La-ngu

In the early days, the majority of La-ngu residents, both Muslim and Buddhist, were bilingual in Siamese (southern dialect) and Malay (Kedah dialect), but did not understand the Malay spoken in the Pattani area. Newcomers to the area, however, and second-generation Malays, could speak only Siamese. By 1980 almost no Muslim resident of La-ngu could speak Malay.

As will be seen when we consider the case of Teluban, it is clear that language separates the Muslims of La-ngu in Satun province from those in the province of Pattani. In the entire province of Satun, less than two percent of the population of 159,176 can speak and understand even the Kedah Malay dialect, let alone that of Pattani, which differs markedly from it. We were told by one informant in Satun province that members of the separatist movement from Pattani had attempted to persuade Muslims in Satun to participate in their struggle, but that they had been unsuccessful, largely because of communication problems.

Education in La-ngu

All of our informants agreed there was no system of instruction in La-ngu in the early days. Local Muslims acquired their basic knowledge of Islam either from their parents or from the Imam on Fridays, and there were no *pondok* (religious) schools for Muslim youth. Prior to 1909 both Muslim and Buddhist residents of La-ngu were apparently illiterate. After the passage of the Primary Education Act in 1921 instituting compulsory education throughout the country, a few children were sent to school in the provincial town of Satun. It was not until 1924, however, that the first primary school in the province was opened; this was at Ban Taloh Sai, about two kilometers from the Kuala Bara seaport. The first teacher of that school, who is still living close to the original school site, said that both Muslim and Buddhist pupils attended. He was not aware of resistance by Muslim people to modern education, and pointed out that:

> Of course, some Muslim parents did not want to send their children to school, but this was true for some Siamese parents also. The reason was, however, not religious but economic. These people could not afford to send their children to school because they needed them to help on the farms and at home. Furthermore, for many of them, the school was too far for them to walk.

Modern education was introduced quite slowly into La-ngu. In 1960, there were only twenty-six primary schools and 3,384 pupils in La-ngu, according to the census taken that year. By 1979, there were still only forty-four primary schools and one secondary school. Today, many schools are still seriously short of teachers, and school buildings are in poor condition. Some Muslim parents send their children to study at *pondok* schools in Pattani, Yala, and Narathiwat. They choose the *pondok* schools in these provinces mainly because most, if not all, Muslims in Satun (and other southern provinces for that matter) believe that Islam as taught and practiced in the Pattani area is "purer" than that in other provinces in Siam. The *pondok* schools in the Pattani area are not popular, however, among the Muslims of La-ngu because classes there are conducted in Malay. There is still no *pondok* school in La-ngu.

In summary, the educational structure in La-ngu has changed little since the district first became an administrative unit. The only educational system which has ever existed in the district is the one provided by the central government. The introduction and expansion of the modern (secular) education system have not been considered threats by any ethnic group. Muslims seem to be as supportive of the system as the Siamese Buddhists. When we turn to the case of Teluban, however, we find a completely different situation.

The Case of Teluban

Teluban (Thai: Saiburi) is a district of Pattani province, situated to the southwest of the provincial town of Pattani. It has an area of about 350 square kilometers and is bounded by Panareh district to the north, Mayo district to the west, the Gulf of Siam to the east, and Bachoh (Narathiwat) province to the south. According to the 1979 census, the total population of the district at that time was 52,004, with a population density of 148 persons per square kilometer. The census shows 80.8 percent of the population as Muslim and 19.2 percent as Buddhist.

Political and Economic History of Teluban

Despite lack of agreement among historians on the origin of Pattani State (not to be confused with present-day Pattani province, of which Teluban is now a district), Pattani seems once to have been an independent entity with its own political, economic, and cultural structures. Politically, Pattani was ruled by its own rajas during successive dynasties that lasted for long periods of time. Eventually it was divided into several small states, and was finally conquered by, and incorporated into, the Siamese kingdom. Culturally, the population of Pattani was overwhelmingly Malay, and its people subscribed to the Islamic religion.

As no annals were kept for Teluban in early times, an account of its political and economic history must rely on fragmentary evidence from secondary sources as well as inferences based on conditions in other Malay states. Teluban was one of the gulf ports under the jurisdiction of Siam as early as the thirteenth and fourteenth centuries (Wheatley 1961:302, 391). It may have had some political and economic importance, as Teluban became one of the seven Malay states of Siam, headed by a Malay raja, that emerged during the division of the Pattani kingdom in 1786.

When Teluban became one of the seven Malay states, its district chief and members of his entourage remained more or less independent in their conduct of the internal affairs of the state. They now had to deal directly with non-Moslems for the first time, however, as Siamese families were brought in from Pattalung, Songkhla, and other provinces to settle in the area, changing the ethnic composition of the population slightly. Teluban appears to have become an outlying district under the protection of Pattani, but to have continued to have its own political structure, for "the Sultan ... did not, in most states of the nineteenth century, embody any exceptional concentration of administrative authority. Powerful district chiefs could and sometimes did flout his wishes with impunity; some of them were wealthier than he was" (Gullick 1958:44). The key office in the political system was the district chief, who, though appointed by the Sultan, held his district by his own strength (Gullick 1958:95–96), and administered it through an entourage of kinsmen and village appointees.

In 1885 Teluban was placed under Monthon Pattani,* and Malay district officials began gradually to be replaced by Siamese. By the late nineteenth century, Teluban had become an important regional trading port. The population remained overwhelmingly Malay, although it also included a few Chinese, Arabs, Siamese, and Javanese (see Annandale 1903:505–23; Skeat 1953:64–73). The ruling class, whose members were recruited by birth, was comparatively homogeneous. The majority of the rest of the population engaged in agricultural activities and fishing. Some Malays engaged in trade, but most business activities were in the hands of Chinese. Malays were involved in agricultural activities, fishing, boat-building, and administration. Other ethnic groups engaged in agriculture and fishing. For these subject classes the most important element of political cohesion was their common relationship to powerful masters.

Significant changes in the local economic structure began to take place as roads connecting Teluban to other towns in the region were completed during the first decade of the twentieth century, and as a railway from Bangkok to Singapore was built in the 1920s. The port declined as trade moved from Teluban and Pattani to other ports. Fishing methods became

---

* A *monthon* is an administrative unit which included a number of provinces. It was abolished after the 1932 Revolution in Siam [ed.].

more technically advanced, but these changes failed to work to the advantage of the Muslim-Malays, as they had neither the technical skills nor the financial resources to compete with the Chinese in large-scale enterprises. Many Malay fishermen became wage-workers on large boats owned by local Chinese or by Siamese newcomers. Malays were less well prepared than the Siamese and Chinese to take jobs in new service areas such as banking, the telephone system, or the medical field. Chinese continued to dominate the business sector except in the operation of small businesses at local and village levels, which were often run by Malays. By the 1970s, fewer than ten percent of the shop-houses in the town of Teluban were owned and run by Muslims, and of these, about half were owned by Pakistanis.

Malay political power, particularly that of the raja, was seriously shaken when the seven provinces were placed under the Thai Area Commissioner in 1901 in an effort to "modernize" the country by bringing outlying provinces and vassal states under the direct control of the central government. A Siamese judge and a tax collector were appointed to "assist" the raja, while a Siamese official was appointed to rule jointly with him. In 1908, the appointment of the first Siamese governor in Teluban marked the end of the political power of the Malay ruling class. Responsibility for local administration was taken almost completely out of the hands of Muslim-Malays when Teluban was demoted to the status of a district (*amphoe*) and joined to the province of Pattani in 1931.

Since 1932 the political structure of the district has remained basically unchanged (see Sutton 1962), under the control of the district officer, or *nai amphoe*, appointed by the Ministry of Interior. According to a retired Muslim official, most of the district officers have had to rely on interpreters (usually Malay teachers) at meetings with villagers. At the sub-district and village level, the headman of the sub-district (*kamnan*) and the village headman (*phuyaiban*) are elected, subject to the approval of the district officer. As of 1980, all sub-district headmen were Muslim-Malays but there were a few Siamese village headmen.

Despite occasional government concessions to the Malays, such as declaring Friday an official holiday, allowing the study of Malay in primary schools, and reinstating Islamic family and inheritance laws, the Malays of Teluban feel deeply that they have been "conquered." Group solidarity among these Muslim-Malays may be attributed mainly to the sense of being "Muslim" (Gullick 1958:135). Indeed, being Muslim is equated with being a Malay; the expression for conversion to Islam is *"masok melayu"*—to enter into the Malay culture. They seem determined to restore their political autonomy, if not full independence (see Seni *et al.*, 1977). The "Great

Pattani protest" of 1975 which lasted for forty-two days in late 1975 was initiated at Teluban. Malay feelings are illustrated in the following poem, written in Teluban in Malay by the author A. M. Murba:

Today we shout to the world,
Telling them our bitter experience
In passing through the century.
Today we talk to you, friend,
About our cries until we are buried in the grave.
Listen, friend,
Our crescent moon has been covered by dark cloud.
Its light is dull as our heart is full of sorrow.
Our blood and flesh were punished without justice;
Judgment has been dead here.
Listen, friend,
Today we stand
Not to take revenge.
Today we search
Not [for the] enemy.
We are searching [for] justice and freedom.

(*Suara Siswa*, 1970:32; translated by the author)

This nationalistic feeling among the Malays in Teluban was also observed by Suthasasana, a Pattani Muslim sociologist. He writes:

... The Teluban residents are the most historically conscious people in the four southern provinces. Tengku Yala Nasae, the one who allegedly had connection with various separatist groups in the south, was an heir of the late Teluban Sultan. In addition, Teluban has been serving as headquarters for many terrorist movements. (1979:138)

Members of the old Malay ruling class retain the loyalty of their Muslim-Malay village constituency, despite loss of power and despite insults to their cultural pride, particularly during the Phibul Songkram regime. A continuing sense of loyalty to the old Malay ruling class may be illustrated by the landslide victory of the son of the late raja of Teluban over a locally-born Chinese incumbent in the 1980 election for the position of Mayor of Teluban Municipality. Certain Malays and Siamese commented prior to the election that:

Even though [he] is economically less powerful, and has limited formal education, he will definitely get many votes from the Muslim Malays who still remember his father and how [badly] he was treated by the Siamese.

In the 1980 elections, not only the mayor's position but the three seats for Teluban in the Provincial Council were won by Muslim-Malays.

Malays have been much less well-equipped by education than the Siamese to accept jobs in the expanding modernized bureaucracy. In 1980, of approximately 700 government officials in the district, only 291 were Muslims, about two-thirds of whom were primary school teachers; most of the rest were employed as public health personnel or police officials. Only a very few Muslims occupy positions as even low-level officials at the District Office, and some of these are not from Teluban, but from other, "non-Muslim" regions.

The Expansion of Modern Education into the Malay-speaking Province of Pattani

A modern (Western) education system was first adopted in Thailand in 1871, during the reign of King Rama V. Prior to this period, traditional education in Siam was conducted through Buddhist monasteries (see Wyatt, 1969). Initially the modernized system was implemented only in Bangkok. The idea of expanding the education system to outlying provinces was first proposed in 1890, but was not actually initiated in Pattani until 1898. The first provincial schools were established in monasteries with the assistance of the Monthon Commissioners.

Two schools opened in Pattani in 1898, both in monasteries; one was in Nong-chick, the other in the town of Pattani. Fifty-five pupils were registered, but there is no information as to how many of them were Muslim-Malays. Since schooling was not compulsory, few people sent their children to government schools. In 1906 the government realized that without strong measures, Muslim-Malays in the area would not send their children to schools. Consequently some changes were made in the administrative structure at the regional level aimed at rapid expansion of public education in the Malay-speaking areas, and in 1909 a third government school was opened in Pattani province.

TABLE 1: NUMBER OF PUBLIC SCHOOLS, TEACHERS AND PUPILS
IN PATTANI AREA IN 1909

| Location | Pupils | | | Teachers |
	Boys	Girls	Total	
Pattani (town)	156	—	156	2
Nong-chick	85	—	85	3
Yaring	78	—	78	1
TOTAL	319	—	319	6

Source: Department of Education, Second Report of 1909.

There is no information as to how many of the 319 pupils in school in
1909 were Muslim-Malays (see Table 1). Probably very few, if any, Malays
attended government schools, however, as is indicated by the report of a
meeting of the education division of Monthon Pattani on September 23,
1910:

The people in Monthon Pattani are overwhelmingly Malays; the
Thai and Chinese are few. The Malays get their "education" at
private homes and at the mosques. They learn mainly Islam.
The Thai and the Chinese get their education from the Buddhist
monasteries. At the beginning, the provincial educational office
tried to encourage the Muslim leaders (Imams) to teach reading
and writing Malay in the mosques with the hope that when instruction has taken place in the mosques, modern subjects and
Thai language may be introduced. Expectedly, instructions at
various mosques will gradually be grouped together and become
a school.[2]

Government attempts to expand modern education (and of course control the Malay-speaking communities) continued. The number of primary
schools increased from three to fourteen in 1910 and the number of pupils
from 319 to 643. Instruction of Malay children in the Thai language was
particularly emphasized, as indicated by the statement made by the Minister of Interior when he visited Pattani in 1911: "Education in this region

must aim at teaching all Malay children to speak Thai as the Mons* in Pak Kret or Pak Lad, Bangkok."[3]

One of the approaches employed by the education office in Monthon Pattani was to organize Thai language classes in the mosques where Quranic education was carried out. The qualified teachers were all (Buddhist) Thais and were paid by the government. The program moved very slowly, however. From 1910 to 1912 there were only three mosques where Thai was taught. By 1912 the number of government schools in the area had increased to twenty and the pupils to 1,528. Yet only a small percentage of all school-aged children attended school; the actual number of children in the district between the ages of eight and seventeen years was reported to be 59,034.

In 1913 another attempt was made to have Thai taught in the mosques and at the *pondok* schools. It was not successful because cooperation from the local Malays was not obtained. In 1916, the number of pupils in Pattani rose to 2,037, representing 3.5% of all school-aged children. Despite various efforts, the Commissioner of Pattani reported that compelling people to attend schools had been made many times, but it was like "putting crabs in a flat container." They showed their interest only at the time of active law enforcement, he reported, and then gradually failed to show up at school again. It was because the parents had no interest in the Thai language, and did not encourage their children to learn it, the Commissioner concluded. Consequently he proposed to the Ministry of Education that:

> If the government was to be successful in implementing educational policy and in providing opportunity for the officers to fully utilize their potential, the government must enunciate a Compulsory Education Act so that every school-aged child will attend primary school.[4]

The Primary Education Act was finally passed in 1920, and took effect in 1921 during the reign of King Rama VI. The teaching of Thai was still emphasized, but implementation was restricted to only a few schools because of a lack of qualified teachers. Once the Act took effect, there was a dramatic increase in the number of schools and of pupils attending them in Pattani. In 1922 there were 127 schools with 11,329 pupils, of whom 10,314 were in the first grade. After this first surge, however, the number of pupils

---

* While the Mons speak a language belonging to a language family very different from that of the Thai, the fact that they are Buddhists and share many cultural traditions with the Thai made assimilation much easier than it has been for the Malays [ed.].

began to drop off. In 1923, there were 9,692 pupils, in 1924 9,560 pupils, and by 1925 the number had fallen to 7,448. As can be seen from Table 2, only 21.8% of school-aged children attended schools in 1924, dropping to 18.6% in 1925.

TABLE 2: SCHOOL-AGED CHILDREN IN MONTHON PATTANI AT-
TENDING AND NOT ATTENDING SCHOOL IN 1924–1925

Ages	Total		Attending School		Not Attending School	
	1924	1925	1924	1925	1924	1925
7–8	5,691	5,961	138	159	5,553	5,802
8–9	4,848	5,451	295	271	4,553	5,180
9–10	4,389	5,167	522	367	3,867	4,800
10–11	5,621	5,475	1,470	1,221	4,151	4,254
11–12	5,888	5,609	1,894	1,501	3,994	4,108
12–13	6,038	5,665	1,991	1,779	4,047	3,886
13–14	5,735	6,522	2,030	2,150	3,705	4,372
TOTAL	38,210	39,850	8,340	7,448	29,870	32,402
			(21.8%)	(18.6%)	(78.0%)	(81.3%)

Sources: National Archives. Doc. MOE 44/52 and MOD 44/80 1924–1925. Reports on Education in Monthon Pattani.

Malay-speaking parents, in particular, deliberately avoided sending their children to government schools. The reports of the Commissioner of Monthon Pattani stated: "Since the parents have no interest in education, [we] have to constantly watch out and motivate them lest the children will eventually disappear from the schools. [But] to enforce the law strictly may cause trouble to many people. Therefore, the policy has to be somewhat relaxed."[5]

The attempt to expand modern education in Monthon Pattani thus continued, but with limited success. It is clear from Table 3 that the percentage of school-aged children who attended government schools was very low (15.5%) by 1925. This percentage remained virtually unchanged until 1932, when the absolute Thai monarch was replaced by a constitutional system, leading to changes within the country's education system.

TABLE 3: SCHOOL-AGED CHILDREN IN MONTHON PATTANI AT-
TENDING AND NOT ATTENDING SCHOOL IN 1928

Total		Attending School		Not Attending School	
Boys	Girls	Boys	Girls	Boys	Girls
23,137	19,266	5,826	711	17,311	18,555

Sources: MOE, Reports of Ministry of Education, Issue 21, 1928, p. 21.

Education in Pattani after 1932

Prior to the administrative changes in 1932, the central government consciously attempted to educate young Malay-speaking people in Monthon Pattani to speak Thai, but teaching in Malay was also permitted. This policy was changed in 1933; teaching in Malay was no longer allowed. The change created resentment among certain sectors of the Malay-speaking population. In 1947, the government acceded to the demand of the Malay-speaking people and again permitted Malay to be taught in primary schools. This policy was abolished in 1951, however, during the Phibul regime.

Whether or not Malay was taught in schools, efforts to force Malay-speaking people to send their children to government schools met with minimal success. The majority continued to send their children to *pondok* schools where Islamic principles and the Malay language were studied and where Malay was used as the medium of instruction. It was estimated that, in 1947, illiteracy in Thai was as high as 81.2% in Monthon Pattani, while the national average was 59.9%. In 1960 it was estimated that 67% of the total population of the Pattani area were illiterate in Thai, while the national average was only 29.2%.

Another move by the central government to extend control over educational activity in the Pattani area was made in 1961 (the beginning of the National Economic Development Plan), when an attempt was made to incorporate the *pondok* schools into the national educational system. The measures used were quite subtle when compared with those used to abolish Chinese schools at an earlier period. According to the new policy, any *pondok* school which followed the measures laid out by the Ministry of Education was eligible for government subsidies and "gifts" from His Majesty the King.

In 1965 the newly improved *pondok* schools were "encouraged" to adopt the Ministry of Education curriculum. A year later, it was announced that no new *pondok* schools were legally permitted, and the existing *pondok* schools which had not complied with the government regulations were no longer recognized. Some Muslim leaders suggested to the Ministry of Education that Malay and Islamic studies be included in the primary school curriculum as in 1951, but the suggestion was not accepted. The traditional *pondok* schools have now officially become "private schools teaching Islam."

The Pondok Schools and Responses to the Introduction of Secular Education

There was no lay educational system in Teluban prior to the division of Pattani in 1786 (Gullick 1958:140; Nopadol 1980:25; my own informants). However, two "educational" institutions held sociopolitical and probably economic importance. They were the system of religious instruction and the pilgrimage to Mecca.

Islamic learning was the only avenue for laymen to acquire prestige and higher social status. It was customary for all Malay boys at the time of puberty to be instructed in reading the Quran and the tenets of Islam. In most cases, they learned from the leading divine figure of their village. There were also famous religious teachers whose pupils came from outlying areas and lived at centers during the period of instruction. Under this system, boys were generally taught by rote to read the Quran in Arabic. Only a few progressed to real mastery of Arabic or profound learning of Islamic doctrines; hence the ability to read the Quran well was a source of social prestige.

The pilgrimage to Mecca was normally an expense beyond the resources of ordinary villagers, and, therefore, pilgrims were usually village headmen or members of a leading or wealthy family. A returned pilgrim was always entitled to great respect, and automatically became a Haji, no matter how little or how much he learned on the trip to Mecca. One who stayed in Mecca to improve his knowledge normally became, upon his return, a *to-kru* (*pondok* school teacher).

The status of a *to-kru* in local Malay society rested upon a complete set of beliefs and values. He was viewed as a religious figure who most clearly embodied the wisdom and power of Islam. The *to-kru* provided the link between the center of Islam in the Middle East, the wisdom of which was embodied in religious texts written in Arabic, and the ordinary villager who was barely literate in Jawi (the script used to write Malay), and totally illiterate in Arabic (see Geertz 1963; Nash 1974), and who otherwise had no access to the teaching of Islam. In other words, the *to-kru* was both teacher and cultural broker (Geertz 1963). Since his was the only form of teaching available to rural Malay youth, and since laymen became members of the elite only by rising through this system of education, the *to-kru* and his *pondok* attained significance beyond the immediate community.

The instruction given by the *to-kru* was his Malay interpretation of the Islamic tradition, derived from the *kitab*, or religious book. The *kitab* was usually the Quran, but any of the standard explications of Muslim law, religious duties, or theology were also regarded as being in the category of *kitab*.

It is unfortunately not possible to know how many *pondok* schools existed in Teluban during the eighteenth or nineteenth centuries, and no one could tell me when the first *pondok* school was opened. It is recorded that there were 497 "private schools" in Monthon Pattani by 1916, and in 1919 there were 595 "Islamic" schools (Nopadol 1980:98–99). It is, however, almost impossible to keep accurate records of this type of educational institution for, as Winzeler (1975) puts it, "*pondoks* develop about the guru and frequently do not long survive his death."

Conflict Between Educational Systems in Teluban

The first Siamese state primary school was opened in Teluban at Wat Sakkhi (the Buddhist temple) in 1901 with only eight pupils (Nopadol 1980:30). However, this school closed the following year. The report from the Buddhist abbot to the Ministry of Education said, in part:

> In Teluban, I have been able to have a school opened twice but it lasted less than a year because the people in this Muang (province) have no interest in education. In addition, some of them are too poor to support the school. Furthermore, the majority of the people are Malays. The provision of secular education is possible only to distribute the school text-books to the temples in the district. (Cited in Nopadol 1980:123)

The Compulsory Education Act of 1921 created fear and resentment among the Malay population. Though rigid enforcement of the law made it difficult for them not to send their children to secular schools, many Malays were, according to a retired education officer, even willing to pay fines rather than send them. Some reportedly tried to avoid paying fines by sending their children to school for one day a month (Nopadol 1980:114), although a few Malays, particularly those who worked for the government, did send their children to the secular schools regularly. There was, however, a great deal of pressure not to do so from members of their own community.

As one informant, who was later to be a teacher in a Muslim school, put it: "When we, the Muslim kids, walked to school, our neighbors looked at us with suspicion. Some of them even ridiculed us. We were almost isolated from our Malay peers."

In 1961 the government began to "urge" all the *pondok* schools to register as "educational institutions," and all the existing *pondok* schools were required by new regulations to be converted before 1971 into "private schools teaching Islam." This move was bitterly resented by many *to-krus*. As Geertz (1963:184) put it: "By striking at the *pondok* system such (secular) schools were striking at the very roots of *kijaji* [Javanese term for the *pondok* school teacher] power." Not only the *to-krus*, but also all members of the Malay elite felt gravely threatened, aware that their social status would be lowered as the indigenous system through which they had acquired their education was replaced by the modern educational system. Furthermore, religious education would become irrelevant to modern occupations. A Muslim headmaster of a primary school at Karubi village commented:

> These days, a returned pilgrim to Mecca (Haji) still enjoys social status, but not as high as it used to be and people now begin to question his religious wisdom because most of these Hajis know Islam [only] as much as at the time they left for Mecca. In addition, studying at the *pondok* schools is of great disadvantage because the chances of going on to higher education are very slim and more seriously, there are no jobs for the *pondok* school graduates. Most of the kids return to their villages and stay with their parents. Only those with sufficient funding sometimes go on to study in Pakistan, Indonesia or Egypt, where most of them study higher philosophy or Islamic studies. When they return home, they find it difficult to get a job. Many of them end up being a *to-kru* at the *pondok* schools.

Despite the fears of the Muslim-Malays, almost all *pondok* schools in Teluban were soon converted into "private schools teaching Islam." One *to-kru* of a small *pondok* stated it this way: "Well, we did not like it, but we had no choice, you either close it or convert it. After meeting with other *to-krus*, we decided to comply with the government's decree." Despite the government's attempt to control the *pondok* schools, *to-krus* were still able to exercise a certain amount of freedom in running their schools. A Muslim teacher of Sinhalese descent who was teaching at a big school said:

> In my school, only a minority of the students attend both secular and religious programs. Most of them attend only [the] religious

program. I heard that in other *pondok* schools some *to-krus* pay equal attention to secular courses, but at my school, the *to-kru* does not care and when he teaches the students he can say whatever he pleases.

A Siamese teaching secular subjects in another big *pondok* school put it:

I don't think the government can really control what is taught or what is going on in the *pondok* schools because they (*to-krus*) know when the inspector or the education supervisor will come to school. They know what they are expected to do. But when the inspector leaves they can do whatever they want to do in the classroom. Teachers like us are usually not sincerely welcomed, and we don't know what they teach the students, for we don't know their language.

Perhaps for these reasons, many *to-krus* can tolerate the government policy.

As of 1980, there were twenty-nine *pondok* schools (private schools teaching Islam) in Teluban, fifty secular schools, and one small primary school run by a Siamese-born Chinese. Despite strong resistance, the Muslim-Malays in Teluban have been receiving more secular education than previously. According to the Education Officer at the District Office, almost all Muslim-Malays of the younger generation (under age thirty) have had at least a primary education, and an increasing number have attained a secondary and tertiary education. The statistics at the secondary school show that only 93 Muslim students were enrolled in 1969, but there were 330 at the same school in 1979. According the principal, this figure would be much higher, except that the brighter Muslim students tended to go for study to the provincial towns of Pattani, Yala, and Narathiwat, and even to Bangkok.

An increasing number of Muslim-Malays are now in the teaching professions (teacher-training being the only kind of higher education most Malays can afford), and with the flight of non-Muslims from the district, Muslim-Malays have gradually taken over many primary school administrative positions. However, Malays still feel they are being discriminated against in competitions for teaching jobs. A 1978 leaflet distributed in Teluban says in part:

In the three southern provinces (Pattani, Narathiwat, and Yala), there are many unemployed Malay teachers and the number increases every year. Whenever there is an examination for the openings, either the (Buddhist) teachers from other provinces or the local (Buddhist) teacher usually get assigned to the posts. This is because the "rulers" (government officials) of these provinces have prejudice against the Malays. From now on, we, the Malay teachers, will try to solve this problem by ourselves. We have formed a group, called U.S.P., which has the policy to solve the problem primarily through violent means for we have realized that there are no other peaceful alternatives. (Written in Thai and signed by Abutaha Yi-ngo, with rubber stamp: ALI ZUBAR)

Linguistic Structure of Teluban, Ethnic Organization, and Ethnic Nationalism

By all accounts, a century ago almost all Muslim-Malay residents of Teluban neither spoke nor understood Siamese. By 1980, both Siamese and Malay informants estimated that 45–50% of the Muslim-Malays in Teluban could speak Siamese with some fluency. The figure might, they said, be higher if those who could only understand some Siamese were included. The increased percentage of bilingualism is undoubtedly the result of modernization processes such as educational expansion and the improvement of transportation and communication systems. It might be thought that bilingual Malays would be less supportive of the separatist movement, but the evidence points to the contrary. I suspect that an already high degree of ethnic nationalism among Muslim-Malays in Teluban has been intensified by linguistic competition with Siamese. As Lieberson (1970:11) points out: "By strengthening a tongue through the provision of good educational facilities and programs, a government also weakens another tongue, since, as we observed, the languages are in competition."

For the Malay, the word "Melayu" (Malay) stands for both language and nationality. Consequently, when the Malay language was suppressed, banned, or humiliated, Malays felt not only that their language had been "murdered" (Corkery, quoted in Thomas 1969:73), but also that they were losing their Malay nationality. Thus it is possible that even in a situation where the level of linguistic assimilation is quite high, as in Teluban, ethnic organization based on linguistic identity can emerge as a means to protect economic and political interests (Khleif 1979; Lieberson 1970).

For the Malay-speaking elite, the expansion of modern secular education was particularly threatening to the legitimacy of their traditional roles, as they found themselves no longer the sole possessors of knowledge and authority. Elites thus interpreted the expansion of modern education as an attempt by the Thai state to achieve political incorporation and cultural domination of Malay communities (Mazrui 1975). In their efforts to resist what they saw as unwarranted state penetration, they found that their most effective strategy was to make use of widely-shared Malay customs, for these are difficult and costly for the central state to suppress, and could become effective vehicles for political and socioeconomic action. Thus while the expansion of modern education was not the only variable that created conditions favorable to ethnic organization and ethnic nationalism, it has been a crucial factor.

Conclusions

It has been claimed that state-sponsored education is instrumental in creating a sense of unity or national identity among heterogeneous groupings in society (Coleman 1965; Black 1967; Inkeles and Smith 1974). But it is possible that schools—particularly those at the secondary and tertiary level, since these inculcate in successful students certain "modern" values (such as desire for financial achievement and a better life-style)—actually sharpen rather than diminish ethnic friction. When different ethnic groups come to share the same dominant values and compete for the same ends in a situation of relative scarcity of economic goods or limited routes for social mobility, the more competition between them intensifies, the more ethnicity becomes a factor in the battle (Nash 1974:256). Thus in Teluban, where Malays and Siamese compete for bureaucratic position, the very education that unites them as members of the Thai nation helps produce a high degree of identity and tension.

It is clear, thus, that education can produce unintended outcomes under certain conditions. The expansion of a modern education system into the Malay-speaking communities in southern Thailand shows that, while in La-ngu, where the local Malays speak Thai rather than Malay and where no alternative school system to the one instituted by the central government ever existed, introduction of modern secular education was not perceived as a threat. In Teluban, by contrast, institution of the same education system has had quite limited success in creating loyalty to the nation.

While the Thai state education system provides legitimacy for certain individuals who possess credentials for becoming full members of the nation and occupying certain roles and occupations in society, it inevitably threatens and destroys the legitimacy of competing educational systems—in this case, the traditional Islamic system. The expansion of modern education has also had negative socioeconomic and political implications for the Malay-speaking elite. It is for these reasons that resistance by Malay-speaking people has emerged in southern Thailand, and that the forms of that resistance have developed to a point where ethnicity is used as the basis for political mobilization.

Notes

[1] The Sam-sam were the same as Siamese in everything except religion. Although nominally Muslims, they rarely attended mosque services or observed the hours of prayer. Skeat (1953:133–34) noted that the Sam-sam "were rarely able to write but when they did, [they] generally used the Arabic characters even for Siamese words."

[2] National Archives, Document, Rama V, File Ministry of Education, 42/8, 1910.

[3] National Archives, Document, Rama VI, File Ministry of Education, Department of Education Report No. 4, 1911, pp. 88.

[4] National Archives, Document, Rama VI, Ministry of Education, 44/28, 1917.

[5] National Archives, Document, Ministry of Education, 44/52, 1925.

References

Annandale, Nelson. *Fascicule Malayenses: Anthropological and Zoological Results of an Expedition to Perak and the Siamese Malay States, 1901–2.* New York: Longmans, 1903.

Abutaha Yi-ngo. [Untitled leaflet]. Teluban: Ali Zubar, 1978.

Black, C. E. *The Dynamics of Modernization: A Study in Comparative History.* New York: Harper and Row, 1967.

Coleman, James. *Education and Political Development.* Princeton: Princeton University Press, 1965.

Geertz, Clifford. "The Integrative Revolution: Primordial Sentiments and Civil Politics in the New States." In *Old Societies and New States: The Quest for Modernity in Asia and Africa,* ed. by C. Geertz. New York: Free Press, 1963.

Gullick, J. *Indigenous Political Systems of Western Malaya.* The Anthione Press, 1958.

Inkeles, Alex and D. H. Smith. *Becoming Modern.* Cambridge: Cambridge University Press, 1974.

Khlief, B. "Language as Identity: Toward an Ethnography of Welsh Nationalism." *Ethnicity* 6(1979):346–57.

Lieberson, Stan. *Language and Ethnic Relations in Canada.* New York: Wiley and Sons, 1970.

Lungputeh, Abdulla. *Short History of Satun Province.* Bangkok: Thai Karnpim, 1958 (in Thai).

Mazrui, Ali. "The African University as a Multinational Corporation: Problems of Penetration and Dependency." *Harvard Educational Review* 45(1975):191–210.

Murba, A. M. "Laungan" [Shouting]. *Suara Siswa* (Kuala Lumpur, Malaysia), 1970.

Nash, Manning. "Ethnicity, Centrality and Education in Pasir Mas." In *Kalantan: Religion, Society and Politics in the Malay State,* ed by W. R. Roff. Oxford: Oxford University Press, 1974.

Newbold, T. J. *Political and Statistical Accounts of the British Settlements in the Straits of Malacca.* Vol. 2. London: Oxford University Press, 1971.

Nopadol, Rojanaudomsart. "Problems of Education in Monthon Pattani 1902–1931." Bangkok: Srinakarinwirote. M.A. thesis, 1980 (in Thai).

Seni Madagakul, et al. *The Attitude of the People toward Crimes and Insurgency in Pattani, Yala and Narathiwas.* Pattani: Prince of Songkhla University, 1977 (in Thai).

Skeat, W. W. "The Cambridge University Expedition to the North-Eastern Malay States and Upper Perak 1899–1900." *Journal of Malaysian Branch of the Royal Asiatic Society,* 26(1953), pt. 4, no. 164 (special issue).

Suthasasana, A. "Muslims and Thai Society." Mimeographed. Bangkok: Chulalongkorn University, 1979 (in Thai).

Sutton, Joseph I., ed. *Problems of Politics and Administration in Thailand.* Bloomington, Indiana: Indiana University, Institute of Training for Public Service, Department of Government, 1962.

Thomas, M. Ladd. *Socio-Economic Approach to Political Integration of the Thai-Islam: An Appraisal.* De Kalb, Illinois: Northern Illinois University Center for Southeast Asian Studies, 1969.

Wheatley, Paul. *The Golden Khersonese: Studies in the Historical Geography of the Malay Peninsula before A.D. 1500.* Kuala Lumpur: University of Malaya Press, 1961.

Winzeler, R. "Traditional Islamic Schools in Kelantan." *Journal of Malaysian Branch of the Royal Asiatic Society,* 48.1(1975):91–103.

Wyatt, David. *The Politics of Reform in Thailand: Education in the Reign of King Chulalongkorn.* New Haven: Yale University Press, 1969.

SOCIAL AND IDEOLOGICAL REPRODUCTION IN A RURAL NORTHERN THAI SCHOOL

Chayan Vaddhanaphuti

Introduction

The encroachment of the Thai state into local schools since the beginning of the twentieth century has resulted in an enormous expansion of modern education as well as a bureaucratization of the school system. Primary, education has become compulsory for every child. In almost every village in rural Thailand, primary schools have gradually replaced Buddhist temples which had been the centers of traditional education. Through these primary schools, the Thai state has sought to fulfill certain functions necessary to its aims of national integration and development. It is generally believed that these primary schools teach modern skills, attitudes, and knowledge to village children so that they will become not only more productive economically, but also "good" members of the national community.

Undoubtedly, there is some truth in this view. Rural primary schools do teach children literacy and prepare them to be law-abiding citizens. Rural children learn some basic arithmetic skills, to speak central Thai—the official language—and to fulfill certain civic duties. It seems, however, that rural schools cannot do their job effectively. It may even be that primary schools are inherently ineffective because, in fact, they are supposed to be ineffective. They are schools for children of rural producers who have always been deprived of social and political privileges. If this is the case, it may also be that primary schools provide something other than necessary skills and proper attitudes. As part of the state machinery, schools have always been more concerned with the state's legitimacy and with asserting ideological control than with providing skills and knowledge to the rural population. Thus, they are obviously not the neutral places they appear to be. Schools confer different "cultural capital" with which to make one's way in life upon children of different class backgrounds. Schools sort children out, and maintain their social and economic differences. In these schools, children are imbued with the ideology prescribed by the state and its authorities.

In this chapter I examine the role of a village school in rural northern Thailand, drawing on material obtained during anthropological fieldwork. I discuss how a rural school prepares village children to be agents of production as well as members of their national community. I describe problems inherent in the school that hinder its effectiveness, and argue that, by and large, these problems stem from the centralization and bureaucratization of rural education. I also examine teaching and learning processes that occur within the classroom as well as beyond the classroom context. I attempt to show what school children actually learn from their school, what messages are transmitted, and through what mechanisms. Based on analysis of my empirical data, I argue that the village school serves as the state agent of social and ideological reproduction, preparing village children to accept existing social contradictions and inequalities.

Following King Chulalongkorn's and Prince Damrong's radical administrative reforms at the beginning of the twentieth century, northern Thailand was gradually integrated into the Thai nation-state. One of the attempts by King Chulalongkorn and Prince Damrong to integrate and centralize the outlying territories was "the creation of a network of officials charged with responsibility for territorial administration" (Riggs 1966:139). This new system, called *thesaphiban*, involved the "creation of a regional organization in which half a dozen provinces were combined in a *monthon* under the control of a commissioner" (Riggs 1966:139). Within the regions, each province, under the control of a governor, was divided into districts (*amphoe*). Each district was under the control of a district officer (*nai amphoe*) sent out by the Ministry of Interior. "By this means, the old network of relatively autonomous provincial governors was brought within a control system superimposed from above at the *monthon* level and undermined from below at the *amphoe* level" (Riggs 1966:140).

The penetration of the state into local communities seems to have been slow and gradual in the first half of the twentieth century, but it accelerated after the state launched the First National Economic and Social Development Plan in 1960, a plan aimed at facilitating capitalist development. Increasingly, various state services such as communication systems, irrigation facilities, public health, education, agricultural extension, and services relating to law and order have been extended to local communities. More and more, the state can exert its control over these areas.

Extension of state control, together with the penetration of the capitalist mode of production, have slowly undermined traditional village authority, beliefs, and practices such as relationships between patrons and clients, ancestral spirit cults, and cooperative labor exchange. In particular, village children now receive a modern primary education, whereas their fathers had to depend on traditional education provided through the village temple. Primary education facilitates increased contact between villagers and functionally-specialized state officials—contact requiring command of central Thai. The expansion of capitalism into the countryside generates differential social relations based on the means of production and induces rural proletarianization, while maintaining and utilizing certain elements of *sakdina* (feudal) ideology for its benefit.* The capitalist mode of production has not totally destroyed the pre-existing *sakdina* mode of production, however, nor has the state been able to completely incorporate local systems. Several local communities still maintain relative autonomy from the state.

Ban Chang and Its Primary School

Ban Chang is situated in Mae Taeng District, about 45 kilometers north of the city of Chiangmai. It is located in a small river valley lying between the main lowland floor of the Chiangmai-Lamphun Valley and the peripheral surrounding areas. The village is connected to other villages and market centers in the valley by means of a narrow dirt road, travelled mainly by minibuses and motorcycles.

Ban Chang is an example of a village which has not been deeply penetrated by the state. Several indicators show that it continues to enjoy relative autonomy. For example, villagers still manage their own irrigation system. Many of them, moreover, have occupied, bought, and sold forest reserve land with no interference from the authorities. Ownership of this type of land is largely communally recognized. Illegal teak-logging operations are carried out by a local network without interception by law enforcement officers. The village has become a place where a convict or an ex-*nakleng* (rogue) can hide himself from the law or from a potential avenger. Murder is often settled by the "law of the forest," that is, by another murder. Most of these cases remain unsolved by the police. In the ideological sphere, traditional beliefs in spirit-healing still persist. Sanctions by ancestral spirits are still, to a large degree, an effective cultural means for maintaining the senior-junior relationship, suppressing intra-familial quarrels, and, in general, regulating the social behavior of the villagers.

Even though the state is represented in the village through primary education, agricultural extension, and public health services facilities, the latter are rather ineffective and quite limited in scope. The state officials who reside in the village actively pursue their own interests rather than

---

* The term *sakdina*, literally meaning 'sacred power [associated with] rice fields,' refers to a premodern system of hierarchically-ranked statuses. Every subject acquired a *sakdina* status by virtue of his relationship to the monarch. Most Thai social scientists today use the term *sakdina* as a gloss for what, in English, is called feudalism [ed.].

representing the state. From the villagers' point of view, the state is ineffective in monitoring the behavior of its own officials. Nor does it provide
protection for villagers against these same officials, who hold the law in their
hands, or from local capitalists, who can bend the law by bribing state officials. Ban Chang is not a completely autonomous local community like
certain other villages in the far periphery of northern Thailand. Obviously,
it has been penetrated by, and incorporated into the state, but there are
several spheres over which the central state cannot exert its control.

Because of Ban Chang's physiographical setting in the near periphery
of the Chiangmai-Lamphun Valley, not much paddy land is available to
the villagers for cultivation. Land is fragmented, and there are only three
landowners with more than twenty-three *rai* (9.1 acres) of irrigated land.
The tenancy rate in Ban Chang is not high, however, when compared with
that in lowland areas. In Ban Chang 29.7 percent of all families rent land,
with half of these tenants renting from parents, whereas in several lowland
villages in the Chiangmai-Lamphun Valley floor the tenancy rate averages
50 percent. More importantly, most Ban Chang villagers (80.4 percent) own
land of some sort, even though much of it is not very productive. Thus, land
tenancy and the land rent system are not problems for a majority of the
people. The tenant who pays 50 percent of his crop as land rent is unlikely
to feel exploited because he is renting from a landlord who is either his
own parent or kinsman or his former teacher and spiritual counselor. Such
kinship and personal ties, reinforced by such values as gratitude, diffuse
the discontent of these tenants and neutralize any potential antagonism.
Nonetheless, it should be noted that Ban Chang villagers do face a potential
problem of severe land shortage, because agricultural land around the
village is under forest reserve and cannot be expanded further.

Second, although the capitalist mode of production began to pene-
trate Ban Chang about fifty years ago, the process was gradual, due in
part to the scarcity of cultivable land and in part to the inadequacy of
modern transportation facilities. The only road connecting the village to
the outside world was not completed until 1971, and is still not paved. In
the mid–1970s, peasants in other villages on the Chiangmai-Lamphun valley floor were actively producing cash crops because they were near market
centers and had access to modern transportation. Ban Chang peasants had
been producing tobacco, and after 1971 gradually began to add other crops
for market exchange. During that time most Ban Chang villagers were
heavily involved in illegal teak production and trade. Thus they experienced capitalism differently from peasants elsewhere. Contradictions in the
production process emanating from increasing capitalist production into a

premodern system in Ban Chang began to be intensified in the late 1970s, by which time the capitalist mode of production had come to dominate the village's economy.

Primary education reached the area around Ban Chang in the early 1930s as part of the state's efforts to incorporate outlying provinces. At the beginning, a small school with one teacher was organized in a village adjacent to Ban Chang. In 1939 it was moved to its present location within the village of Ban Chang. In the late 1960s, the Ban Chang school was expanded to accommodate an increased number of students. A couple of teachers were hired to help the school principal. During the late 1970s, the school had an enrollment of approximately 150 and produced between 35 and 40 fourth grade graduates each year. During this period, there were five or six teachers in the local school, most of them freshly graduated from the Chiangmai Teacher Training College with little teaching experience. In 1980, the Ban Chang school opened its upper primary level (grades 5 and 6), and two more teachers were assigned to teach at the school.

Like other rural primary schools in Thailand, the Ban Chang School aimed to teach children the central Thai dialect, various basic skills, certain rules of behavior, and the duties of citizens, or, in other words, certain knowledge and skills deemed necessary for national development. It is true that the school provided some formal education to its children, so they would not grow up illiterate. However, the Ban Chang school was unable to realize its objectives efficiently. Most students left school with little proficiency in central Thai; they carried with them some basic arithmetic skills and some vague ideas about their obligations to their country. However, most of the education the school provided seemed to bear little relation to the real needs and problems of the community.

The failure of the Ban Chang school to fulfill its commitment occurred for several reasons. First, the expansion of the Thai bureaucracy along with the drive for national economic and social development in the previous two decades resulted in an enormous increase in the budget for primary education as well as in the number of people employed in education. These were considered resources which the Ministry of the Interior wanted to control. The Ministry of Interior argued that it was directly in charge of virtually all other affairs in rural areas, and efficiency could be increased if primary education was decentralized and placed under its supervision. The Ministry of Education was unable to prevent the administration of primary education from falling under the control of the Ministry of the Interior. It did, however, manage to retain control over academic content and standards. This arrangement proved to be inefficient and a grave mistake. Primary education became more, rather than less, centralized. Controlled as it was by Ministry of Interior officials who had no professional background in education, the budget for primary education was apparently misallocated, so that textbooks and other materials received at local primary schools were quite obviously of low quality. This was especially evident in the Ban Chang school.

Second, not all primary schools in Thailand suffered from limited budgetary allocation. Several large primary schools in the well-developed lowland areas were able to obtain extra financial support from their communities. Unfortunately, the Ban Chang school could draw little support from its villagers. Therefore, any improvement in the school had to depend largely on budgetary allotment from the state. During the years from 1978 to 1980, there were not enough classrooms or teachers for the children enrolled in the Ban Chang school. Three classes were held in a small temporary pavilion beneath the school teacher's house on the school grounds. There were not enough teaching materials and textbooks for the children; most of the existing teaching materials were paid for from the teachers' own salaries or donated by university students. I was told that each teacher spent about 100–150 *baht* a year from his or her salary to buy teaching materials. These purchases were made without reimbursement.

Third, there was a marked lack of teaching supervision at the Ban Chang school. This was partly because the school principal had to spend more time at the District Office than at the school. Besides attending monthly meetings, picking up salaries on behalf of his teachers, and following up on the school's requests, the principal had to carry out tasks at the District Office which were not at all related to the management of his school. For instance, he was assigned to help the District Office carry out village scout training in other villages and to organize the annual District Winter Fair.

Besides the frequent absence of the principal, there was almost no academic or administrative supervision from the district or provincial supervisors. A school teacher told me that during her five years of service in Ban Chang, she recalled only one time that the academic staff of the District Educational Office had come to visit the school. Even then, they spent only fifteen minutes talking about teaching methods which were supposedly new, but with which the teachers were already familiar. This teacher also recalled that the District Education Officer visited the school only once during that period.

Fourth, in analyzing this rural school's inefficiency, it is necessary to examine the teachers' class backgrounds, training, and expectations. Rural school teachers alone are not to blame for their apathetic behavior and attitudes, because they have been the victims of social circumstances. In the first place, rural school teachers were, themselves, the products of the educational inequality generated by state policies. Since the introduction of modern education at the turn of the century, the state has adopted a policy which provided more educational opportunities for children of the ruling classes and in urban areas, while depriving rural children of the same opportunities. The latter were mainly children of peasants, small merchants, and junior government officials, who could hardly afford the expenses of furthering their children's education beyond the primary level. As a result, these children had less access to advanced schooling, and, therefore, had limited employment opportunities. Most became farmers like their parents.

The expansion of rural education in the last two decades has led to an increased demand for teachers in rural schools and an expansion of teacher education. This has provided a new opportunity for many rural children to attain higher education, as well as to find non-farming jobs. Teacher education, thus, is considered an avenue of upward mobility for many rural children. Once those children became teachers in rural schools, many found, however, that their occupation was neither economically rewarding nor socially prestigious. More and more rural teachers became dissatisfied with their work, but because of their class background and the limited educational opportunities available to them, they had no other career alternatives.

Besides this unequal educational opportunity structure, another factor has added to the problem of teaching in rural areas. In producing rural teachers *en masse*, teacher-training colleges failed to prepare their graduates adequately for service in rural schools. Graduates preferred assignments in urban settings where they could obtain a higher degree that would enable them to choose a better job with better pay. Thus, rural schools in Thailand were generally staffed with teachers who were ill-prepared for the tasks at hand, and who had little motivation for teaching in rural settings. In the Ban Chang school, for example, most, if not all, teachers wanted to be transferred from Ban Chang as soon as they could. Although a few of them agreed to stay on, their motive was to accumulate more teak to build themselves temporary houses which they could sell later for a price two or three times higher than the cost. In some cases, they had to remain with the Ban Chang school because there were no vacant positions in urban schools.

Given the lack of support and attention from the state and the lack of enthusiasm for teaching in a rural school, the Ban Chang teachers were alienated from their work and the community they served. Half of them did not live in the village but commuted to school every day. Quite often, they arrived for school late and left school earlier than they should have. Those who stayed in the village often engaged in various personal businesses, and had a life style different and apart from most of the villagers. Ban Chang teachers were not involved with the community, either in regular activities such as rice planting and harvesting, or in special efforts such as community development work. Their attitude was that their responsibility was only to teach school children, and their expectation was that they would be in this village only temporarily.

All of these problems contributed to the school's failure to fulfill its primary objectives. The school also conveyed a false promise to students and parents that the more education one had, the better occupation and income one could obtain. After students finished their lower primary, which was compulsory, they were encouraged to go to upper primary school, if they could afford it. For most Ban Chang children, however, to continue education beyond the village school was almost impossible. First, there was no upper primary education available in the village until 1980. Second, most parents who might want to send their children on to the upper primary and secondary school could not afford to do so. Those who could afford these expenses found that such an education was insufficient to enable their children to attain better occupations, and that professional training from a vocational school would also be necessary. This meant that parents would have to support their children in school for seven years beyond lower primary education. It was obviously very unrealistic and almost impossible for most Ban Chang parents to support their children to that level.

The experience of Ban Chang children provided a concrete example of how limited educational opportunities resulted in the reproduction of class structure. During the entire period of almost fifty years of public education in Ban Chang, there were only nine children from the village who had attained an educational level as high as, or higher than, upper primary school. During the period I was in the village, one had finished upper primary school and returned to the village; two others were still studying at an upper primary school at the district seat. One was studying at a private secondary school in Chiangmai City and another was pursuing a bachelor's degree. Four had completed vocational programs. All except one of these children came from rich families. Six of them were the children of landlords. One was the daughter of a small peasant who also owned a grocery store. Another was the daughter of a carpenter, whose parents, while not rich, tried very hard to support her, because she was a very bright student.

Before 1980, the Ban Chang school did not offer upper primary education to local children. Parents who wanted to send their children to attain higher education had to spend a large sum of money for both school expenses and boarding fees. The former headmaster of the Ban Chang school, who sent four of his children to upper primary and secondary schools in the city of Chiangmai, bought a house in the city where his children could stay during their schooling. After finishing his secondary education, one of his sons attended the Police Academy in Lampang. Admission to the Academy was highly competitive, for many young men wanted to be policemen, an occupation that afterward could bring them enormous power and resources. To enroll, one needed either a patron or a sizable sum of money to buy entry; the former headmaster admitted he had used the latter to enroll his son. The village headman, who sent his son to a private school in Mae Rim, a district capital near Chiangmai, had to pay for the son's room and board. Those parents who were less economically well-off could afford only to send their children to the upper primary school at the district seat. Their children had to commute to school by minibus every day. This often was unsatisfactory because the minibus which ran between Ban Chang and the district seat was not dependable.

The attainment of additional education was not always as rewarding as expected. For example, the former headmaster's second daughter, after finishing her secondary education, went to the Chiangmai Teacher Training College and later found a teaching job in Mae Jaem, one of the poorest districts in Chiangmai province, located almost 200 kilometers from Ban Chang. This was quite a disappointment for her parents. In spite of the fact that there was a vacant position at Ban Chang school, as well as at several other schools in the local district, she could not be transferred to teach in one of them. Another Ban Chang girl, daughter of a large landlord, also attended the Chiangmai Teacher Training College. She could not find a job after graduation, and so returned to the village for a while. Later she married someone from outside the village and moved away to live with her husband's family.

The Ban Chang school, like most rural schools in Thailand, failed to prepare children to become competent agricultural producers in their local community. Instead, it oriented them toward higher education which most of them could not afford to pursue. On the one hand, the school became an avenue for social mobility for those who could afford to invest more in education. On the other, for those who could not afford such education, the school became a symbol of futility. On the whole, the school became a social mechanism which sorted Ban Chang children into at least three different groups according to their parents' class and status background, namely, the children of large landowners, rich *phǫliang taobaum* (tobacco curing-plant owner), or of the ex-headmaster; second, children of small peasants; and third, children of landless peasants and wage laborers.

The extremely limited number of children in the first group were able to go on to upper primary and secondary schools, and then beyond that stage to vocational schools in the city of Chiangmai. Those in the second group could afford to attend only the lower and upper primary schools in the village. After they finished their schooling, they remained in Ban Chang to help their parents in the fields, and later became farmers like their parents. Children of the third group, even though they were encouraged by the school to finish upper primary school, decided not to do so. This was because their parents needed them to help work in the fields, or to take care of their younger siblings while both parents worked as wage laborers in order to double the family income. In this sense, the Ban Chang school helped perpetuate and reproduce class and status differences.

The Village School and Ideological and Cultural Reproduction

I have already discussed the role of the Ban Chang village school in social reproduction, that is to say in reproducing class relations. The rural school in Ban Chang is a part of the state's effort to modernize and integrate the rural population. It presents itself as a neutral, meritocratic institution rewarding those students who work diligently. It fosters the idea among villagers that the more education one obtains, the more opportunity one has to break away from the back-breaking occupation of farming.

I have argued that, in reality, the Ban Chang school has never been able to deliver on this promise, for the school itself is understaffed, poorly maintained, and inadequately supervised. More than that, such a promise is unrealistic, for most local parents cannot afford to send their children for higher education beyond the village school, and even in those cases where they can, occupational opportunities for young graduates, especially those without well-connected patrons, are rather limited. At best, the Ban Chang school helps children of rich peasants become rural schoolteachers or junior government officials if they want to leave farming. At the same time, most students become rural cultivators and remain in the community. For these, most of what they have learned from the school is not relevant to their occupation or useful in improving agricultural productivity. After four years of schooling, they do learn to speak central Thai adequately (although with a northern Thai accent). Most of these graduates, however, cannot read or write central Thai well. None can read or write northern Thai, as it is no longer taught in either school or temple.

In the following section, I examine the role of Ban Chang school in ideological and cultural reproduction (Giroux 1983:258, MacDonald 1977:8–9, Willis 1981). These functions are as important as, and can be analytically separated from social reproduction. In other words, what I attempt in this section is an investigation of the role of the Ban Chang school in socializing village children into the political and moral order of the larger society to which they belong. My analysis of the process within the village school is limited for two reasons. First, there is a methodological problem in my investigation of the villagers' school experience. Most adult members of Ban Chang whom I interviewed could not recall the nature of their interaction with their teachers during their school years. This means that we know almost nothing about what happened in the Ban Chang school of the past. Thus, I have had to rely upon my observations of the present situation. From these data, obviously, I cannot describe the effects of school experience on the formation of the ideology of today's adult villagers in Ban Chang. What I could observe, however, was the ideological and cultural milieu of Ban Chang's children.

Second, in comparison with other means of ideological and cultural reproduction at the village level, the Ban Chang primary school involves its students for only a short period of time. Because of limited educational opportunities, village children spend only a small portion of their lives attending school. Villagers are required to spend only four years in school as children, while they attend merit-making ceremonies and listen to radio programs throughout their lives. Thus, they have greater exposure to ideological and cultural messages conveyed through the family, the village temple, and the public media. This is not to suggest, however, that the school plays no role in ideological and cultural reproduction. On the contrary, it plays an important part, particularly during the formative years. Its impact on village children cannot be ignored, although it should not be overemphasized.

To understand how the school performs its task of cultural and ideological reproduction, it is necessary to identify two important features: the sociopolitical context in which the school is located, and the kind of ideology and knowledge the school tries to produce and reproduce. The Ban Chang school, like other rural schools in Thailand, was originally designed to incorporate the rural population into the emerging nation-state. Unlike urban schools, which have long since been turning out agents of production for the expanding capitalist-oriented economy and bureaucracy, the Ban Chang school aims simply to produce rural cultivators who will be law-abiding citizens. This is done largely through teaching the central Thai dialect and civic responsibility which emphasizes, for example, the ideology of submissiveness to authority.

Although the capitalist mode of production penetrated the peripheral area, where Ban Chang is located, some time ago, the demand for different types of skilled labor for commercialized agriculture is relatively low. Agricultural production in the area is still largely carried out by simple technology. At the same time, the Ban Chang school provides its students with no agriculturally-related education that could be used to improve productivity. While tobacco production, the major cash crop in the area, requires some technical skills and knowledge to maintain the quality of the product, such skills and knowledge are provided directly by the Thai Tobacco Monopoly. It is only since the formation of the National Education Plan of 1977 that the government has begun to make education a tool of national development as well as of national integration. This new purpose is reflected in the expansion of primary education. Yet, even with the addition of the upper primary level to the Ban Chang school in 1981, education has little relation to the demand for skilled labor in the area.

Aside from the still limited effort to make education relevant to the capitalist economy, the following are considered the goals of education: to create understanding and enthusiasm among the citizens so that they will participate in the country's democratic political system headed by the king; to develop an unswerving loyalty to, and faith in, the nation, the Buddhist religion, and the king; and finally to raise the level of Thai consciousness regarding nationalism, national security needs, and civic responsibility for national defense (Ministry of Education 1977). These goals represent an ideological response to conflicts and tensions in the larger society. The school is used by the state to establish an ideology which will maintain the existing sociopolitical order. This ideological effort is linked with some use of repressive measures, such as the escalation of military operations, particularly against communist insurgency. The ideology itself has its roots in the nationalistic ideas of King Vachiravudh (1910–1924), who found the traditional ideology which was based on the Buddhist doctrine of *karma*, inadequate to justify the sociopolitical order (Chattip and Montri 1981:229–30). It was only later, however, that the school came to be used to produce and reproduce this nationalist ideology.

The ideological premises of the state are clearly reflected in texts and messages taught in the schools. A text used in the third grade, for example, contains passages that emphasize loyalty to the monarchy and belief in Buddhism and nationalism:

> Our country has a democratic government with the king as our national leader. (Ministry of Education 1979:76)

> Our country, Thailand, is so well endowed
> > There is fish in the water,
> > There is rice in the fields.
> > We work on our own land;
> > We build our houses and live together.
> > We live well and happily;
> > We have built our country to its greatness.
> > Thailand, our country, is so wonderful.
> > We love Thailand much more than our lives.
> > > (Ministry of Education 1979:72)

> When the king's automobile passed by, Udorn and his friends jointly paid respect to the king as they had been taught by their teacher. All people who were waiting to see the king also did similarly. Some elderly men and women even joined their palms over their heads; all did this with a deep affection and appreciation and without any prior agreement. (Ministry of Education 1979:96)

These messages express explicitly the dominant, or "theoretical ideology" (Sharp 1980:96), an ideology which is also reproduced by other means as well, such as through the state-controlled media, the village scouts, and so on. Linking the three institutions of nation, Buddhism, and monarchy with the stability and continuity of the existing order implies that the existing order is to be maintained and preserved whatever inequities it perpetuates. In turn, the government views any attempt to change the existing sociopolitical order as a serious threat to the three basic institutions that form the underlying pillars of the society. As a consequence, the national ideology has become a means by which the privileged classes maintain the status quo and keep other classes from challenging the existing order. In imparting this national ideology to the masses, the school becomes a means for perpetuating the existing class structure. It produces docile, submissive and loyal citizens who accept the legitimacy of the social order. I do not claim that the school alone is responsible for this task. Nor do I claim that it can perform this role completely and effectively. Nonetheless, after passing through the school system, villagers are generally convinced that these institutions are highly important and should be championed in order to achieve national security and development.

Having identified the "theoretical ideology" produced and reproduced through education, let us examine the "practical ideology," i.e., the actual ideology that is transmitted in the Ban Chang school. The practical ideology being produced and reproduced in the Ban Chang school fits Sharp's formulation well:

> Within the classroom, pupils are engaged in processes which legitimate and in the last analysis reinforce the concept of the teacher as *the* pivotal authority, having power ... over the allocation of rewards and punishments through the grading and classification system ... pupils ... are encouraged for their diligence, social conformity and deference to the teacher's authority. (Sharp 1980:124)

Before we reach such a conclusion, however, it is necessary to examine some sociocultural specifics of the Ban Chang school. Like the village temple, the Ban Chang school is a domain separate from the rest of the village. It is an official place symbolized by the display of the national tricolor flag on a pole in front of the main school building—a symbol which can be found in all official places. The school is under the control of the state, and run by a group of teachers who are state employees and not villagers. Their responsibility is to transmit certain knowledge considered necessary for village children to become decent law-abiding citizens.

In an attempt to learn about the school experiences of villagers three to four decades ago, I interviewed a sample of older Ban Chang villagers. Most reported that they studied with Achan (teacher) Mi, the only teacher in the Ban Chang village school between the 1940s and the 1960s. Some recalled that Achan Mi did not inspire fear in his students. When I interviewed Achan Mi himself, however, he reported that he often used corporal punishment in order to keep his classroom in order, and that, partly for this reason, his students were generally quite obedient. During his time, he told me, a rural teacher was quite an authoritarian figure for both villagers and their children. Because of his previous experience in the monkhood, his secular knowledge, and his prestigious position, he was highly respected by the local parents and much feared by his students. He was then the only government official residing in the village. He was quite involved with the affairs of the village; one time he was even chosen by the villagers to be their headman, which he accepted for a few days and then decided to resign. Achan Mi married the daughter of a prominent *phǫliang* (economic patron) in Ban Chang and thus, became a member of the kinship network of the village. To his students, he was not only a schoolteacher, but also a relative and full member of their village community. While they were somewhat in awe of him, they also respected and loved him as their close relative. This relationship is drastically different from the one between the present Ban Chang schoolteachers and their students.

The present Ban Chang school is quite different from the one a few decades ago. It has expanded in physical structure as well as in the number of its teachers, owing to the increased demand generated by the gradual demographic growth in the area. In the late 1970s, the teaching staff consisted of five teachers and a headmaster who also helped to teach whenever he could. The number of the teaching staff increased to seven in 1981, when an upper primary class (Grade 6) was added. As mentioned earlier, the Ban Chang schoolteachers tend to remain aloof from the villagers. Unlike most villagers, they are educated and have a different life style. For example, they do not participate in agricultural production. Moreover, they draw their income from their monthly salaries, and are economically better off than most villagers. They wear official uniforms or urban style clothes rather than simple village clothing, and this, plus their ability to speak the central Thai dialect fluently sets them off from local people. The fact that most teachers do not reside in the village serves to reduce further their contact with villagers.

The school is a very different environment for children from their family home. This is not only because the school is an official place run by teachers, but it also emphasizes a new type of unequal and official relationship between children and adults. The adults, that is the teachers, possess legitimate knowledge which the children as students must learn. This adult-child relationship is not mediated by kinship ties. Nor is it a relationship based upon the concept of the traditional teacher who is supposed to transmit knowledge without expecting monetary return. This new relationship stresses the role of the teacher as the representative of state authority. In the school, then, students gradually learn how to interact with the teachers; they learn norms and definitions of social interaction. It is the social knowledge, or "habitus" (MacDonald 1977:35), internalized from day-to-day interaction with these teachers, that becomes a basis, a set of "constitutive rules" (Apple 1979:86), for interacting with other authorities in the larger society.

When village children are eight years old, their parents are required by Thai law to enroll them in the village school where they entrust them to the teachers. Once these children are in school, they gradually change their day-to-day pattern of behavior. When they become students, children dress in school uniforms (white shirts and khaki pants for boys, white blouses and navy blue skirts for girls) which distinguish them from their younger or older siblings who are not enrolled in school.

As students they are supposed to arrive at school before 8:00 a.m., gather in columns according to grade and sex in front of the school flagpole, and listen to the school headmaster—a school authority. After he makes announcements for the day, all the school children sing the national anthem and recite a Buddhist chant (*suatmon*). Those who arrive at school later than 8:00 a.m. will be reprimanded or disciplined. After "paying respect" to the national flag, the students enter their classrooms and study subjects which are prescribed by the state.

During the school day, which ends at 3:30 p.m., students cannot leave the school site except during the lunch break when they are allowed to go home for lunch. At 3:15 p.m., they once again gather in front of the flagpole to listen to messages or directives from the school headmaster or a designated teacher before they are dismissed for the day.

For school children, all of these activities are new and different from what they have experienced at home. There are school authorities whom they must respect and to whom they must listen, and there are new symbols to which they must pay respect. They are also taught to behave similarly toward other authorities outside school. They are taught to remember the names of, and show respect to, a few important local and national authorities, such as the village headman, the commune headman, the district officer, the governor, the minister of education, the prime minister, and the king. The titles and names of these authorities are written on a blackboard located in the corridor of the main school building. In this way, village children gradually learn to interact with the school authorities as well as with other authorities they may meet in their social world.

As mentioned earlier, the Ban Chang school has always been understaffed. There were more classes than teachers, and the headmaster was usually engaged in activities outside the school. As a consequence, the six classes for the four grades of the lower primary level were taught by four teachers. This meant that the teachers often had to leave children in one classroom doing assignments while giving instruction to children in another classroom. Due to the shortage of teachers and the inadequacy of teaching materials, most of the time teachers had to depend on the blackboard for presenting lessons. Once they had written the lessons or assignments on the blackboard, they could leave to teach the other class. Even though some teachers tried very hard to teach two classes simultaneously, it was obviously impossible to give close attention to all of the children. There certainly was not enough time for them to deal with children who had special problems.

The structure and context of the classroom, when compared with the realities of everyday life, confront children with a number of contradictions. For example, while their teachers are authority figures possessing the knowledge they are supposed to learn and having power they fear, frequently they are not present to assert their authority and power. Children are left alone to study from the blackboard with a threat of punishment if they do not follow instructions. When they do not understand the problems, there is usually no teacher in the classroom to ask for help. One can argue that, in many ways, the classroom situation reflects the larger society of which they are becoming members. In the larger society, as in the school, there are many authorities who possess knowledge and power, but these authorities, like the schoolteachers, are not easily accessible to the citizenry.

A second contradiction, it can be argued, is that while children are taught to be nationalistic and decent law-abiding citizens, they often come in contact with adults who are neither nationalistic nor law-abiding citizens. In their everyday life, they see illegal teak-trading in the village. They know that some of their relatives, teachers, and other local authorities are involved in this law-breaking activity. They see that the law often can be circumvented by money and power. They see government officials taking advantage of their relatives and their friends' parents. They are taught that their country is wonderful and that fish is in the water and rice in the field, but at the same time, many live in poverty, and several come to school without lunch to eat (a few depend on bananas and papayas which grow wild on the school site for their lunch). They are taught to love their country more than their lives, but they are neglected by the government and their country. They are often told by their teachers that their school does not receive an adequate budget to buy teaching materials. During my fieldwork in Ban Chang, I noticed that there was a lack of basic physical education equipment (for instance, soccer balls) for the children to play with at school. I was told that all the schools in the entire Ban Chang commune received a single soccer ball for the academic year. Thus it had to be rotated to each of these schools periodically, but before the Ban Chang school had its turn, the ball was no longer in any condition to be used.

The point here is not whether the children perceive, and are fully aware of, these contradictions. By and large, children in primary school may be too young to recognize explicitly such contradictions or even their own poverty. Some may not feel at all that they are neglected by the authorities or the government, for they have never been treated otherwise. Many are often too shy to admit that they are from poor families, despite the fact that many of these children wear old and shabby uniforms without shoes and some have to skip lunch. The point is that these students must confront contradictions at school as well as in their larger society, and that they will eventually see discrepancies between what they are taught and the reality in which they live.

The unequal relationship between teachers and students is apparent in the classroom situation. In the classroom, teachers are the authorities in charge. They have knowledge to transmit to the students and legitimate power to decide whether or not the students actually have learned what they are supposed to learn. They make sure that the students follow the school rules and regulations; they have the power to administer physical punishment to those who violate these rules. The students, on the other hand, are supposed to listen, cooperate, and obey; they are in the classroom to learn from the teachers and to do what they are told to do. More than that, they are supposed to behave properly toward the teachers, that is, to remain at their seats while listening to their teacher or studying their lessons, to obtain permission from their teacher before leaving the room to visit the toilet, and so on. They are supposed to talk with their teacher in the (official) central Thai dialect. They address their teacher by title and refer to themselves by central Thai pronouns which are markedly different from those of northern Thai. Boys are supposed to bow, and girls are expected to join their palms together and bow their head in showing their respect to their teachers. Outside of the classroom, whenever they see a teacher pass by, they are expected to stop, stand still, and show respect. Those who violate these expectations are reprimanded and labeled as ill-mannered students. Those who conform to the rules are rewarded with praise.

Most students in the Ban Chang school came from poor peasant and tenant families. A few were children of rich peasants and village merchants, and these dressed, behaved, spoke, and performed in class quite differently from the others. I do not have quantitative data linking students' class background and school achievement, but I was told by the teachers that children from well-to-do families tended to do better. From my own observation, these children seemed well equipped with books and school materials, and they were more likely to answer their teacher's questions in central Thai (though with some accent) than those who came from poor families. They also tended to be obedient and diligent students, that is, they tended to do their assignments and not play around as much as the others. By contrast, those from the poorer families were slow in answering questions (in central Thai). They tended to sit at the middle or far end of the class-room, and boys in particular tended to talk with their peers or play around rather than study. The teachers also treated students who were diligent and attentive differently from those who were not. These students were often given warm personal attention, allowed to go outside the classroom earlier, or entrusted to do personal errands for the teacher. Those who did not conform to the teachers' norms tended to be treated coldly or sometimes even ridiculed. In other words, students whose values fit with those of the teacher tended to receive better treatment.

Conclusion

It is generally believed in Thailand that four years of primary schooling should produce Thai citizens who have basic skills in arithmetic and can speak, read, and write central Thai, who are loyal to the nation, Buddhist teachings, and the king, and who will be decent, economically productive, and law-abiding citizens. In this chapter we have observed that in one rural school (and by extension in rural schools in general) these presumed goals of modern primary education can be accomplished only partially.

In Ban Chang during the research period there were only four teach-ers to look after six classes; the principal had to be away from the school much of the time; there was no effective supervision at the district level; school supplies were inadequate. These problems were built into the struc-ture of the education system. At the national level, removing the bud-get for primary education from the Ministry of Education and placing it under the control of the Ministry of Interior meant that those in charge of education were not educators. Thus they were unlikely to see the di-version of the principal's time and the lack of supplies, for instance, as problems needing correction. Ill-paid, ill-trained, overworked and with lit-tle supervisory help, the teachers could not but be demoralized. Of ru-ral background themselves, they believed that their training should bring them more respect and wider opportunities than farming. Thus they did not identify themselves with the community of Ban Chang, but instead viewed their jobs as steppingstones to better positions. Finally, gener-ally speaking, those students who were able to get the most from their primary education in Ban Chang were the children of the well-to-do. Be-cause further education is not free and most of the families of Ban Chang are poor, most students had little possibility of continuing their educa-tion beyond four years, regardless of their potential. Despite this, stu-dents were taught to value the idea of further education. The educa-tion they actually received was not designed to be especially relevant to the occupation the majority of them were likely to follow, that of farming.

When all the above factors are considered as a systematic whole, it appears that the true function of rural education in Ban Chang is to produce docile citizens who accept the inequities of the expanding Thai capitalist economy and remain loyal to the three aspects of the Thai state (king, Buddhism, and nation) without reflection on their own situation. Whether this is to the advantage of Thailand in the long run is an unanswered question.

References

Apple, Michael. *Ideology and Curriculum*. London: Routledge & Kegan Paul, 1979.

Chattip Nartsupha and Montri Jenvidyakarn. "Wiwattahakan Udomkan Nai Sangkhomthai" [Ideological development in Thai society]. In *Setthasat Kab Prawattisatthai* [Economics and Thai history], by Chattip Nartsupha et al. Bangkok: Samnagpim Sangsan, 1981.

Giroux, Henry. "Theories of Reproduction and Resistance in the New Sociology of Education: A Critical Analysis." *Harvard Educational Review*, 53.3(1983):257–93.

MacDonald, Madeleine. *Knowledge, Ideology and the Curriculum*. London: The Open University Press, 1977.

Ministry of Education. *Baeprian suemsang prasopakanchiwit chan p.3* [Text for improving and building experiences of life, third grade]. Bangkok: Rongpim Khurusapha, 1979.

Riggs, Fred W. *Thailand: The Modernization of a Bureaucratic Polity*. Honolulu: East-West Center Press, 1966.

Sharp, Rachel. *Knowledge, Ideology and the Politics of Schooling: Toward a Marxist Analysis of Education*. London: Routledge & Kegan Paul, 1980.

Willis, Paul. "Cultural Production is Different from Cultural Reproduction is Different from Social Reproduction is Different from Reproduction." *Interchange*, 12.2–3(1981):48–67.

THE CONTRIBUTIONS TO RURAL CHANGE
OF MODERN VIETNAMESE VILLAGE SCHOOLS

Alexander Woodside

Introduction

Revolutions characteristically precipitate a large enthusiasm for education and for new educational systems, both among the revolutionary leaders and the people they lead. As Danton put it during the French revolution, after bread, education was the first need of peoples. A revolutionary ethos has obviously pervaded Vietnam since World War II. In the early 1940s, the tribunes of the Viet Minh proclaimed "ten great policies" (reminiscent of the ten great policies of the Chinese communist party at Yanan in August 1937), one of which was the creation of an educated citizenry through the eradication of illiteracy and through general, compulsory education at the primary school level. Probably few Viet Minh policies were more popular in the villages. A residual desire for schools has been an incontestable feature of Vietnamese rural life, and has itself been crucial to the expansion of popular education in Vietnam in the past four decades.

The certain touchstone of this popular craving for schools has been the Vietnamese communist government's ability to pay for education, in part, through the strenuous and extraordinary mobilization of village resources. In the late 1950s, for instance, people's councils in "many" villages in the north built schools by quite uninhibitedly squeezing extra cash and days of labor out of the villagers. Some villages required each family in the village, whether the family had school-age children or not, to contribute thirty to fifty piasters in money, and ten to twenty days of labor, in just one school year, to support the village school (Vo Thuan Nho et al., 1980:99). Certain special Vietnamese schools, such as the Hoa Binh school of young socialist workers, a pilot school located in a mountainous region populated by minorities, not only financed their own operations completely but also fully repaid the loans from the state bank which had first enabled them to come into existence (Thai Quang Nam 1979:95–97).

Lest this be thought to be merely evidence of the coercive powers of the Vietnamese government, and no evidence at all of the authentic popularity of schools, it is a fact that village educational ambitions have been so powerful that they have seriously confounded the efforts of the Hanoi Ministry of Education to establish a well-balanced distribution of schools, classes, and teachers throughout Vietnam. Impetuously and without au-

thorization, some localities—it is not clear how many—have opened schools
on their own, and then aggressively searched for teachers for them (Nguyen
Thi Binh 1982:5). The government can, in fact, take for granted the village willingness to make greater economic sacrifices for schools, as it did in
1981 when it promoted the appearance of new "school sponsorship funds,"
to be jointly regulated by the Ministries of Education and Finance, which
would solicit further contributions from the people (*Nhan dan,* January 19,
1981:1). Villagers are evidently even willing to tolerate the arbitrary collection of examination fees, to pay for food and for the welcome ceremonies
for examiners at the annual general school graduation examinations, although the amount of the fees collected per pupil may vary markedly and
capriciously within a single province.[1] In sum, education—unlike, perhaps, medicine, or the dissemination of news, or the facilitation of athletic
competitions—is one sphere of life in which the Vietnamese people have
strong natural expectations of state action.

What I propose to do in this essay is to look, all too thinly, at the
history of the "general schools" (*truong pho thong*) in Vietnamese villages
and at some of the ways, subtle and unsubtle, by which such schools may
try to stimulate cultural and economic change. I shall isolate the general
schools from the more comprehensive history of rural education in communist Vietnam, which has also included heroic literacy campaigns, adult
education or "cultural supplementation" (*bo tuc van hoa*) schools, and "half
work half study" schools. My justification for doing so is that the general
schools, which are divided into three levels—elementary primary school,
meaning grades one to four before the 1979 educational reform and grades
one to five after it; higher primary school, which was grades five to seven
before 1979 and grades six to nine after it; and middle school, more urban
than rural, which involved grades eight to ten before the 1979 reforms and
grades ten to twelve after it—have increasingly become the foundation of
village education, during Vietnam's sometimes tormented evolution away
from the "guerilla style" (*kieu du kich*) of mass instruction of the 1940s
and 1950s. As Vietnamese educators, and others around the world, have
increasingly come to see, the mere possession of a literacy inculcated by informal, blitzkrieg literacy drives may not change the cultural and economic
attitudes of the peasantry nearly so much as certain social processes, mediated and renewed by permanently established schools, which accompany
the diffusion of literacy in a regular classroom. (Literates left to themselves
may not read; venturesome illiterates may have newspapers read to them.)
Hence the organization, and the classroom emphases, of Vietnam's 11,400
general schools (as of 1980) undoubtedly influenced their nearly twelve mil-

lion pupils (as of 1980; out of an official population of 52.7 million) almost as much as the actual contents of the textbooks such pupils were taught to understand. As of 1975, every village in northern Vietnam evidently had at least one general primary school.

Readers should be aware, however, that what follows is not the whole story of rural education—or cultural change—in Vietnam. My approach involves at least two kinds of distortions of village history. The first one is that the general schools, as the need for the three major reforms of 1950, 1956, and 1979 attests, have not been undefiled success stories in the eyes of their creators. Their shortcomings have recently even raised spiritually expensive anxieties about the magnitude of the differences between Vietnamese society and the societies of the USSR and of eastern Europe from which some of the features of these schools have been borrowed, and anxieties also about the chronic unpreparedness of the schools' hundreds of thousands of yearly graduates for productive work in the Vietnamese countryside. The purest educational triumphs of the Vietnamese revolution are probably to be found, not in the general schools, but in the more exhilarating pedagogical fever of the often improvised and spontaneous guerilla-like literacy crusades. These crusades apparently imparted at least a rough passive literacy to more than sixteen million people between 1945 and 1981. Serving as their homespun teacher virtuosi during their last big manifestation, in the Vietnamese south from 1975 to 1978, the crusades assembled members of society as diverse as a septuagenarian woman in Minh Hai province who taught literacy to almost one hundred people, and the Khmer monks who opened literacy classes in their temples in Hau Giang (Ngo Van Cat 1980:172; also see Woodside 1983b).

A second distortion is that the general schools have evidently played very little part in directly influencing either the cultural outlook or the economic practices of the people who dominate the rural labor force, especially the basic production brigades of the agricultural cooperatives of the north: middle-aged peasant women. Females accounted for 65 percent of the entire agricultural labor force in 1981 (*Nhan dan*, March 8, 1981:1). In certain places of concentrated farm work outside ordinary villages, such as state farms, their preponderance was even greater. At the Binh Lieu state farm in Quang Ninh province, for example, females were 90 percent of the work force in 1982, and their meager marriage prospects in such a context had become an important issue (*Nhan dan*, December 1, 1982:3). Two social psychologists who surveyed the village of An Binh in Hai Hung province southeast of Hanoi, in 1980, discovered that while most of the village's communist party members, who were male, had at

least completed higher primary school, the village's ordinary farm workers
(nearly 70 percent female) had rarely gone as far as grade two (Nguyen
Duc Uy and Bach Van Tho 1980:3). This makes it obvious that a synop-
tic picture of the agencies of cultural change in Vietnamese villages would
have to include radio broadcasts, film shows, and theatrical performances,
as well as general schools. Moreover, the slow transformation of Red River
Delta villages from relatively self-centered enclaves surrounded by bamboo
hedges, to supposed "open systems" (*he thong mo*, a Vietnamese adoption
of the Western social science jargon) in which many villagers, the majority
of whom are male youths with relatively good educational backgrounds,
may leave, raises another question. To what extent must the economically
harassed Vietnamese state tolerate its villagers supporting and helping finance the general schools for the wrong reason—not the desire to assimilate
a new world view, but the ancient reason that schools are a "ladder" to a
better life as a white collar official in the cities?

The Transition from Confucianism to Communism in Village Schools

Until the end of the nineteenth century, Vietnamese village schools,
as is well known, taught Confucian moral discipline, literacy in classical
Chinese or Sino-Vietnamese, and elite literature. They did so in such
a way as to educate potential examination-taking literati (called *cu tu*)
who aspired to become court officials. They were privately established
by their teachers or by village households, which then hired the teachers.
Teachers were generalists rather than specialists. Michel Duc Chaigneau,
who lived in the Hue area in the early nineteenth century, reported that
schoolteachers there customarily combined the functions of teachers, public
scribes, and physicians (Chaigneau 1867:73). If the curriculum which the
great blind southern schoolteacher, physician, and poet Nguyen Dinh Chieu
(1822–1888) imposes upon his fascinating fictional hero, Luc Van Tien, is
at all representative, more mature teenaged pupils might also study ancient
works on military strategy. The traditional village school might therefore
take in everything from very young male pupils, who spent their time
practicing how to write Chinese characters on wooden boards covered with
soil or clay, to older male pupils, who read the Confucian classics, pored
over the Chinese dynastic histories (which were the public administration
textbooks of the premodern era), and memorized model compositions of
rhymed prose (*phu*). Older pupils also had to learn a variety of compulsory
literary punctilios. These included the avoidance of "taboo" characters
(characters which appeared in the names of Vietnamese rulers) and the

respectful elevation of words spoken or written by emperors in characters raised above all others in the margin at the very top of the page.

This sort of education, or clerical training, led unfalteringly towards the bureaucracy. It led away from the villages. Pupils who wished to pass the various levels of civil service examinations sought to move quickly from the private village schools to the government-sponsored district schools (known colloquially as *nha huan*, and led by district school directors, or *huan dao*), to the prefectural school (*nha giao*, led by prefectural directors of school or *giao thu*), and, ultimately, to the provincial schools (led by provincial educational commissioners, or *doc hoc*). The bureaucratic standardization of such schools was so intense—as a prelude to the standardized life of the civil service—that even their sizes (computed in "beam sections," or *gian*) were carefully prescribed by the Nguyen court, as well as the rest of their architecture. Centuries of history have therefore conspired to make the Vietnamese people think of education as a single track enterprise whose final destination is the university; or, in nineteenth-century terms, the imperial college (*Quoc tu giam*), the Hue metropolitan examinations, and the career of a mandarin.

The needs of the peasants who had to remain in the villages were never addressed. As I have suggested elsewhere (Woodside 1983a:26–29), educational forms and theories in Confucian societies belonged to the most heavily ritualized realms of public discourse. They were peculiarly paralyzed by antiquarian precedents and models, so much so that the very notion of a vocational "school" which had no connection with government service was far less tolerable in China or Vietnam than it would have been in premodern Europe. The real educational curricula of the rural common people were those syntheses of moral stipulations and communal restraints which were known as the village codes (*khoan uoc*). Researchers in Vietnam are just now beginning to look at these important documents. But they apparently inculcated attitudes, such as industriousness, rather than knowledge (of things like farm techniques). Preliminary investigations of the traditional codes of villages and hamlets of several northern provinces— codes which were drawn up in the seventeenth and eighteenth centuries, and recopied towards the end of the nineteenth century—have shown that they inveighed against laziness, stressed the need to obtain the maximum harvests from the land, and reminded all peasants that they were eternally obliged to renew the dikes of the artificially flood-proof agriculture their ancestors had bequeathed them. Such village codes enforced a collective work discipline, based upon moral principles, which is at first sight almost reminiscent of that of the Protestant ethic in Europe. But they were, in fact, quite remote from any Protestant spirit. Instead of relying primarily upon the inner compulsion of newly emerged religious values, Tonkinese village codes merely threatened their peasants with the mechanical external sanctions of the corporate village: money fines for inadequate dike maintenance, for instance, or ostracism of the funeral processions of households which had betrayed communal economic requirements (Nguyen Danh Phiet 1978:259–75).

Deprived of literacy themselves, the most tatterdemalion peasants were nonetheless rarely ignorant of the link between literacy and village self-esteem. For Vietnamese villages commonly had village associations, known as *tu van* (roughly "orthodox culture") groups, which transcended family ties, and which incessantly celebrated the moral and social splendors of literacy. The *tu van* associations embraced all village males who had won exemption from corvée because of their literacy, and who were accordingly known as *ong nhieu* (very roughly, "mister exempt"). Such males included degree-holders, examination-eligible students, and, occasionally, rich peasants who had bought their exemption from corvée. Many of them might be the same men as the village elders. But their purpose as members of the *tu van* group was at once more theatrical and more educationally promotional than that of the elders' councils. On the one hand, the *tu van* associations wrote and conducted most of the sacrificial orations at the village meeting hall and at its Confucian shrine. Such sacrifices had a recreational aspect (involving extraordinary costumes and the playing of many different kinds of musical instruments) as well as a religious one. On the other hand, the *tu van* associations maintained fields known quite aptly as "study fields" (*hoc dien*), from whose income they financed ambitious but poor village pupils, and paid the teachers who were instructing village children.[2]

Nor was this the end of the worship of literacy as a village asset. Phan Ke Binh (1875–1921), a celebrated Confucian classicist writing before World War I, even nostalgically claimed that many precolonial Vietnamese villages had annually assembled all their pupils and given them unsolicited examinations—known as "advance and benefit tests" (*khao tien ich*)—and had, as well, punished households which had school-going children, but from which the sounds of studying at night could not be heard (Phan Ke Binh 1970:152–54). What is of great interest here is that in traditional China, associations of literate males were far less village-centered. The Chinese celebration of literacy was far more commonly an expression of lineage pride, or pride of association with a specific school or academy. By the standards prevailing in the other great nineteenth-century Confucian society with mandarinal examinations and without a fully hereditary system of social statuses, therefore, the Vietnamese cult of literacy conveyed an extraordinary obsession with the economic and cultural success or failure of the village.

If the strong connection between the possession of literacy and the fate of the village must have moved some poor rural Vietnamese to try schooling, there was another difference between Vietnam and China which may also have helped. Scholastic barriers to widespread literacy, if not social and economic barriers, were undoubtedly weaker among the Vietnamese. Elites in both societies agreed, in theory, that literacy was not as important as proper moral indoctrination, and that literacy that was not preceded by careful moral training would produce decadence. (Hence the maxim in Vietnamese village schools: "First one studies rites, afterwards one studies literature.") Reading was not supposed to be a technical quest for information. It was supposed to be a sort of moral gymnastic, in which the pupils who were the readers tried to copy and acquire the moral "skills" (cong phu) of past sages. Zhu Xi, the twelfth-century architect of Neoconfucianism, had taught generations of Vietnamese, as well as Chinese, Japanese, and Koreans, the moral importance of a prolonged, meditative, chanting approach to the understanding of texts, known as "ripe reading" (thuc doc). Such an approach was obviously a huge practical obstacle to mass education, because it consumed so much time. Yet traditional Vietnamese pedagogues never shared their Chinese counterparts' fondness as well for linguistic and phonological fundamentalism as a means of recapturing the essence of ancient teachers. They were less inclined to deny penetration of the educational system to students who had not mastered various historical forms of calligraphy (ancient script, small seal script, Han dynasty square script, and so on), or the comprehension of pronunciations of words in various historical periods. The traditional Vietnamese educational world, being smaller, was less specialized and less sharply divided between esoteric academicians and more humble village instructors. It was more of a scholastic—although not a social—democracy.

For these reasons or others, some poor Vietnamese villagers did become quite literate. And, more than literate, some became highly cultured. Even a Vietnamese Marxist historian as hostile to the nineteenth-century Confucian social order as Tran Van Giau must concede that thirty to forty percent of the men who passed civil service examinations in Vietnam in the 1800s were the "sons of the poor." But Giau also observes (Tran Van Giau 1973:23–24) that their triumphs meant a smooth passage out of the peasantry into the ranks of the exploitative landlord-bureaucrat class. In contrast to the situation in Vietnam's Theravada Buddhist neighbors, the acquisition of a significant literacy usually led to an irreversible transformation of social status. Literacy and manual labor, it is certain, remained utterly divorced.

There is perhaps no need to labor all the inadequacies of French colonial education in Vietnam, which have become commonplaces among scholars. J.S. Furnivall (1956:111) estimated in the late 1930s, that a smaller percentage of the population of French Indochina was attending school than that of any other Western colony in Southeast Asia, including the Netherlands Indies. Although the total number of pupils in all elementary primary schools, superior primary schools, and middle schools in Vietnam may have increased from 163,110 children in 1923 to 546,111 children by 1942, almost all these children were attending primitive elementary primary schools which the villages, and the pupils' families themselves, financed. The colonial government appears to have spent more than twice as much money on courts, police, and prisons in 1942 as it did on education (Nguyen Anh 1967:31, 42–43). Apart from the extraordinary smallness in numbers of school-going children, the other prominent feature of Vietnam's colonial educational system was its reverence for the French language and for French history rather than their Vietnamese equivalents, especially in the superior primary schools (known in French as the *écoles primaire de plein exercice*) and the middle schools. When the "national language" (*quoc van*) was taught in the superior primary schools, it was an undiscriminating mixture of Chinese and Vietnamese words. Indeed, at least until the early 1980s, there was evidently a subterranean bias against teaching "purely Vietnamese words" (*tu thuan Viet*), as opposed to Sino-Vietnamese words and words with Chinese roots, in even some of the village schools of communist Vietnam (Trinh Manh 1981:9). The official explanation of this was the existence of an assumption—much criticized—that pupils already understood purely Vietnamese words. But it is hard not to see the practice as a ghostly legacy from the colonial era.

Literacy and illiteracy are words with vast circumferences. We must not completely surrender all judgment when we contemplate the communists' official statistics about illiteracy in Vietnam in 1945. According to such statistics, 95 percent of the population was illiterate, including 97.2 percent of all females in localities where there were primary schools and 99.8 percent of all females in localities where there were none (Ho Truc 1975:30). Yet, undoubtedly, a very large gulf did exist, in cultural interests and in worldviews, between the tiny number of highly literate Vietnamese who read and wrote an amazing variety of books and tracts, and whose lives centered upon the written word,[3] and the millions of peasants whose lives instead were dominated by a hypnotically rich oral culture.[4]

It would be disingenuous to suggest that colonial education had not brought progress of a kind. By introducing the notion that the present was superior to the past, colonial schools inevitably had an anti-feudal effect. They demolished the absolute respect for ancient sages and Confucian philosophers which had so stultified critical inquiry in precolonial villages. Perhaps the most positive contribution of the colonial schools, as Dang Thai Mai (1974:10–11) has asserted, was that they domesticated in Vietnam the modern pedagogical insight of industrial Europe that children have different mental and imaginative capacities at different ages, with which school curricula must properly coordinate themselves. But, altogether, French colonial education did not give Vietnamese villagers either the knowledge or the critical consciousness with which to participate effectively in twentieth-century economic change.

The reasons for this are both obvious and not so obvious. As to the less obvious ones, no significant body of messianic economists existed in western Europe before 1940 to persuade French colonial officials that education might help to increase economic productivity in colonies or even in the mother country. The conventional view of education was merely that it was a form of public good. In this respect, the Soviet revolution was almost unique in acquiring an early interest in the expansion of education as a means of indirect investment in economic growth: the writings of S.G. Strumilin (which influenced the first Soviet ten-year plan, with its relatively large expenditures on schools) epitomized this interest in the 1920s and 1930s. And the strong influence of this early Soviet faith—that education might explain whatever economic growth could not be accounted for purely by accumulations of capital—was one of the things which most sharply separated the Vietnamese communist approach to schools from that of their erstwhile colonial masters and enemies. As early as 1945, Ho Chi Minh declared that the purpose of the new communist schools must be to ensure that "the people are strong and the country is rich." References to Strumilin appear even now in Vietnamese economics journals.

The more obvious reason for the deficiencies of colonial education in Indochina may be found in the public pronouncement, made in 1925 by the French chief of the educational service in Cambodia, that schools should speak to "small Asiatics" much less "about their rights, which they have a tendency to exaggerate, than about their obligations" (Pujarniscle 1925:104). The communists, well aware that a popular revolution could only be based upon a profound consciousness of "rights" which had been violated, accordingly made political education—topics such as the differences between monarchism and fascism and communist "new democracy," the importance of participating in elections for a national assembly—the centerpiece of the mass education campaign they launched in Vietnamese villages from September 1945.

The dominant passions of the early communist educational creed were populist ones, partly borrowed from China. The Chinese communists' experiments at Yanan, in north China, between 1937 and 1945, undoubtedly helped to shape the early Vietnamese communist schools, which came into existence in the late 1940s, during the first years of the Viet Minh struggle with France. Certainly the 1943 announcement of the central committee of the Indochina Communist Party—that education must from now on be governed by the three forces of nationalism, science, and the masses (*dan toc, khoa hoc, dai chung*)—very obviously originated in Mao Zedong's theoretical formulation of the "new democracy" stage of the Chinese revolution in January 1940. Probably the struggling communist republic's dramatic educational reform of July 1950 marked the apotheosis of Mao's thought among Vietnamese educational theoreticians, even if an exposition by the then undersecretary of the education ministry, Nguyen Khanh Toan, entitled "Educational problems" (*Nhung van de giao duc*) was the actual Vietnamese blueprint for these reforms. At any rate, the 1950 reform required the unequivocal politicization of education. Schools in Viet Minh-controlled areas could not be "neutral." They had to be the "instrument" of a "definite social class."[5] The 1950 reform shortened and simplified education. The number of years in the Viet Minh general school system was reduced to nine. Barriers which had daunted upward progress in the colonial educational system were removed. Pupils would have to pass only one "light" graduation examination, instead of the former three. School subjects which were not "necessary" to the successful prosecution of the resistance war— such as foreign languages, music, world geography, ancient history, and classical literature—were abandoned or reduced in scope, in favor of "new" subjects such as current events, citizenship training, and the promotion of economic production. As another reverberation from Yanan, the 1950 educational reform sought to lower the ancient prestige of the schoolteacher as a miniature sage whose authority could not be challenged. "Administration councils" were established in the higher primary and middle schools, composed of teachers, parents, and pupils, all of whom would enjoy equal privileges of discussing and voting upon school issues, "on a level with each other" (*ngang nhau*) (Vo Thuan Nho 1980:38, 42–46).

But the pendulum began to swing away from Mao's thought after 1954. Ho Chi Minh himself denounced "guerilla education" at a March

1956 conference of Vietnamese educators. Vietnamese schools, Ho said, must abandon the guerrilla style they had previously cultivated, and must turn instead to "regular rules" and to planning.

The substance of the reform of 1956 lengthened general education to ten years, reversing the tendency of 1950. And the "Regulations for General Schools" (*Dieu le nha truong pho thong*) which the Education Ministry belatedly issued in 1976, and which had the force of law, were designed to attack the slack discipline and the exaltation of personal "convenience" in Vietnamese schools which had earlier been encouraged by the "guerrilla" atmosphere, as well as by the preindustrial habits of the villages. The "Regulations" now greatly fortified the power of principals and teachers, in contrast to the policy of 1950. Teachers received the legal authority to demand that other people respect them (something which had hardly been necessary in the Confucian era) and the legal authority as well to "guarantee" the hours when classes should begin, an important right in a rural society whose peasant children and their parents did not always share the state's bureaucratic sense of time (Ho Truc 1976:4–6).

But probably the definitive farewell to the educational legacy of the resistance war, and the inspirations from China which had accompanied it, came with the educational reform of 1979. The politburo resolution which announced the 1979 reform complained that the content of education in the general schools was not comprehensive enough, particularly with respect to technical knowledge; that teaching methods were simplistic and old-fashioned, and failed to pay enough attention to productive labor; that the scientific and cultural information which the schools communicated was out of touch both with Vietnamese realities and with contemporary science; and that schools did not prepare their pupils either to enter useful vocations or to "love" the vocations in which they eventually found themselves (Nghi quyet 1979:4–5). The 1979 reform itself, which had only begun to be implemented in the early 1980s, and which may influence Vietnamese education for the remainder of the century, lengthened general education again, this time to twelve years. It proposed compulsory education for all children in the country between the ages of six and fifteen years, another extension. Breaking at least temporarily with previous egalitarian impulses, the reform also anticipated the provision of special schools for children with unusual aptitudes in such subjects as foreign languages, art, physical training, literature, mathematics, biology, physics, and chemistry.

The Uses of Schools in the Struggle for Cultural Reform

So much for the history of the transition from Confucian schools to communist ones. The rulers of Vietnam, since 1954, have suffered from three recurrent anxieties about their schools. One is the fear that educational growth is outstripping national economic capacities, with an attendant evil impact upon educational quality.[6] Another is the fear that links between the schools and the overwhelmingly rural society around them (80.83 percent of the Vietnamese people lived in villages rather than cities or towns, according to the 1979 census) are not intimate enough. The third is the fear that schools, as unique institutions, will resist firm political control in many subtle ways. Behind this third fear lurk a number of factors. The underground presence of the old Confucian view that teachers were custodians of ultimate values who had the duty to advise enlightened governments and to admonish poor ones, may still make some Vietnamese educators unwilling to accept wholeheartedly the statement in the 1976 school regulations that the schools are now no more than the "instruments" (*cong cu*) of the proletarian dictatorship. Apart from that, schools are generally a law-giver's nightmare. Even the Marxist-Leninist canon has few certain guidelines about how to run them. It is not obvious whether principals, for example, should have great power, or very little. It took the Vietnamese government, by no coincidence, more than three decades to devise the regulations for its general schools, far longer than it took to draw up national constitutions. A further consideration is that in both Confucian and communist Vietnam, schools have tried hard to be microcosms of the values which the society at large consecrates.[7] The lack of any spectacular contrast between school practices and those of the polity beyond the school suggests that any "group of rotten pupils" (*nhom hoc sinh hu*) which becomes alienated from the school is also likely to be alienated from the social system as a whole; hence the political conditioning of the schools' populations acquires a huge significance.

In spite of that, the evidence suggests that Vietnamese general schools, at least until the 1979 reform, preserved more of a traditional academic separateness from politics than might be thought. Political education was given a subordinate classification in the schools, along with music, art, and physical training; it was not categorized as a "fundamental culture" (*van hoa co ban*) subject like history, geography, mathematics, literature, and the natural sciences. In such a status-ridden environment, a subordinate classification could have a devastating effect. Because few teachers wished to specialize in politics, its courses were commonly assigned to history teachers to teach on the side. The small group of unabashed politics teachers who did exist could expect, if they were good and fortunate, to be quickly transferred from the classroom to "management organs." Those who were not so good or so fortunate could expect discriminatory treatment, like being assigned to guard their schools in the summertime while the more privileged "fundamental culture" teachers were given professional reinforcement training (Nguyen Phu Boi and Ngo Van Dau 1978:23–25).

The extent of the schools' influence upon village culture must be examined cautiously, and from many angles. Primary schools, after 1954, continued to be established upon a village basis, rather than upon the basis of any other administrative or social unit. For this reason, ironically, they lost the intimacy of the village schools of the Confucian and colonial periods. For farm collectivization and bouts of administrative reorganization in the countryside had expanded the population of villages, and had done so unevenly. In 1978, as a representative example, the "reorganized" district of Nam Ninh, in the coastal province of Ha Nam Ninh south of Hanoi, had nine administrative villages (*xa*) with over 10,000 people in them, nine with 8,000 to 10,000 people, and only four with fewer than 6,000 people. Not surprisingly, bloated primary schools, which covered grades one to seven and which had as many as sixty classes of pupils in them, were relatively common in this district (Nguyen Trong Hoe and Nguyen Gia Quy 1978). Even if schools of this extraordinary size still remained socially effective enough to introduce decisive cultural changes, they were no longer the only beacons of cultural leadership in the countryside, as they had been in much of prerevolutionary Vietnam. Army units, cooperatives, and libraries, and even stores were now regarded as "organs" (*co so*) with the obligation to diffuse and organize culture. After 1975, when the communist government discovered that it now ruled highly commercialized Mekong delta villages with 40,000 to 50,000 inhabitants per village, and with daily district, village, and hamlet markets (as opposed to the primary and secondary cyclical markets of the rural north), it made the south's markets the favored places for the propagation of new cultural messages and procedures (Nguyen Van Hieu's article in *Nhan dan*, June 5, 1982, p. 3). Schools, in other words, now have a cultural role which is both diminished and more specialized. Confucian emperors had never formally regarded markets as major places for transmitting the orthodox culture, even if local markets as well as schools had influenced the popular culture in the traditional period.

Moreover, generalizations about the paramountcy of schools in the diffusion of new cultural meanings and values are likely to founder upon the extreme variety of Vietnamese social and economic life. The Educational Sciences Institute made a comparative study, in the late 1970s, of a Ho Chi Minh city ward and of a village (named Xuan thoi son) located a mere 25 kilometers from Ho Chi Minh city center. The study revealed striking educational discrepancies between the two communities. As one example, the percentages of school-age children between the ages of twelve and fifteen who had quit school rose year by year from 8.2 percent to a relatively low 28 percent in the ward, but from 22.2 percent to a steep 60.1 percent for the same ages in the village. An important reason for such an acute difference in school attendance rates within just 25 kilometers or less was, of course, the availability of employment. Job prospects were poor in the city. But the village had a handicraft industry (the weaving of container bags for export) which paid even children a daily income of more than one piaster. That was enough to unravel universal education in Xuan thoi son (Nguyen Ngoc Dung 1978:18). All this may confirm in a new manner the recent findings of European economic historians, that the first superficial establishment of literacy and of universal education occurs more easily in economically stagnant areas than in industrializing ones. But what it certainly makes clear is that a true reconstruction of the cultural impact of schools in Vietnam requires an exhaustive appreciation of even the most minute variations in that country's economic geography. No such appreciation can be offered here.

Since the late 1940s, the communist schools have committed themselves to an assault upon the traditional separation of mental and manual labor in Vietnam. This is one of their greatest contributions to social and cultural revolution. In October 1961, the "two goods" (*hai tot*) movement was introduced, in which schools were encouraged to compete with each other for the honor of being publicly declared to have good teaching and good studying. One of the model primary schools which emerged triumphantly from this competition was the Bac Ly school in Chung ly village, Ly Nhan district, Ha Nam Ninh province, as already mentioned on the delta coast south of Hanoi. The Bac Ly school still sets the standards for village education in Vietnam. The combination of labor with booklearning at the Bac Ly school has gone through a number of phases. For many years, labor education was used merely to train pupils in a few skills, such as breeding fish. Later the Bac Ly school changed its emphasis, from the transmission of skills to the use of labor to teach rural pupils how to think, especially about traditional economic pastimes of their locality which they were physically and psychologically capable of exploring. For the first time, village economic activities were in effect formally graded in terms of their closeness to adulthood. Grade five pupils served as members of groups which planted vegetables (or looked after the village "martyrs' cemetery," if that was assigned to the school for supervision); grade six pupils served in carpentry or handicraft or fish-breeding groups; only in grade seven could pupils move into the school groups which handled machinery or transplanted rice (Phung Huy Trien 1981:12–13). Just how much such school procedures consolidate the traditional dominance of rice in the Vietnamese economy is difficult to assess. The schools' greater social mission, so far incompletely fulfilled, is to banish the old specter of the literate males who grew long fingernails to dramatize their membership in a leisured ruling class—a phenomenon which the Jesuit missionary, Christopher Borri, personally observed in south central Vietnam as far back as the early seventeenth century.

The rural school has taken on another sensitive task. It has tried to serve as an outpost of communist rationalism and secularization in a society whose village markets, even in the Red River delta, still openly sell paper elephants and packets of paper "underworld money" (tien am phu), at lunar New Year's, for peasants to burn as a means of succoring the souls of their dead ancestors (see the letter of Dang Xuan Ngung in Nhan dan, March 5, 1981, p. 3). The scientific, and scientistic, doctrines which the communist revolution has imported from the West have hardly won a secure foothold in much of the Vietnamese countryside. There is a vast reservoir of religious beliefs, accumulated over centuries, whose relationship to the purposes of the communist state superimposed upon them is ambiguous. The nineteenth-century village school coexisted uneasily with the amazing parade of professional specialists in sometimes "heterodox" religious practices who circulated around it, themselves bearing the title of "teacher" (thay): people like astrologers (thay so), physiognomy interpreters (thay tuong), blind soothsayers (thay boi), and, in the north, mountain shamans (thay mo). Communist schools, as far more extreme agencies of secularization in a formidably unsecular society, cannot coexist with such "teachers." Instead they must attempt to undermine the "superstitions" which supposedly nourish them.[8]

In struggling with the traditional peasant religion, Vietnamese schools are simply repeating a crusade which the Protestant reformation and the seventeenth-century English revolution originated, and which twentieth-century revolutionaries from Leningrad to Havana have necessarily inherited. Its archetype was the campaign against medieval saints' days which interfered with the work discipline of an industrializing society, and which were thought to rob laborers of earnings which they might otherwise have accumulated and invested. Nor should the economic motive in the Vietnamese attack upon the old folk creeds be discounted. The privatization of fortune-telling, as a result of its public repression, has meant that fortune tellers working unseen in their own homes could charge peasants, in 1981, an alleged minimum of five piasters (perhaps four days' income) each

time they threw their medieval metal coins into the air and requested the
yin and *yang* principles to reveal their influence in the way the coins fell
(again, see the letter by Dang Xuan Ngung in *Nhan dan*, March 5, 1981, p.
2). But although there is nothing surprising or unprecedented about the
Vietnamese revolution's determination to make the popular culture less sacred, it is striking that, in this effort, the schools are made to be more
secular than the revolutionary state to which they belong. Because of the
old-fashioned nature of Vietnamese patriotism, which is not wholly modern
or secular, but which the communist government does not want to see die
out, the battle front between the culturally orthodox and the culturally
heterodox must be moved inside the traditional or sacred sphere, with the
state accepting some features of life within this sphere and rejecting others.
For the school, however, the battlefront remains entirely outside the sacred
sphere. The point might be demonstrated in a preliminary way by a brief
look at the management of time in modern Vietnam.

The public calendar of the precolonial period was a lunar calendar
issued by a court agency known as the Imperial Observatory (*Kham thien
giam*), which exercised the emperor's prerogative of deciding when New
Year's day occurred. Years calculated according to this lunar calendar bore
names which recurred every sixty years.[9] But the Imperial Observatory
at Hue was abolished in 1945. The Viet Minh showed no interest in
performing its "feudal" functions. As a result, private printing houses
in the north and south continued to print their own unauthorized and
uncoordinated lunar calendars. These did not agree with each other in
such crucial matters as the date of New Year's day, or the calculation
of intercalary months. The disappearance of a single authorized lunar
calendar had an unsettling effect upon the Vietnamese village economy. The
cycles of rural markets, which were based upon the lunar calendar, became
confused. The critical transplanting of rice for the fifth month harvest
was done too late or too early, because peasants married to the ancestral
slogan "transplant before New Year's" found themselves in a calendrical
limbo. In 1967 the Hanoi government, while insisting upon the exclusive
use of the solar calendar in the planning of farm operations, nevertheless
belatedly published its own reformed lunar calendar, and decreed that
the lunar calendar could continue to determine holidays and ceremonial
days (such as New Year's) and, equally important, the historical days of
remembrance so vital to Vietnamese nationalism: the anniversaries of the
Hung kings, of the Trung sisters, of Tran Hung Dao.[10] Since 1967, in other
words, the Vietnamese state has officially embraced two systems of time:
political-economic time and ritual-festival time. It has attempted to share

the ritual apparatus of the old village culture, while seeking to disenthrall peasants from "superstition" at the same moment. But rural schools are not allowed to embrace both systems of time. The otherwise broad-minded August 8, 1967 decree which tried to reestablish state control over time, by legitimizing the lunar calendar, pointedly confined schools entirely to the solar calendar (Nguyen Xien 1976).

In this and in other respects, the school takes a more rigorously secular approach to Vietnamese popular culture than does the Vietnamese state. The village school also relies more heavily than do more purely political agencies upon elite-produced written literature as a catalyst of proper cultural behavior. As a means of documenting this distinction, let us consider the quest of the village people's committees, since 1954, to transform, as well as reduce in scope, the traditional religious festivals. One of their notable targets has been the spring boat races, which used to attract tens of thousands of peasants, peddlers, religious specialists, gamblers, and actors to riverine cantons in Thai Binh and other northern provinces.[11] The procedure of the people's committees has been to place the building of the boats under government patronage (which enables the government to shrink the sizes of the boats and their crews) and to make collective economic enterprises, such as handicraft cooperatives, the official owners of the boats, rather than traditional units of religious solidarity like hamlets. But one of the most important changes involves literature. Before the revolution, the signal callers in rural boat races sang out signals derived from the stanzas of Vietnam's most brilliant classical poems, such as the early nineteenth-century *Tale of Kieu* (*Truyen Kieu*) or the eighteenth-century *Song of a Soldier's Wife* (*Chinh phu ngam*) or *Lamentation Inside the Royal Harem* (*Cung oan ngam khuc*). In postrevolutionary Vietnam, on the other hand, the signal callers have been compelled to abandon classical poetry and guide the races instead by new folk songs created by the people of the locality, under the committees' surveillance (Pham Duc Duat 1981).

It is hard not to be struck by the contrast between this and the procedures of the village primary schools. For even the alphabetical studies primer which the schools use at the grade one level teaches Vietnamese children how to recognize letters and sounds precisely by means of "lively" lines of classical poetry by Nguyen Trai, Nguyen Du, Nguyen Khuyen, and others (*Nhan dan*, September 8, 1981, p. 3). And "ancient literature" accounts for at least 10 percent of the classroom time devoted to literature in primary schools, under the 1979 reform curriculum. This requirement gains added significance from the fact that medieval Vietnamese writers rarely wrote for children, and hardly thought of children's literature as being a special art form (Nguyen Hue Chi 1982).

Of course the contrast, or contradiction, between the village people's committees and the village schools is more apparent than real. The schools may be trying to inculcate a knowledge of classical literature while the people's committees, the organs charged with administering and reforming culture outside the schools, seem bent upon reducing that literature's application. In fact, both types of institution are engaged in the same process, which is the preservation of classical literature as a national cultural legacy, but the suppression of its use as the imaginative furnishings of uncontrollable popular religions.

The schools, however, have received the more conservative task. Why is this so? One reason might be that the school, with its examinations and its standardized curriculum, is still necessarily too much the product of a prerevolutionary elite era to participate very flexibly in enterprises of drastic mass cultural conversion. As long as the village school has even the vaguest association with the notion of training and choosing talent for a limited number of high status positions, it may be that it will have, in structure and in form, a certain irreducible conservatism. As a corollary of this, the school is less representative of the village population than the special committees which the communist party establishes to obtain radical cultural change quickly: for example, the "civilized way of life committees" (*ban nep song van minh*), full of the middle-aged females who are so uninvolved with the schools, which have been set up to change village wedding and funeral practices. The necessarily greater social representativeness of improvised outside organizations means that the school is often overshadowed in the struggle against the cultural "remnants" of "feudalism."

The schools' loyalty to their past elitist archetypes may be seen in their academic programs. Communist cultural theoreticians like Ha Huy Giap have supplied the Vietnamese people with properly modern definitions of culture, for example, that culture is the system of knowledge and morality which people create to satisfy material and spiritual needs in definite social contexts. But the schools' relationship to written literature suggests that the literal prerevolutionary meaning of the Vietnamese word for culture (*van hoa*)—"the change that literature brings about"—has not been completely obliterated. The single subject of Vietnamese language and literature occupies about 40 percent of all the hours of teaching in Vietnamese elementary primary schools (grades one through five). Small children entering primary school at the age of six are already expected to know about 2,500 words of their extraordinarily rich language. When they graduate from elementary primary school, they must know at least 10,000 words. Popular literature, which includes proverbs, folk songs, riddles, fables, legends, and myths, occupies 30 percent of the literature studied in the 1979 reform curriculum; ancient literature, as already noted, occupies some 10 percent; "contemporary literature," which the curriculum significantly differentiates from popular literature, represents the remaining 60 percent. As another aspect of the painstakingly literary approach taken to education in Vietnam, extracurricular reading is prescribed, on paper, for the pupils of even the poorest village primary schools. Such pupils are supposed to read—despite a shortage of books and paper—a minimum of thirty books outside their classroom textbooks, before they graduate (Trinh Manh 1981).

The belief that literature, if read in certain ways, could exercise an enormous power—far beyond providing the reader with conscious knowledge—was of course widespread in Confucian Asia. Good literature was even thought to have a beneficial physiological effect, such as curing illness. The famous and moving description of the Vietnamese philosopher Le Quy Don's boyhood education (his young body was allegedly warmed by reading the *Dich kinh* or *Classic of Changes*) in the eighteenth century *Literary Text Collection of the Ngo Lineage* (*Ngo gia van phai*)—shows a little of this for Vietnam. The persistence of part of this belief in contemporary Vietnam might be detected in communist schoolteachers' creed that a poor line of poetry is an immoral line of poetry, that the active effect of textbook readings will be lost on children if aesthetic education and its link to morality are not stressed. But two of the most important effects which the literary exercises in Vietnamese village schools are designed to obtain are thoroughly untraditional. One is peasant respect for science. The other is peasant respect for what one might call the benign manageability of nature. The diffusion of these two attitudes is crucial to the success of a planned economy.

The importance of science is heavily invoked, even in grade one, symbolically and otherwise. Instructors in methods of personal hygiene, for example, do not offer their pupils "health" classes, but rather classes in "general knowledge science" (*khoa hoc thuong thuc*). More important, the primary schools are to try to supply the first components of what they call a "worldview" (*the gioi quan*) which assumes a knowledge of general mathematical concepts, rather than simply the techniques of counting. Pupils are supposed to become "independent, creative people" (*con nguoi doc lap, sang tao*) through the use of "direct observation" teaching techniques and experiments in such mathematical activities as the geometrical measurement of circumferences and angles, rather than being confined to the memorization of announced orthodox rules as in the past. This is not, of course, to say that the government wants pupils "independent" enough to question the political order. But it does seek pupils capable of enough autonomous conceptualization, from an early age, to enable the rate of learning in Vietnamese schools to be accelerated—compared to the Confucian and colonial periods—because of the tension between the global knowledge explosion and the fact that schooling, prolonged in both the 1956 and 1979 reforms, cannot nonetheless be prolonged indefinitely. There is no more important an event in the Vietnamese educational revolution than this struggle to vernacularize a wholly new empirical education in the villages. So far, however, village mathematics teachers have been accused of being relative failures in this struggle: they have been criticized for being too formalistic, too unappreciative of the need to get their pupils to think mathematically rather than merely add and subtract, too unwilling to break their pupils' overwhelming reliance upon printed textbook material and mechanical memorization (Pham Thi Dieu Van 1981:16–18).

As for nature, the new *Grade One Practice Readers* (*Tap doc lop 1*), in use in primary school classrooms since September 1981, devote 50 percent of their lessons to "nature" and the "national country" (*thien nhien* and *dat nuoc*, significantly the same educational category). The old grade one readers devoted only 15 percent of their lessons to this theme. Pupils are encouraged to think of nature in terms of their own self-restraint.[12] The new grade one reader thus contains a linguistically elaborate story about a rose with silky petals "floating before the wind," growing in a luxuriant garden drenched in dew; a child trying to pluck the rose is reproved by its mother, reads a sign forbidding any plucking, embraces its mother and promises not to pluck any more flowers. But children are also induced to regard nature as being friendly and amiably anthropomorphic. Another story in the new grade one reader, this one about "smiling" water buffaloes, and about ricefield crabs which make "surprised" looks with their eyes, seems intended to have this effect.

The official explanation for the more sentimental style of the new reader is that many years of destructive war coarsened Vietnamese peasants' attitudes to the environment, and that primary school texts of the 1980s must therefore strengthen "humanitarian" attitudes to nature (see the excellent discussion in Dao Van Phuc 1982). More fanciful historians cannot overlook the possibility that textbooks which exalt the scientific and the homely aspects of nature are designed to undermine a traditional millenarian view of natural phenomena as arcane, magical, and fate-ridden. There would certainly be social grounds for this: Vietnamese newspapers reported that, in 1982, even in northern provinces, traders, former soothsayers and temple watchmen, but also youths, students, and some party cadres, showed a strong appetite for astrology, occult prophecies, sacred mushrooms, and "new doctrines" bearing the "strange" title of "the dragon flower assembly of the Maitreya Buddha" (*hoi long hoa di lac*), a reference to the far from new Vietnamese millenarian belief that the messiah Buddha would descend to earth and spread enlightenment, and thus salvation, under a tree whose branches were dragon-like (Hoang Hien 1982). Obviously it is premature to predict how deeply the reformed textbooks will alter the cultural consciousness of Vietnamese villages.

The Limits of Schools as Incubators of Economic Change

The twin gospels of public ownership of the economy and the organized redistribution of the population through migration have propelled Vietnamese villages—especially northern ones—into a new era. The introduction of "socialist" cooperatives into northern villages began at the end of 1958, and was essentially completed by the spring of 1961. By 1961, some 88 percent of all peasant households in the north belonged to more than 35,000 cooperatives. The birth of these cooperatives was not accompanied by any technological revolution. It was rather a political act of faith which anticipated such change: mechanized irrigation by electric pumps and the replacement of water buffaloes by small tractors were still dreams rather than realities. Only 9,100 of the 35,000 cooperatives of 1961 were as large as a single hamlet; and only 146 were as large as a single village. Under American bombing from 1965 to 1968, cooperative agriculture was not abandoned; it expanded. The cooperatives' scale increased. Their numbers dwindled. More of them became "high rank" units in which all production materials and tools belonged to the collectivity. By 1977, close to 72 percent of the cooperatives of the northern delta and midlands were as large as single villages; since 1965, their production has been prescribed and directed by the district governments above the villages.[13]

None of this, when combined with population growth and with the brutal devastations of the war, enabled Vietnam to grow enough food to feed itself. Nor was cooperativization an infallible guarantor of communal altruism and enlightenment. Thinly disguised land wars continued in rural Vietnam, featuring the usurpation of publicly owned property, sometimes not just because of greed but because of the survival of the old Confucian culture. Early betrothals and marriages of infant children, for example, popular in the old days as a way of cementing alliances between families, were a prime cause of land encroachment (because of their stimulation of excessive housing needs) in northern Vietnam more than two decades after the arrival of collectivized farming (letter in *Nhan dan*, October 1, 1982, p. 2). Poor land management—such as taking good land out of cultivation in order to build roads—added to the effect of such cultural tide-rips, meaning that, in many places in the north, the amount of farm acreage actually shrank after 1961. As one instance, the quantity of cultivated land in Thai Binh, an overcrowded coastal province southeast of Hanoi, declined by 12.6 percent between 1960 and 1973 (most of the above data is from Dinh Thu Cuc 1977).

As a result, peasants were encouraged to migrate to "new economic zones," in the mountain regions and in the south, where population pressure was less and where new farm lands could be cleared. Between 1976 and 1980 alone, some 600,000 Vietnamese farm workers and 1,100,000 more of their relatives and dependents were assigned to the new economic zones: their numbers included 160,000 northern peasants who were migrating to the south (article by Nguyen Van Kien of the Hanoi Finance Ministry in *Nhan dan*, June 26, 1980, p. 2). Only its exportation of some 44,000 of its peasant families, or 256,000 villagers, between 1961 and 1981, enabled the province of Thai Binh to keep its population relatively stable (at 1,506,235 people in 1979), despite its high birth rate (Phan Quang in *Nhan dan*, November 2, 1981, p. 3).

Western sociologists have argued that schools in the Third World work to eliminate "resistances to development" which are based wholly upon defense of traditional values or perspectives (see, for example, Berger 1976:199–202). With schools functioning in circumstances as socially and politically tumultuous as the ones just described, this theme does not take us very far. For it is possible to imagine a school in such a situation seeking to eliminate peasant resistance to migration, for example, in one of two dramatically different ways. The school might teach that the supposed costs of a permanent departure from the old village are exaggerated and the product of reactionary thought. Or, the school might acknowledge those costs and try to palliate them by nourishing new forms of community spirit that will compensate peasant children for the potential disruptions of their lives outside the school. How have Vietnamese schools managed this difficulty?

The question is related in part to the outcome of a struggle in Hanoi between two sets of educators. They might be called economic idealists and economic realists. The idealists believe that village schools should train modern-minded "polytechnical people" (*nguoi bach khoa*), well versed in all "contemporary technological principles," who will be capable of rapid deployment anywhere in all sorts of new economic enterprises after they graduate. The realists believe that such schools should instead dispense the most immediately applicable vocational training in status quo occupations (weavers, carpenters, iron workers) which already have a long history in rural Vietnam (Dang Quoc Bao 1982:53). The controversy implies that each village school has to make a choice. The school can be a forcing-house of new economic expectations and techniques; this might encourage an exodus, either desired or undesired, from villages which cannot live up to such expectations. Or it can be a parochial promoter of the virtues of the existing "special features" (*dac diem*) of the economy of the village to which it belongs; this might dampen enthusiasm for migrations elsewhere, but would also help dissuade restless youths from fleeing the countryside to "besiege the universities" (*bao vay dai hoc*).

Not surprisingly, rural primary schools have mostly functioned as tiny strongholds of the realist point of view. According to the social psychologists who recently studied life in rural Hai Hung province, there are more specialized groups (*nhom*) in Vietnamese villages now than there were before the revolution: villagers' identities depend more upon their membership in manual labor groups, skilled work groups, machinery work groups, as well as student groups, demobilized and wounded soldier groups, and retired village worker groups. Primary schools simulate their own versions of village groups which are economic units. Hence, for example, the elementary primary school in Nghia Dong village in the hill country of Nghe Tinh province in north central Vietnam, a model school with highly praised achievements in career guidance and labor education, took advantage of one "special feature" of its village's economy—many natural ponds—by organizing the thirty-eight pupils of its grade 6A class into a fish-raising brigade, subdivided into teams (*to*) and groups whose children would be responsible for feeding corn meal and cassava leaves to the school's own collection of pike and perch. The Nghia Dong school also had an industrial arts brigade. It also, apparently, was more of a simulation of the village status quo than an agency of change or a symbolic alternative: it was headed by a male teacher (whereas a female teacher headed the school brigade for planting rice), and it had far fewer pupils in it than did the school's fish and rice units, just as villages themselves have far fewer machinery workers than simple manual workers (Kim Dung 1982).

The primary schools, in other words, have been essentially concerned with preparing their pupils for middle school, or for the existing employment chances of the local collectivized economy. They have not been parochialism-smashing institutions concerned with preparing pupils for incorporation into very much larger, or different, economic systems. One reason for this is the assumption that the most important force for real economic change in the villages will not be the primary schools, but two institutions outside the village: the army (where village youths will be taught the newfangled skills of doctors, mechanics, and car drivers), and the district tractor stations (to which village youths will circulate as apprentices). The soldiers and the tractor mechanics who later return to their villages are then supposed to become "central personages" (*nhan van trung tam*) who will "transplant" the behavior of the more advanced worker class to their less advanced rural neighbors (Nguyen Duc Uy and Bach Van Tho 1980).

This should not imply that rural primary schools have introduced no tangible economic changes at all. In 1976, for example, pupils at the Nghia Dong primary school just mentioned pioneered wet-rice farming in their village, which had previously been accustomed to growing only dry, low-yield hill rice. In transplanting the rice seedlings, the pupils and the young female mathematics teacher who directed them tried to set their village another important technical example. They transplanted the seedlings in an east-west alignment, so that the amount of sunlight they received would be equal. But it must be noted that the Nghia Dong school was able to contribute to this improvement of village agriculture only after a decisive change had occurred in the local economic environment with which the school had nothing to do (an irrigation canal was completed in 1973 which allowed the village to change from maize and sweet potatoes to wet rice); and only because the school had a politically skillful principal whose mastery of village relationships allowed him to tap scarce resources (he persuaded the village to give the school land, rice seeds, and even the services of an agricultural engineer, all of which are coveted in rural Vietnam). What was more, the school's excursion into wet rice farming in 1976 presupposed that its pupils would remain in the village after graduation, as its next generation of farmers, so that they would eventually impose upon their elders, by sheer force of numbers, the new agricultural methods they had learned in school (Kim Dung 1982).

When primary schools have undermined village parochialism, they have done so only indirectly. They have not played much of a direct part in the mobilization for migrations to new economic zones. Such migrations have undoubtedly bewildered the inhabitants of many old villages, and it would be reasonable to assume that preparation for the migrations has placed a severe strain upon what even the communists now like to invoke as "the ties of friendship and honor of the village" (*tinh nghia xom lang*).

The peasants who do not migrate must, among other things, put a precise and public cash value upon the feelings of solidarity they are supposed to have for their departing neighbors, by deciding how much money and food to give them, and how evenly or unevenly to spend the money which the government has lent the cooperatives to enable them to repurchase the gardens and dwellings of the peasants who are leaving. But it is the village party committees which supervise this delicate process. They show films which extol the homelike merits of other provinces of the "ancestral land" (to quoc). They conduct the exhaustive preliminary discussions with youth groups, women's groups, village elders, wounded soldiers, and army members (but not teachers). They contribute their own members to the migration as volunteers (sometimes by having party cells draw lots).

The schools' contributions to what one might call the psychological acceptance of migration are more oblique. They lie in the creation of detachable, or one might even say "portable," forms of organizational life and striving which do not need a firm association with local geographical units, although they do not rule this out. Vietnamese schools—like Soviet or Chinese ones—work tirelessly to involve their children in many peer organizations. These might include the children's brigades (Doi thieu nien) or the Red Star brigades (Doi Sao do) which are designed to control the behavior of school pupils, supply them with irresistible peer models, and give them what Bronfenbrenner (1973:149–56) has called "superordinate goals" to which to dedicate themselves. Character building is no longer the concern merely of the pupil, his father and older brothers, and the teacher, as it was in prerevolutionary Vietnam. It has become collectivized, in a way that was unknown in the past, when the only pupil peer groups were the disciple associations (hoi dong mon, associations of pupils who studied within "the same gate") of individual teachers. Confucius has been supplanted not just by Marx but by A. S. Makarenko, the Soviet educator of the 1920s who specialized in the development of group-oriented discipline and socialization methods. And as part of the intense group cultivation of "selfmanaged roles" (vai tro tu quan), Vietnamese school peer organizations in such migration-conscious provinces as Thai Binh deliberately teach their pupils types of play which will accommodate mobility and change, such as camping, or such as the simulation of "sprouting cooperatives" (Kim Dung 1980). Indeed, types of children's play which became popular during the restless period of guerrilla resistance to the French, and which stressed loyalty to the nation rather than to the village, have been carefully preserved in Vietnamese schools, in spite of criticism of other aspects of the guerrilla style of education. The outstanding example is the game known as "the work of Tran Quoc Toan" (*cong tac Tran Quoc Toan*), which can be traced back to 1948 (Vo Thuan Nho 1980:40). It invites Vietnamese children to imagine their participation in the life of a self-reliant thirteenth-century general who fought Mongol invaders with his own army of relatives and servants, because he was thought too young at first to be entrusted with a royal command.

Vietnam must be one of the few countries in the world whose schoolchildren play games recalling events some seven centuries old. But what is more important is that the peer modeling which informs these games encourages pupils to think that they must repay the favor (*bao on*) of the nation, not of the village. The all-important Confucian virtue of reciprocity survives, but more unequivocally than ever before transcends village loyalties.

Notes

[1] For examples from Han Nam Ninh in 1981, see *Nhan Dan*, May 11, 1982:2.

[2] For a somewhat idealized view of the *tu van* groups, see Nhat Thanh (1968:471–73).

[3] David Marr (1981:414) suggests that there were about 10,000 of these people in 1945.

[4] As an instance of its richness, in Ha Bac province northeast of Hanoi, researchers in 1972 discovered the existence of some 500 different folk songs, of one famous type known as *quan ho*, within one rural area of less than 250 square kilometers.

[5] Many patriotic but not very communist teachers and students had fled from the cities to the Viet Minh base areas during the war with France. For example, the staff and pupils of the Viet Bac Resistance Middle School, when it began its school year in 1947–48, were drawn from the Chu Van An and Nguyen Trai middle schools in Hanoi. As in Yanan a decade before, the political indoctrination of such people had become a sharp necessity.

[6] Such a concern is of course pervasive in the Third World.

[7] A contrast here might be with American or Canadian high schools, which purvey the values of democracy in their teaching, but which themselves are relatively undemocratic, with minimal student participation in school management.

[8] The religious practitioners themselves are asked to sign written documents pledging to renounce their occupations. Village governments confiscate their paraphernalia, such as the turbans and the imperial robes favored by rural sorceresses.

[9] Hence, the famous Tet offensive was known to Vietnamese as the offensive of *Tet Mau Than*, *Mau than* being the lunar calendar year name for 1968.

[10] Interestingly, the lunar calendar does not enjoy this widespread a sanctioned use in the People's Republic of China, which is not so dependent upon the Vietnamese kind of historical folk patriotism.

[11] On the importance of Dragonboat Day in nineteenth-century Vietnam, see Woodside (1971:36–37).

[12] Northern Vietnam suffers, among other things, from deforestation caused in part by the peasant search for firewood.

[13] The cooperatives themselves nevertheless reproduced the bureaucratic structure of the district with their own administrative committees,

which might include—for example—one chairman in charge of planning and the calculation of profits and losses, four assistant chairmen, one director of the cooperative's production teams, one director of its subsidiary occupation teams, one director in charge of animal husbandry, and one director for building materials.

References

Berger, Peter L. *Pyramids of Sacrifice: Political Ethics and Social Change.* New York: Anchor Books, 1976.

Bronfenbrenner, Urie. *Two Worlds of Childhood: U.S. and U.S.S.R.* New York: Pocket Books, 1973.

Chaigneau, Michel Duc. *Souvenirs de Hué.* Paris, 1867.

Dang Quoc Bao. "Mot so van de ve kinh te giao duc" [Some problems with respect to education economics]. *Nghien cuu kinh te (Journal of Economic Research)*, Hanoi, February, 1982, pp. 4–53, 79.

Dang Thai Mai. "Ve viec day van trong nha truong" [On the work of teaching literature in the schools]. *Tap chi van hoc (Journal of Literary Studies)*, Hanoi, 2(1974):1–14, 23.

Dao Van Phuc. "Ve van de giao duc tu tuong, dao duc trong sach giao khoa" [On the Problem of Morality and Thought Education in Textbooks]. *Nghien cuu giao duc (Journal of Educational Research)*, Hanoi, 9(1982):14–17.

Dinh Thu Cuc. "Tim hieu qua trinh tung buoc cung co va hoan thien quan he san xuat xa hoi chu nghia trong cac hop tac xa san xuat nong nghiep o mien Bac nuoc ta" [Towards understanding the step-by-step process of strengthening and perfecting socialist production relationships in the agricultural production cooperatives in the north of our country]. *Nghien cuu lich su (Journal of Historical Research)*, July–August, 1977, pp. 37–50, 76.

Furnivall, J. S. *Colonial Policy and Practice: A Comparative Study of Burma and Netherlands India.* New York: New York University Press, 1956.

Ho Truc. "30 nam xay dung nen giao duc Viet Nam" [Thirty years of building Vietnamese education]. *Hoc Tap (Study and Practice)*, Hanoi, 9(1975):30–36.

——. "Nghiem chinh chap hanh dieu le nha truong pho thong" [Seriously carry out the regulations of the general schools]. *Nghien cuu giao duc (Journal of Historical Research)*, 9(1976):4–6.

Hoang Hien. "Ai bay tro me tin va ai me tin?" [Who fabricates superstitions and who is superstitious?]. *Nhan dan*, June 19, 1982, p. 3.

Kim Dung. "Giao duc dao duc o cac truong cua Thai Binh" [Moral education in the schools of Thai Binh]. *Nhan dan*, December 1, 1980, p. 3.

———. "Huong nghiep o Nghia Dong" [Career guidance in Nghia Dong village]. *Nhan dan*, July 1, 1982, p. 3.

Marr, David G. *Vietnamese Tradition on Trial, 1920–1945*. Berkeley and Los Angeles: University of California Press, 1981.

Nghi quyet. "Nghi quyet cua Bo chinh tri ve cai cach giao duc" [Collective resolution of the politburo with respect to educational reform]. *Dai hoc va trung hoc chuyen nghiep (Universities and Specialized Middle Schools)*, Hanoi, 7–8(1979):2–16.

Ngo Van Cat. *Viet Nam chong nan that hoc* [Vietnam resists illiteracy]. Hanoi: Nha xuat ban giao duc, 1980

Nguyen Anh. "Vai net ve giao duc o Viet-Nam tu sau dai chien the gioi lan thu I den truoc cach mang thang 8" [A few basic points about education in Vietnam after World War One to before the August Revolution]. *Nghien cuu lich su*, 102(September, 1967):29–46.

Nguyen Danh Phiet. "Giao duc lao dong trong cong dong lang xa" [Work education in the village commonality]. In *Nong thon Viet-Nam trong lich su* [The Vietnamese village in history]. Vien su hoc (*Historical Studies Institute*), comp., vol. II, pp. 259–75. Hanoi: Nha xuat ban khoa hoc xa hoi, 1978.

Nguyen Duc Uy and Bach Van Tho. "Nhung bien doi ve mat xa hoi o nong thon va kha nang cachmang to lon cua lop tre" [Changes with respect to social aspects in the villages and the great revolutionary capabilities of the young]. *Nhan dan*, August 13, 1980, p. 3.

Nguyen Hue Chi. "Van de tho co cho cac em" [The problem of ancient poems for children]. *Tap chi van hoc*, 4(1982):81–93.

Nguyen Ngoc Dung. "Dieu tra tinh hinh thuc hien pho cap giao duc o 2 don vi thuoc thanh pho Ho Chi Minh" [Investigating the situation of the implementation of universalized education in two units belonging to Ho Chi Minh City]. *Nghien cuu giao duc*, 6(1978):16–21.

Nguyen Phu Boi and Ngo Van Dau. "May kien nghi ve mon hoc chinh tri" [A few proposals about the school subject of politics]. *Nghien cuu giao duc*, 1(1978):23–25.

Nguyen Thi Binh. "Xay dung doi ngu giao vien dap ung yeu cau cua cai cach giao duc" [Establishing a corps of teachers in response to the demands of educational reform]. *Tap chi cong san (The Communist Journal)*, Hanoi, 8(1982):4–10.

Nguyen Trong Hoe and Nguyen Gia Quy. "Buoc dau tim hieu ve to chuc va quan li truong pho thong cap I–II hop nhat" [First steps towards understanding the organization and management of unified elementary and higher primary general schools]. *Nghien cuu giao duc*, 1(1978):13–14.

Nguyen Xien. "Cau chuyen ve ngay Tet va am lich" [A talk about New Year's and the lunar calendar]. *Nhan dan*, January 28, 1976, p. 3.

Nhat Thanh. *Dat le que thoi: phong tuc Viet-Nam* [Particular local habits and procedures: the customs of Vietnam]. Saigon, 1968.

Pham Duc Duat. "Bai tru me tin trong tuc boi trai co truyen" [Eliminate the superstitions in the traditional boat race customs]. *Nhan Dan*, November 28, 1981, p. 3.

Pham Thi Dieu Van. "Khac phuc tinh hinh thuc trong day va hoc toan cap I" [Overcome the formal quality in teaching and studying elementary primary school mathematics]. *Nghien cuu giao duc*, 4(1981):16–18.

Phan Ke Binh. *Viet-Nam phong tuc* [Vietnamese customs]. Saigon, 1970. (Originally published in 1915).

Phung Huy Trien. "To chuc tot lao dong san xuat cua hoc sinh de nang cao chat luong tri duc" [Organizing the productive labor of pupils well in order to raise the quality of their mental education]. *Nghien cuu giao duc*, 3(1981):12–13.

Pujarniscle, E. "Instructions relatives à l'enseignement primaire supérieur et de l'enseignement secondaire local." *Bulletin général de l'instruction publique*, Hanoi, December, 1925, pp. 101–04.

Thai Quang Nam. "Education et travail productif au Vietnam." *Canadian and International Education*, London, Ontario, 8.2(1979):92–99.

Tran Van Giau. *Su phat trien cua tu tuong o Viet-Nam tu the ky XIX den cach mang thang Tam* [The development of thought in Vietnam from the nineteenth century to the August Revolution). Hanoi: Nha xuat ban khoa hoc xa hoi. Volume One, 1973.

Trinh Manh. "Nhung diem moi cua mon tieng Viet va van hoc o cap I" [New features of the school subject of Vietnamese language and literature in elementary primary school]. *Nghien cuu giao duc*, 12(1981):8–10.

Vo Thuan Nho et al. *35 nam phat trien su nghiep giao duc pho thong* [35 years of development of the enterprise of general school education]. Hanoi: Nha xuat ban giao duc, 1980.

Woodside, Alexander. *Vietnam and the Chinese Model.* Cambridge, Mass.: Harvard University Press, 1971.

——. "Some Mid-Qing Theorists of Popular Schools: Their Innovations, Inhibitions, and Attitudes toward the Poor." *Modern China*, January, 1983, pp. 3–35.

——. "The Triumphs and Failures of Mass Education in Vietnam." *Pacific Affairs*, 56.3(1983):401–27.

CONTRIBUTORS

Chayan Vaddhanaphuti received his Ph.D. from Stanford University, and has carried out extensive research in rural northern Thailand. He is currently Assistant Professor, Faculty of Social Science, Chiang Mai University, Chiang Mai, Thailand.

Jean-Paul Dumont has written widely on symbolism and the construction of meaning. His earlier works include books about the Panare Indians of Venezuelan Guiana; a study of a Stanley Kubrick film; and a work about a nineteenth-century coded French manuscript. His recent work has focused on the island of Siquijor in the central Philippines, and he is currently preparing a monograph based on fieldwork experience on this island. He is the Clarence J. Robinson Professor of Anthropology, George Mason University, Fairfax, Virginia.

Sidney Jones has carried out research in Java and has worked for the Ford Foundation in Indonesia and New York. She has worked for Amnesty International in London and is currently head of Asia Watch and is based in New York City.

Charles F. Keyes has carried out extensive research in mainland Southeast Asia, especially in Thailand. He is author of *The Golden Peninsula: Culture and Adaptation in Mainland Southeast Asia* (1977) and *Thailand: Buddhist Kingdom as Modern Nation State* (1987), and editor of *Ethnic Change* (1981), *Karma: An Anthropological Inquiry* (1983), and "Peasant Strategies in Asian Societies: Moral and Rational Economic Approaches—A Symposium", *The Journal of Asian Studies* (1983). He is currently Professor of Anthropology and Director of the Northwest Regional Consortium for Southeast Asian Studies, University of Washington, Seattle, Washington.

Resil Mojares is Director of the Cebuano Studies Center of the University of San Carlos, Cebu City, the Philippines. He has a Ph.D. in literature from the University of the Philippines (1979), and teaches history and literature at the University of San Carlos. Mojares is the author of *Origins and Rise of the Filipino Novel* (1983), *Casa Gorodo in Cebu: Urban Residence in a Philippine Province, 1880–1920* (1983), *Theater in Society, Society in Theater* (1985), and *The Man Who Would Be President* (1986).

Uthai Dulyakasem received his first degree from Chulalongkorn University and worked as a secondary school teacher for several years in southern Thailand before continuing his studies at Stanford University. He carried out field research in southern Thailand and, after receiving his Ph.D. from Stanford in 1981, assumed a position on the Faculty of Education at Silpakorn University, Nakorn Pathom, Thailand. He has served as dean of this faculty and is currently a lecturer. He is also currently Assistant Manager of the Foundation for Children and Co-chairman of the Pridi Banomyong Institute in Thailand.

Alexander Woodside is Professor of History, University of British Columbia, Vancouver, B.C. where he has taught Chinese and Southeast Asian History since 1971. He is the author of *Vietnam and the Chinese Model* (1971) and *Community and Revolution in Modern Vietnam* (1976), and recently co-edited with David Wyatt, *Moral Order and the Question of Change: Essays on Southeast Asian Thought* (1982).

OTHER PARTICIPANTS IN THE CONFERENCE ON "CULTURAL CHANGE AND RURAL EDUCATION IN SOUTHEAST ASIA"

James Brow, Professor of Anthropology, University of Texas, Austin, Texas, served as a discussant at the conference.

Dinh Gia Khanh, Professor and former Director of the Institute of Folklore, Hanoi, Socialist Republic of Vietnam, presented a paper at the conference on "Vietnam's Rural Culture: Traditional and Modern."

Lim Teck-Ghee, who was formerly affiliated with the Centre for Policy Research, Universiti Sains Malaysia, Penang, Malaysia, served as local organizer and was a discussant at the conference.

Zuraina Majid, member of the faculty, School of Social Sciences, Universiti Sains Malaysia, Penang, Malaysia, presented a paper at the conference based on her research in Sarawak.

Moeljarto Tjokrowinoto, affiliated with the Rural and Regional Research and Studies Centre, Gadjah Mada University, Yogyakarta, Indonesia, presented a paper at the conference on "Community Organization for Nonformal Education: Using Village Solidarity for Enhancing Village Productivity."

Ramli Mohamed, member of the faculty, School of Humanities, Universiti Sains Malaysia, Penang, Malaysia, presented a paper at the conference on "The Use of Local and Religious Resources for Rural Extension and Education: The Experience of the Muda Agricultural Development Authority, Malaysia."

David Szanton, Staff Associate, Social Science Research Council, New York, served as coordinator and discussant at the conference.

Yoshihiro Tsubouchi, affiliated with the Centre for Southeast Asian Studies, Kyoto University, Kyoto, Japan, presented a paper at the conference "On the Decline of *Pondok* Education in Rural Kelantan, Malaysia."

Le thi Nham Tuyet, Professor, Research Center on Women, Social Sciences Committee, Hanoi, Socialist Republic of Vietnam, presented a paper at the conference on "Changes in the Cultural Life of Rural Vietnamese Women."

Christine Pelzer White, formerly affiliated with the Institute of Development Studies, University of Sussex, Brighton, England and currently Professor of History, University of Hawaii, Honolulu, Hawaii, presented a paper at the conference on "State, Culture and Gender: Continuity and Change in Women's Position in Rural Vietnam."

INDEX

expansion of 59, 157
Java 22, 24, 29, 104–106
needs of 5
Thailand 101, 121, 157–158,
163
the Philippines 6, 59
Vietnam 174, 177–178
Burma 4, 5–6, 8, 9, 13, 119
business 56, 94, 137
calendar, lunar 189
calendar, school (see *school calendar*)
Cambodia 8, 119
capital (monetary) 23
and education 180, 182
capitalism, expansion of 95, 153–
157, 164 (see also *market
economy*)
capitalist mode of production 155,
156, 163–164
Catholic priests 6, 12, 45, 70, 93,
188
Catholic schools 6, 14, 53
Catholicism (see also *missionaries, Catholic* and *Roman
Catholicism*)
Cebu, island in the Philippines
70, 42–64
Cebu City 44, 59
Cebuano language 70, 71, 72, 76,
79, 81, 83, 84
celebrations (see *food and feast-
ing*)
certification, of teachers (see
teacher education)
child labor 2, 22, 24, 59, 74, 162,
187
children, economic value of 2, 59,
74–75, 162
Chile 1

Chinese immigrants 7, 24, 133
Chinese language 5, 6, 9, 123
Chinese mestizo (*mestizo sangley*)
44
Chinese schools (in Thailand) 7,
143, 145
Chinese temples 132
Chinese traders 44, 133, 136
Christian schools (see *Catholic
schools* and *missionary
schools*)
chu nom (Vietnamese demotic
script) 9
Chulalongkorn, (Rama V) king of
Siam (1869–1910) 7, 95, 139,
154
citizenship 1, 4, 6, 11, 115, 116,
153, 157, 164, 165, 166, 169,
174, 183
civil servants (see *bureaucracy,
employment in* and *officials,
state*)
class (see also *social order*)
mobility of rural people 8, 11,
33, 75–79, 94, 122, 153,
159, 160–162, 177
socioeconomic 3, 5, 11, 45, 75,
153, 158–162, 165
structure and education 2, 93,
153, 159, 161–162, 183
classroom
as reflection of larger society
100–103, 153, 169
structure of 99–102, 158, 169
clergy (see *Buddhist monks,
Catholic priests, imams*)
code-switching 80–81
coeducation (see *female education*) 160
colleges 53, 146, 159, 160–161